A CENTURY OF ENGLISH FARCE

A CENTURY OF ENGLISH FARCE

By LEO HUGHES

PRINCETON, NEW JERSEY
PRINCETON UNIVERSITY PRESS
1956

Publication of this book has been aided by
a grant from The University of Texas Research Council

Printed in the United States of America
by Princeton University Press, Princeton, New Jersey

PREFACE

✦✦

"Humor can be dissected, as a frog can," suggests E. B. White, "but the thing dies in the process and the innards are discouraging to any but the pure scientific mind." I acknowledge the soundness of his remark but, without laying claim to a pure scientific mind, I confess to finding some innards fascinating. Or to obviate the charge of cruelty implied I might suggest that what is involved here is not so much dissection as exhumation—of the archeological rather than the grisly sort.

This probing into some of the dimmer recesses of English drama began as a study of farce in the Restoration theatre. As anyone who has read more than casually in the period will have observed, the term *farce* is bandied about with vigor in the theatrical literature after 1660, usually serving as a convenient weapon with which rival dramatists can belabor each other. Some of the vigor is accounted for, to be sure, by the fact that the term was a newcomer to the English vocabulary but not all of it can be laid to mere novelty. Some investigation of the genre, of its alleged causes and effects, seemed to me to be warranted. Then, too, there appeared to be a gap in the very full literature on the theatre in that virtually no one had directed his attention specifically to the genre, though there could be no question of its vitality and wide popularity—whatever its esteem among critics.

I had not pursued my studies very far, however, before I became aware that any arbitrary limitation to the period 1660-1700 would be impracticable. In fact, the decade around the turn of the century gave promise of being the most interesting span of all. So I pushed forward until, to make the story brief, I was eventually led on to the middle of the eighteenth century, by which point farce as a distinct dramatic genre seemed well set upon its course.

· v ·

In this study I have not attempted to support any new or striking thesis. Instead I have been content to buttress what must be almost a commonplace: the idea that farce is involved far more directly and intimately in the business of the theatre itself than any other dramatic form, that it cannot profitably be thought of apart from the theatre in which it was produced. For this reason I have found it necessary to devote much space in the following pages to the fortunes of the London theatres, to actors and companies, to bills and box-office receipts.

So many persons have assisted in the gathering of materials for this book that I cannot name, or even recall, all of them individually. My thanks are due the staffs of the Boston Public, Chicago, Folger, Harvard, Huntington, Illinois, Library of Congress, Newberry, New York Public, Texas, and Yale libraries; I wish also to thank the authorities of the University of Texas for material assistance. A few persons I do wish to single out in special gratitude. I regret that one, my old friend and teacher Harold Newcomb Hillebrand, is now beyond the reach of my thanks. I am deeply indebted to my former colleague and collaborator A. H. Scouten. My greatest debt is to my wife for her helpfulness and patience during the long period while this study was being developed.

L. H.

Austin, Texas
September 1955

CONTENTS

Preface   v

1. A Problem in Definition   3

2. Structure and Devices   21

3. Farce and the Afterpiece   60

4. Rival Entertainments: Pantomime,
    Burlesque, Satire, Sentiment   94

5. Sources and Influences   130

6. The Actors   153

7. Fairs and Strollers   203

8. Some Representative Farces   232

9. Conclusion: The Status of Farce   272

Bibliography   286

Index   293

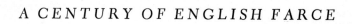

A CENTURY OF ENGLISH FARCE

CHAPTER 1

A PROBLEM IN DEFINITION

++

It is one of the maxims of the civil law, that definitions are hazardous. Things modified by human understanding, subject to varieties of complication, and changeable as experience advances knowledge, or accident influences caprice, are scarcely to be included in any standing form of expression, because they are always suffering some alteration of their state. . . . Comedy has been particularly unpropitious to definers; for though perhaps they might properly have contented themselves, with declaring it to be "such a dramatic representation of human life as may excite mirth," they have embarrassed their definition with the means by which the comic writers attain their end, without considering that the various methods of exhilarating their audience, not being limited by nature, cannot be comprised in precept.—RAMBLER, No. 125 (May 28, 1751).

++

ANY attempt to treat the history of a dramatic genre for a century and more must necessarily begin with definition if there is to be a common ground upon which writer and reader may meet. The terms *comedy, farce, burlesque,* and the like—none too readily distinguishable in the abstract— become almost unmanageable when applied to a body of dramatic material, unless and until some common definition has been agreed upon.

We might of course resort to the practice of following the usage current in the period itself. The late W. J. Lawrence has insisted on our doing just that. In an article published thirty years ago in the *Musical Quarterly* he condemns as utter pedantry the attempts to arrive at a precise nomenclature: "Theatrical nomenclature . . . must be taken at its face value. It is not the function of the musico-dramatic historian to throw classifications of old on the Procrustean bed and maim them in accordance with some hard-

and-fast principle. Nothing but confusion can ensue from such a course. No matter how unscientific many of them now appear, the labellings given by bygone authors to their works must remain sacrosanct."[1]

While I find it possible to respect the principle upon which Lawrence's requirement is based, I shudder to think of the confusion which would follow any attempt to carry it out—at least in the case of the term treated here. His mandate seems to me to imply two conditions: first, that bygone authors labelled their works with some care; second, that the labels had a fairly definite meaning to the author's contemporaries. So far as the use of the word *farce* in the Restoration and the first half of the eighteenth century is concerned, neither of these assumptions is sound.

To take the first, the accuracy or the consistency with which a piece was labelled, how may we classify a given play when it bears one label on the title page and another in the preface or prologue or dedication? I have noted some two dozen plays in the period so labelled. Again, what are we to do with a piece entitled comedy in one playbill and farce in the next? In the early part of the 1715-16 season the newspapers carried bills for Bullock's *Woman's Revenge* first as "the last new Farce," a little later as "the last new Comedy," and before the end of the Christmas season as merely "Play."[2] Or what shall we call *The Stage Coach*, issued as farce in 1704 and comedy in 1705? Or where shall we list at least a few pieces, such as the anonymous *Wit of a Woman* (1704), which bore no label on title page or elsewhere?[3] Other examples could be added, but these should serve to indicate the hopelessness of depending upon author or publisher for help in classification.

[1] "Early Irish Ballad Opera and Comic Opera," *Musical Quarterly*, VIII (1922), 397.
[2] *Daily Courant*, October-December 1715, various dates.
[3] Other plays without label are Jevon's *Devil of a Wife* (1686), Theophilus Cibber's *Auction* (1757).

Luigi Riccoboni, famous eighteenth-century actor and historian of the drama, cites an interesting case of similar confusion from an earlier century. In his study of the Italian theatre he speaks of the state of affairs in comedy before the end of the fifteenth century. Modern commentators, he remarks, "reckon all the Pieces written in the preceding Ages to be no better than so many *Farces*, tho' they are very long, and divided into five Acts. Some Pieces of this kind are called in the Title-Page *Farces*, and others, *Comedies*. It is likewise remarkable that a great many others in the Title-Pages are named *Farces*, and in the Epilogue, *Comedies*. From this, it is plain, that their ancient Poets by these two words, understood the same thing."[4]

Nor is it possible to discover any very precise meaning which the term conveyed to the author's contemporaries. Perhaps, to borrow Sterne's remark, "They order this matter better in France." Perhaps a student of French farce is able to accept the terms as he finds them, though I doubt it. For even the French found it difficult to keep their genres carefully distinguished, as any examination of the works of Molière and his contemporaries will reveal. Observe the struggles of modern students of the period to keep their nomenclature meaningful. Professor Lancaster tries hard, without attaining complete success, to distinguish between such terms as *farce* and *petite comédie* in his monumental study of the drama of the age of Louis. And the distinguished French literary historian Gustave Lanson quarrels with Molière's own labels, as, for example, in the case of *les Précieuses ridicules*: "L'auteur, en les publiant, les intitule comédie, et nous rejetons le nom de *farce*, par respect pour lui. Mais l'etiquette n'y fair rien: regardons la pièce." And his examination reveals numerous marks of the farce.[5] Ashton, on the other hand, finds *Sganarelle*, even though

[4] *An Historical and Critical Account of the Theatres in Europe* (London, 1741), pp. 38-39.
[5] "Molière et la farce," *La revue de Paris*, III (1901), 139.

in verse, to be "nearer farce" than the prose *Précieuses ridicules.*[6] Obviously, then, we find no assurance of carefully fixed terminology in France though there seems to be less confusion in French drama than in English.

Never so careful in the use of literary labels as their neighbors, the English were at the additional disadvantage of being forced to work with a new term since *farce* had taken its place in dramatic nomenclature only with the Restoration.[7] Perhaps the attitude adopted by Sir Robert Howard is a trifle too John Bullish to serve as wholly typical but it does have a certain representative quality about it. Speaking, in the preface to his *Great Favourite* (1668), of the difficulty of pleasing current taste, he refuses to condemn the people who prove so whimsical but falls upon "the unnecessary understanding of some that have labour'd to give strict rules to things that are not mathematical, and with such eagerness persuing their own seeming reasons that at last we are to apprehend such argumentative Poets will grow as strict as Sancho Pancos Doctor was to our very Appetites; for in the difference of Tragedy and Comedy, and of Fars it self, there can be no determination but by the Taste."[8]

Without attempting an exhaustive survey of contemporary definitions or usages, we may profitably spend a little time in attempting to discover how the eighteenth century

[6] *Molière* (New York, 1930), p. 42. Though I can claim no real familiarity with the popular drama of Spain, I judge from the studies of scholars like Crawford, Jack, and Northup that a similar difficulty of distinguishing among such labels as *entremés* and *paso* exists in Spanish literature.

[7] On the adoption of *farce* as a term in the English theatre, see my article "The Early Career of *Farce* in the Theatrical Vocabulary," The University of Texas *Studies in English*, 1940, pp. 82-95.

[8] Dryden, in his *Defence of an Essay of Dramatique Poesie, being an Answer to the Preface of The Great Favorite, or the Duke of Lerma*, attacks his kinsman and opponent for so abject a surrender to anarchy. Unfortunately his attempt to provide the distinctions which Howard despaired of supplying applies to tragedy and comedy only.

employed the term. Such an inspection, I may say in advance, will lead to the conclusion that while *farce* meant somewhat the same thing it does now, there is no very consistent use and very few earnest attempts at definition. Here and there the emphasis is placed upon what Johnson insisted on as truly basic in a definition of comedy, that is, *purpose*; usually, however, one of the more accidental or incidental features is stressed.

In spite of what seems a fairly common misapprehension in our day, farce was not distinguished from comedy on the basis of length. The following statement from a modern textbook, for example, very much oversimplifies the case: "In fact, in the Restoration when the word farce was introduced, it was not used to refer to a special type of comic technique at all, but to the short humorous play which was coming into popularity at the time, a play of three acts instead of the customary five."[9] Or, to give one other example, Professor Gagey informs us that "The eighteenth century made a broad and rather careless distinction between pieces of three acts, which were called ballad operas, and pieces of one or two acts, which were labelled ballad farces."[10] To indicate just how "broad and careless" the distinction was, if it can be said actually to have existed, I cite the evidence of no less than twenty ballad operas of the 1730's in one or two acts which were *not* labelled farce.

While it is true that most pieces labelled farce ran to less than five acts and most plays in one act only were labelled farce, even this rule has some interesting exceptions. Mrs. Behn's *False Count* (1682) was labelled farce, even though in five acts; four one-act pieces around 1740, Garrick's *Lethe* and James Miller's *Hospital for Fools*, *Picture*, and *Camp Visitants* (possibly Miller's; see *Larpent Catalogue*), are not called farces. Breval's five-act *Play Is the Plot* (1718) is

[9] F. B. Millett and G. E. Bentley, *The Art of the Drama* (New York, 1935), p. 121.
[10] *Ballad Opera* (New York, 1937), p. 101.

labelled comedy on the title page, but the author in his very candid preface admits that the play is "of too low a nature for anything but Farce." In dozens of cases plays in two or three acts were labelled indiscriminately farce or comedy. For purposes of illustration we may return to the critical period around 1704-05. Two out of three three-act plays which appeared in 1704 were labelled farce; but every one of four three-act plays appearing in 1705 was labelled comedy. Or we may drop back to 1703 to discover two authors with completely different attitudes toward the relation between length and label. On the one hand, Mrs. Centlivre says in the preface to her *Love's Contrivances* that she had planned a three-act farce but was prevailed upon by her friends to change it to a five-act comedy. On the other, the author of the five-act *Sir Giddy Whim* (1703) apologizes in his prologue for calling his piece comedy:

> The Author begs you wou'd accept his Show
> He has a hundred Presidents, you know,
> To call it Comedy, 'tho 'tis not so.

And what is true of practices at the beginning of the century is just as true half a century later as may be seen in Murphy's labelling two out of three of his two-act plays farce and one comedy, or in Garrick's applying *comedy* to his farcical adaptation of *The Taming of the Shrew* and to his non-farcical *Guardian*, both two-act pieces.

The position of the play in the bill has some effect on its classification, though here again there is no great consistency. A few examples taken from either end of the century of theatrical history covered here will serve to indicate some disposition to label all material added to the main piece in an evening's bill as farce. Take Pepys' curious use of the term. In an entry for 2 May 1668 he records his boredom with Shadwell's *Sullen Lovers*. The evening was not altogether wasted, however, for "a little boy, for a farce, do dance Polichinelli, the best that ever anything was done in the world, by all men's report: most pleased with that, beyond anything in the world, and much beyond all the play." Shadwell's stage directions indicate the position of this edifying spectacle in the bill, for at the very end we get: "Enter a Boy in the habit of Pugenello, and traverses the Stage, takes his Chair, and sits down, then Dances a Jigg." At least one other entry in Pepys (19 January 1669) suggests that this usage had some currency early in the period, but a glance at the other end reveals that it was much more common then. Without citing any of the numerous examples I may say that an examination of the requests for licenses now preserved in the Larpent collection reveals how common a practice it was for John Rich and Garrick or Lacy to label any piece which was designed to close the evening's bill as farce, whether it had anything actually farcical about it or not. Or, to cite one specific example from this time, we may take the entry for Coffey's most famous farce in *The British Theatre* (London, 1752): "*The Devil to Pay* . . . was performed in Three Acts without Success, but when formed into one, as a *Farce* [i.e., when shortened and offered not as a main piece but as an afterpiece], has been performed everywhere with Success."

The majority of afterpieces in dialogue were farces, but by no means all of them were; nor were they always called farces. Perhaps two striking and widely separated instances will serve to demonstrate how little dependence may be placed upon position as a criterion. In 1703 a bill in the *Daily Courant* offered "A Farce, call'd *The Cheats of Scapin* [in three acts]. And a Comedy of two acts only call'd *The Comical Rivals, or the School Boy*."[11] Twenty years later we find a bill in the *Daily Post* offering "A Farce of Three Acts, call'd *Cartouche*. . . . To which will be added, a Comedy of two acts, call'd, *The Country House*."[12] I may perhaps call attention here to the fact that in each of these

[11] April 29, 1703.   [12] June 3, 1723.

bills not only the former piece but also the longer piece is labelled farce, and also to the fact that Vanbrugh had originally called his *Country House* farce.

In the *Rambler* essay from which the lines which head this chapter are taken, Johnson scoffs at his contemporaries for another absurdity in classification or definition, the custom of distinguishing between tragedy and comedy on the basis of the social level of the characters, a distinction which was supposed to have the august support of Aristotle. Johnson was not the first or the only commentator to deny that Aristotle had meant rank to distinguish comedy and tragedy. Congreve in his *Amendments* (1698) and the author of the *Dissertation on Comedy* (1750) specifically deny that μίμησις φαυλοτέρων had any connection with rank and both render the phrase as imitation of the worst sort of people in respect to morals or manners, a translation virtually identical with that of such modern translators as Lane Cooper and A. H. Gilbert.[18]

This adherence to a supposedly Aristotelian principle is evident in the treatment of farce also. Particularly in the period following 1728, when the vogue of *The Beggar's Opera* brought great numbers of underworld characters onto the stage, there were frequent attempts to tie up farce and "low life." Some writers outdid Aristotle or his commentators and provided an extra stratum for the dramatic form. The author of *The City Farce* (1737), for example, says he recently fell to wondering, "Whether it would be blameable to make a new Essay toward reviving the Spirit of our English Farce, which was designed to yield some Benefit as well as Diversion, by exposing those Follies which affect chiefly the Middle Station of Life, and

[18] Cooper, *Aristotelian Theory of Comedy* (New York, 1922); Gilbert, *Literary Criticism: Plato to Dryden* (New York, 1940). Professor Gilbert gives a clear picture of how the notion of rank crept into the interpretations of the Poetics in such commentaries as those of Trissino, Cinthio, and Guarini; see especially pp. 508, 513.

are therefore beneath the Province of Comedy, which is principally confined to the Genteel Part of Mankind." And Fielding seems at one time to have held a similar view, for he begins the prologue to his *Lottery* (1732) in this way:

> As Tragedy prescribes to passion rules,
> So Comedy delights to punish fools;
> And while at nobler game she boldly flies,
> Farce challenges the vulgar as her prize.

In spite of these and other instances[14] of attempting to confine farce to the vulgar and the vulgar to farce, this principle was never really well established. There are numerous characters from the lower classes in plays not labelled as farces and not a few members of the gentry, particularly of the rural gentry, in farces.

Another trait which seems to be quite characteristic of farce in any age, improbability or extravagance, provided yet another cause for confusion, though this time the confusion is more often between farce and what we now call burlesque.[15] One of the cardinal principles of eighteenth-century criticism was of course the requirement to follow nature. As applied here it meant that the writer of comedy was obliged to stay within the limits of probability. When he failed to do so he was often charged with descending to farce. Since the writer of burlesque also went beyond na-

[14] Perhaps as telling a way as any to show how widespread this idea was would be to cite the example of an artist in another field, William Hogarth. H. B. Wheatley quotes the artist's statement of his common method, which reads, in part: "I therefore wished to compose pictures on canvas, similar to representations on the stage. . . . Let the decision be left to every unprejudiced eye; let the figures in either pictures or prints, be considered as players dressed either for the sublime,—for genteel comedy, or farce,—for high or low life." *Hogarth's London* (London, 1909), p. 45.

[15] In the "Translator's Foreword" to *Aristophanes: the Eleven Comedies* (New York, 1943), p. xii, there is a very interesting and enlightening comparison between the work of Aristophanes and modern burlesque and other comic forms. The quotation from Lucas Collins is especially apt.

ture, his work commonly received the same label. The first dramatic burlesque of the period, *The Rehearsal* (1671), was usually referred to as a farce though it bore no label at all in editions I have seen which were published within a century of its premiere. Fielding adds to the confusion of terms by titling his first burlesque *The Author's Farce*, though it is clear from his prologue to that piece that the title is meant to be ironic.

Burlesque was a sufficiently familiar term in the eighteenth century, but it was not much used in the drama. Only ocasionally does one find it in a context which clearly suggests the theatre. The authors of *A Complete Key to the . . . What D'ye Call It* (1715) call Gay's piece, which he had labelled "Tragi-Comi-Pastoral Farce," a burlesque; and in 1719 Mrs. Aubert described her *Harlequin Hydaspes* as a burlesque in the preface to that piece, though the title page says "Mock-opera." Even by mid-century there was no settled use of *burlesque* as a dramatic term, so that Foote in the dedication to his *Taste* (1752) finds it necessary to use two terms, *farce* for plays, *burlesque* for nondramatic literature: "I look upon Farce to hold the same Rank in the Drama, that Burlesque does in other Poetry. It is employ'd either in debasing lofty Subjects, or in raising humble ones. Of the two Kinds we have Examples in the *Tom Thumb* of Mr. F——, and a Travesty of the *Ulysses*."

Though Foote's preface gives us no help in distinguishing farce and burlesque, it is important in its refusal to accept any term less than *comedy* for his short satirical pieces. In this connection it may be well to note that in the earliest editions Foote's plays were labelled comedies, though they were later issued rather commonly as farces. The sole exception which I have noted is that of *The Englishman Return'd from Paris* (1756); it was published as a farce, even in spite of its being merely a sequel to *The Englishman in Paris* (1753), which was originally labelled *comedy*. It is

A PROBLEM IN DEFINITION

perhaps superfluous to add that *The Englishman Return'd from Paris* is neither more nor less farcical than the others. Extravagance, going beyond nature, appears in plays other than burlesque and farce. For example, the highly improbable situation which provides most of the fun in *She Stoops to Conquer* caused Johnson to describe the play as bordering on farce.[16] Yet Johnson thought Goldsmith's a very fine comedy indeed. A comment made a few months after the one just referred to takes us back to the *Rambler* essay, written twenty years before: "I know of no comedy for many years that has so exhilarated an audience, that has answered so much the great end of comedy—making an audience merry." Horace Walpole was of another opinion. Goldsmith's play was too "low" for his refined taste; it was in fact "the lowest of all farces."[17] Then there are dozens of instances, where writers are not, as in the case of Goldsmith and Johnson, on friendly terms, in which comedies or even tragedies which approach the improbable or fantastic are labelled farce. I do not, however, wish to be distracted into a pursuit of *farce* as a term of derogation or invective.[18]

Most of the examples hitherto given represent definition by chance or implication only. The more deliberate attempts to define the term precisely yield slightly better results. The dictionaries do not, however, provide much help. Blount expanded the definition of *farce* in the second edition of his *Glossographia* (1661) to include "A fond and dissolute Play, or Comedy, also the Jig at the end of an Interlude, wherein some pretty knavery is acted."[19] Phillips

[16] *Boswell's Life* (Hill-Powell), II, 205-206.
[17] *Boswell*, II, 233.
[18] For some examples of the use of *farce* in invective before 1700 see my article, "Attitudes of Some Restoration Dramatists toward Farce," *Philological Quarterly*, XIX (1940), 268-287. It is perhaps sufficient, however, to cite the classic example, Rymer's use of the phrase "bloody Farce" to describe *Othello*.
[19] Blount's definition was taken practically verbatim from Cot-

made no mention of theatrical usage until his fourth edition of 1678, in which he added to the earlier definition, "A sort of Comical Representation, less Regular then a Comedy, but stuffed with rambling and extravagant passages of wit." Coles, Bailey, and Johnson follow the lead of Blount and Phillips. Perhaps the only notable features of these definitions are the obvious moral and esthetic disapproval, shown in *knavish, fond, dissolute,* etc. and the devotion to etymology, which leads to the stress on *stuff.*

It is only in the less compact definitions found in an occasional preface or critical essay that we get any very full or adequate attempts to define, and these are few and late. Dryden was evidently the first to undertake to treat *farce* fully in English, but what he says is not too satisfactory as he seems more intent on disparaging than on defining. In the preface to his *Evening's Love* (1668) he tells us that "Farce . . . consists principally of grimaces. . . . Comedy consists, though of low persons, yet of natural actions and characters; I mean such humours, adventures, and designs, as are to be found and met with in the world. Farce, on the other side, consists of forced humours, and unnatural events. Comedy presents us with the imperfections of human nature: Farce entertains us with what is monstrous and chimerical." So Dryden continues for some lines, producing a definition which is more notable for its rhetorical qualities than for its usefulness. Yet his definition is referred to by several later writers.

Even more unsatisfactory is a definition which appeared two years later in Edward Howard's feeble production called *The Womens Conquest.* Little can be made of his prolix and confused account. According to him, "Farce . . .

grave's French-English dictionary of 1611. Werner Klemm is of the mistaken notion that Bailey, in the 1721 edition of his dictionary, was the first lexicographer to devote an entry to the noun *farce* in the theatrical sense. *Die Englische Farce in 19. Jahrhundert* (Bern, 1946), p. 3.

consists of Mimickry and other ridiculous Gestures mingled together, for which it may properly enough bear the denomination, though it is no more of kin to a Play, then a Mule is to a Horse, in having somewhat longer Ears."

Dryden was instrumental in provoking another writer into attempting a definition, not by the influence of the preface quoted above but by his play *Amphytrion*. The unknown author of *A Comparison between the Two Stages* (1702) has one of the speakers in that book introduce Dryden's piece for discussion. Sullen, the professed critic in the group, falls upon the play unmercifully: "I think it as very and substantial a Farce as *Scapin*, or the *Emperor of the Moon*." When the first speaker calls attention to the fact that Dryden labelled his play comedy, Sullen is not abashed.

> *Sul.* I care not what he calls it; if he called it a Tragedy, he had assurance enough to bear it out in a Preface, but let him call it what he will, 'tis still as vile a Farce as ever he rail'd against, and everything that is so repugnant to Truth or Possibility is the same.
>
> *Ramb.* Is that all the difference between Comedy and Farce?
>
> *Sul.* Not all; there is in the contexture of one and the other a very great difference; for in Farce the Author is not tied to the same Rules as in Comedy; Farce is more loose and disengaged, not cramp'd by Method or measure of Time or other Unity. . . .

Among early eighteenth-century commentators John Dennis probably devoted more attention to the genre than any other writer though his remarks are too scattered and too self-contradictory to help fix the term. In the well known exchange of letters with Congreve over the place of "humour" in comedy he remarks: "For this seems to me, to constitute the Essential Difference betwixt Farce and Comedy, that the Follies which are expos'd in Farce are singular; and those are particular, which are expos'd in Comedy.

These last are those, with which some part of an Audience may be suppos'd infected, and to which all may be suppos'd obnoxious. But the first are so very odd, that by Reason of their Monstrous Extravagance, they cannot be thought to concern an Audience; and cannot be supposed to instruct them."[20] He clearly means here, as his further remarks and illustrations show, not satire on actual individuals but such peculiar and far-fetched idiosyncrasies as that of Morose in Ben Jonson's *Silent Woman*.

Yet Dennis employs a totally different set of critical principles in distinguishing farce and comedy in the preface to his *Plot and No Plot* (1697) in which he explains how he had changed his original plan of writing a farce and turned the play into a "low comedy" instead. Here the distinction seems to rest on somewhat broader grounds: the unities are preserved, the scenes linked, and so on. Still later, in a letter written in 1717 to Henry Cromwell, he implies that still another distinction is possible when, in speaking of the Roman mimes, he says: "They were low Farces, compos'd on purpose only to make people laugh."[21]

Only at the end of our period, or really just beyond it, do we find any very satisfactory attempts to set the limits of farce. In his *Dissertation ... on the Provinces of the Drama* (1753) Bishop Hurd approaches, so long as he remains on general grounds, a sound and reasoned distinction. The aim of comedy is, in his judgment, "the sensation of pleasure arising from a view of the truth of characters, more especially their specific differences," whereas the "sole aim and tendency of farce is to excite laughter."[22] After this promis-

[20] *Critical Works of John Dennis* (ed. E. M. Hooker, Baltimore, 1939-1943), II, 385.
[21] *Critical Works*, II, 165.
[22] The *Dissertation* was appended to Hurd's edition of Horace's *Art of Poetry*. I have used the third edition, Cambridge, 1757, rather than the first edition, four years earlier. Both Hurd and Dr. Johnson seem to have looked upon the sort of dramatic satire in which individuals are attacked, the plays of Aristophanes among

ing beginning, however, he becomes exceedingly prolix and confused and can be followed only with difficulty, and with little or no profit. His tendency to look backward toward the Ancients and toward earlier English writers rather than those of his own day renders his account even less useful to the present study.

The fullest and in many ways most adequate contemporary definition I have met with comes within the same decade as Hurd. It too reverts to Dryden's definition of roughly a century before but adds to that definition and descends to particulars. In Wilkes' *General View of the Stage* (1759) a whole section is devoted to farce:

> Farce is founded on chimera and improbability; the events are unnatural, the humour forced, and it is, in the opinion of Dryden, a compound of extravagancies, fit only to entertain such people as are judges of neither men nor manners: it appeals entirely to the fancy; delights with oddity, and unexpected turns: it has in one thing indeed the same effect as Comedy, viz. it produces laughter; but it is not a laughter founded upon reason, excited by the check given to folly, the reproof to ignorance, or the lash to corruption.

After a few more remarks in the same vein the writer gets around to illustration by analyzing two highly popular farces of the period, *A Duke and No Duke* and *The Devil to Pay*. He then takes up some more recent plays, Garrick's *Lethe* and Foote's *Englishman in Paris* and *Englishman Return'd from Paris*, to show how inapplicable the label *farce* is for them. Clearly he would not use the label for burlesque either.

In the absence of any adequate definition provided by contemporary writers—the most satisfactory one given so far falls outside the strict limits of our period—one may be

---

the ancients, those of Foote among moderns, as farces. For Johnson's views on this subject see *Boswell*, II, 95.

justified in attempting to arrive at a satisfactory working definition. It should be obvious from what has already been said that no useful purpose can be served by trying to include in this study every piece which at one time or another—by author's or publisher's whimsy or critic's pique—bore the label *farce*. I have no intention, for example, of treating burlesque drama. The burlesque has already been given considerable attention, though the dramatic variety deserves still more.

In order to speak a common language, then, I shall confine my study to those pieces which would commonly be labelled farce today. Perhaps this last point, the signification of the term in our day, requires our attention for a moment. It must be admitted that we occasionally employ the word somewhat loosely. I do not think, however, that there is any important disagreement over studied definition. I have seen Wycherley's *Country Wife* referred to on two or three different occasions by careful students of the drama as farce.[23] Yet I am sure that not one of them would be tenacious of his usage if hard pressed. In each case the context shows clearly that the term is used to emphasize the lightness or cleverness of what has also been called our finest comedy of manners. In short, I am satisfied that few would quarrel with this definition from a highly authoritative source:

> *Farce* is a form of the comic in dramatic art, the object of which is to excite laughter by ridiculous situations and incidents rather than by imitation with intent to ridicule, which is the province of burlesque, or by the de-

[23] Nicoll, A *History of English Drama*, 1600-1900, I, 238, calls Wycherley's play "a bright and glorious farce." Palmer, *Comedy of Manners* (London, 1913), p. 22, refers to it as "perhaps the most perfect farce in English dramatic literature," repeating the identical phrase later, p. 128. Thorndike, *English Comedy* (New York, 1929), p. 300, all but says the same thing.

lineation of the play of character upon character, which is that of comedy. . . .[24]

Perhaps some elaboration on this concise statement, particularly elaboration in terms of theatrical practice, would not seem gratuitous. The key to the whole matter, it seems to me, lies in the phrase "to excite laughter." The chief, even the exclusive, business of farce is to stimulate the risibilities of the audience. The distinction between farce and other kinds of comic drama must then rest upon the nature of the laughter elicited by each. The laugh, the smile, the smirk with which an audience receives high comedy or the laughter tinged with scorn which greets the jibes of the burlesque writer differ appreciably from the nonreflective guffaw with which the antics of the farceur are received.[25] As Petit de Julleville says in describing medieval French farce, "Son seul objet est de faire rire par une représentation frappante, énorme, du ridicule. La gaieté y déborde sans arrière-pensée ni sous-entendu; sans retour amer ou sérieux sur nous-mêmes, sur nos défauts, sur nos vices, dont elle s'amuse à rire, sans perdre temps à se'n plaindre, et sans prétendre à nous corriger."[26]

It might be more judicious, however, to close this attempt to set the limits of my survey by focusing attention upon current rather than past usage, on English rather than foreign practice. Here, finally, is a clear marking of the boundaries of farce made by one of our eminent dramatic critics, a keen student of current theatrical fare, Mr. John

---

[24] *Encyclopædia Britannica,* 11th edition, s.v., *farce.*

[25] On occasion, even in the eighteenth century, there were attempts to distinguish among the various kinds of laughter or, perhaps better, among the various degrees of the risible. See, for example, Beattie's fairly consistent discrimination between the *ludicrous* and *ridiculous, Essay on Laughter and Ludicrous Composition Written in the Year 1764* (first published with *Essay on Poetry and Music,* 1776).

[26] *La Comédie et les mœurs en france au moyen age* (Paris, 1886), p. 11.

Mason Brown: "Farceurs belong to a race apart. They have as little in common with comedians as comedians have with tragedians. The sky is the limit so far as they are concerned. No holds are barred. Every trick or stunt is legitimate if only they can get away with it. And why not? The sole point and justification of a farce is that it be funny. It is a comedy written with a slapstick rather than a pen. Its business is to make us accept the impossible as possible, the deranged as normal, and silliness as a happy substitute for sense."[27]

Perhaps it would be wise to close this chapter with a disclaimer. My purpose in this study is in no sense normative. It would be an act of presumption even to wish to bring about a greater uniformity in the usage of *farce* than we have. Attempts at a scientific taxonomy in literature have always been as ill-fated as they have been visionary. I do wish, however, to make my own objective clear. No real harm is done to the reputation of a play or its author by the loose classification which too often marks histories of the theatre. But such looseness frequently confuses an issue which may not be really so very complex. To take a familiar example, the practice so often followed of lumping together *Pasquin* and *The Intriguing Chambermaid* as farces by Henry Fielding obliterates a distinction between the plays that the most superficial glance at their impact on theatrical history will disclose. The effect of a dozen *Intriguing Chambermaids* on the fortunes of the theatre could have been no more than a possible increase in receipts; the effect of one *Pasquin,* or a comparatively few plays of the type, was to bring about the Licensing Act with its far-reaching effects on the English theatre.

[27] *The Saturday Review of Literature,* 24 March 1951, p. 26.

CHAPTER 2

STRUCTURE AND DEVICES

+++

Let those that play your clowns speak no more than is set down
for them.—HAMLET

+++

IF THE ESSENCE of farce is its dependence upon mere laughter, as opposed to comedy and its treatment of moral problems, that dependence will be seen to have a profound effect upon the structure of farce. Laughter is by its very nature transient, even fitful. The hearty, unreflective variety is especially dependent upon surprise and cannot therefore be long sustained. Correspondingly, the kind of drama which has as its chief aim the eliciting of this sort of laughter must itself be fitful, full of shifts and surprises, in terms of structure, episodic. To use the Italian term made popular in the seventeenth century, farce is chiefly a matter of *lazzi*.[1]

As good an example as any may be found in the collection of commonwealth drolls known as *The Wits*. The very slight plot of *Simpleton the Smith* runs somewhat in this fashion: Old Simpleton prevails upon his loutish son to marry a wealthy but shrewish neighbor, called simply "Doll a Wench" in the list of characters. Young Simpleton would much prefer being left to his victuals instead of going courting. He submits, however, and we soon find him singing

[1] Gherardi, in the preface to his *Théâtre italien*, undertakes to define *lazzi* but with results more amusing than helpful. After suggesting that the term is equivalent to *tour* or *jeu italien* he illustrates: "Après avoir repeté deux ou trois fois le même lazzi, c'est-à-dire, après avoir fait deux ou trois fois le même jeu italien." For a more adequate definition see Nicoll, *Masks, Mimes, and Miracles* (London, 1931), pp. 219-221. What it all boils down to is "pieces of stage business," though verbal *lazzi* are suggested by analogy.

and fiddling under Doll's window. After being frightened by a pair of rivals passing in the darkness he gets Doll's attention—and a full *pot de chambre* on his head. Despite this inauspicious beginning the next episode finds him already married and in grave danger of being made a cuckold. The pair of rivals come in Simpleton's absence to court Doll but are interrupted by the unexpected return of Simpleton, who is looking for a pair of bellows. Doll hides the callers behind her skirts and sends her husband off with a promise that she will procure some bellows for him. However, Simpleton again returns, this time so suddenly there is no opportunity for concealment. So Doll quickly orders her lovers to "play bellows" and then blandly turns to Simpleton saying she has already acquired what she had promised. Just how the suitors complied with her order is not told. The scanty stage directions leave much to the actors' creative talent, and to the reader's imagination; obviously the most ridiculous kind of horse play was called for. Nor is it quite clear just how the play closes; since the disillusioned husband calls in old Simpleton we may assume that it ends in a scuffle and beating.

Obviously this brief piece is not a carefully constructed play with protasis, epitasis, catastrophe—all of the machinery reputedly to be found in the well-made play of classical mold. It consists rather of two quite distinct episodes linked only by having certain characters in common. The second episode does nothing in the way of developing character or theme. Either episode could exist without the other. Other episodes could be added without destroying any unity for there is none, except the unity of purpose.

I have chosen *Simpleton* not only because it is so typical of the structure of farce at an elementary level but because it represents something atypical also. For the period in which it appeared, though falling chronologically in the direct center of the development of the English theatre, is actually a period outside the stream of tradition. Legally at any rate there was no English theatre; the tradition had been suspended by decree. *Simpleton* is not a canonical play but a droll, a crude production of some surreptitious company performing outside the law. Under such circumstances it was impossible to develop or maintain the standard repertory of five-act plays. What the droll troupe needed instead was a few short pieces, requiring few actors, the most elementary properties and costumes. At a moment's notice of the approach of the Round-Head constabulary they must be able to suspend activities and steal off with their scanty belongings. One of the ironies of theatrical history is that it is chiefly because they did not always get away that we know so much detail about these companies.[2]

I call attention to these commonplaces of theatrical history simply to emphasize that while the droll just analyzed does provide an illustration of farce untrammeled by any higher purpose than provoking hearty laughter it cannot serve to illustrate the development of the structure of English farce under more normal conditions in the theatre. From the middle of the sixteenth century, with such plays as *Ralph Roister Doister* and *Gammer Gurton's Needle*, there had been no place in the repertory for the short play. Moreover, there was another tradition—often scarcely observed—that a comedy must have some unifying structure of intrigue or character revelation. Farce, if it was to find a place at all, could hardly have been developed in the fashion I have suggested, from the simple ludicrous episode many times compounded. Instead it was obliged to serve as episodic relief, as comic filler—in short, as *farce* in its original sense of stuffing.

Up to the time of the Restoration there had been only one opportunity, during the interregnum of 1642-1660, for farce to stand alone. With the Restoration and a return to

[2] For details on theatrical activities during the interregnum see the works of Elson, Hotson, Baskervill, and Rollins listed in the bibliography.

the standard repertory, farce was reduced once more to an ancillary status. In time, as the next chapter will show, it again attained something like the independence of the short droll, but for several decades the farceur was obliged to be content with a minor share of the stage. Whatever the terms under which it operated, however, the structural pattern of farce was much the same, and it is with this basic pattern that I am at present concerned.

Before plunging into an analysis of the pattern of farce in the full-length play after 1660 I wish to call attention to two quite opposite aspects of farce writing and acting in the whole period covered here. On the one hand, the restrictions imposed upon the farceur of this age, as compared with the freedom of a more tolerant day, are striking. Whether tied to the full-length play, often with a serious main plot, or allowed the greater freedom of the short, often almost wholly farcical play of a later day, he was still obliged to keep some semblance of the traditional intrigue, usually one involving marriage. Note, for example, that even the slight farce of *Simpleton* treats both sides of this major event in man's life. On the other hand, it is equally interesting to observe how the farce writer or player managed to introduce so many of the devices which had been developed in the trial and error of theatrical performance and handed down through generation after generation.

Clearly enough, the structure of farce is readily divisible into two phases or levels: the framework and the details or, an even better figure, the thread and the separate beads. Of the two the former has little interest for us. Almost any form of intrigue or chain of incidents will serve to link the *lazzi* which are the real stuff of farce. In turning, then, to the actual farces of the Restoration period I shall pass over *The Duke and No Duke* (1684), which uses intrigue supplemented by magic, and over *The London Cuckolds* (1681), which is little more than a five-act concatenation of largely discrete episodes, to take a play somewhat less conventional but decidedly more useful in showing the essential relationship of the thread to the episodes strung on it and in establishing more clearly the parallelism between the structure of the farce of an earlier age with that of our own times.

Something less complex and distracting than romance or jealousy would serve better to link farce episodes. The ideal thread is, I suppose, the chase, so fully exploited in more recent times. The chase has the advantage of providing suspense without at the same time distracting our attention too much from the discrete episodes. At the same time it allows the dramatist to maintain a pace too fast for the leisurely examination which the wildest flights of fancy do not readily survive. The suspense-packed movies of Mr. Hitchcock, to cite a parallel case, have exploited the advantages of fast pacing to forestall a too close scrutiny of motivation. Professor Greig has even suggested a similar benefit from the same device on a somewhat higher literary plane: our acceptance of evil in a Falstaff or a Gargantua, he believes, is earned so easily simply because the vigorousness or the furious pace does not permit us to examine the darker side of our ambivalent attitude too closely.[3]

Most important of all, the chase provides motivation for introducing the many devices so basic to farce: concealment, with all the possibilities of disguise and posture; repetition, which may be exploited to whatever limits the cir-

---

[3] *The Psychology of Laughter and Comedy* (London, 1923), pp. 147-149. It is interesting to see an eighteenth-century commentator make much the same point. The author of *The Actor* (1750) points out the necessity of overplaying certain parts: "The judicious player will always swell out his voice, and be very free with his gestures in the principal parts of the characters of the first and second sort that we have mention'd, because they are in themselves heightenings upon nature; and he will do the same in those of the third kind [i.e. characters not based on real life], because it is his business to amuse and confound the spectators with noise, that they may not be at liberty to examine whether the author has not now and then exceeded the bounds of probability." pp. 243-244.

cumstances warrant; perhaps most significant, violent physical action, tumbling, beating, noise.

Though no exhaustive use was made of the chase in Restoration farce, it was used, particularly in the plays of Durfey and Mrs. Behn. Such a play as *Rover*, Part II (1680) of the latter playwright makes considerable use of pursuit and evasion. The possibilities on the Restoration stage are limited, however, both by the weight of the tradition virtually to require the use of the love or marriage theme and by the physical limitations of the stage itself.

It seems reasonable to suppose, incidentally, that one very great advantage the pantomime had over the older dialogue-farce was the greater possibility of employing this very device of the chase. The pantomime was a machine play and therefore more resourceful in the use of complex structures on the stage (windmills, castles, and the like), pseudo-magic transformations to add to the possibilities of disguise and concealment, even flight in the literal sense of the term. With all these aids pantomime was more than a match for farce. An interesting parallel is to be found in our century. The early Keystone-style movie, which exploited the chase to the fullest, has now been virtually replaced by the animated cartoon. The basic reason, I submit, is not that the Keystone chase had grown stale from overuse or that producers found it cheaper to mass-produce drawings but that the earlier movie, itself so much more resourceful than the stage, could not compete with a medium in which even the law of gravity is suspended, in which miraculous changes call for only a limited imagination and an inexhaustible supply of graphite.

As an example of a full-length play with a generous mixture of farce we may choose Lacy's *Old Troop, or Monsieur Raggou* (1665). Here is a play in which the controlling interest would appear to be in the extremely coarse and realistic scenes taken from the recent civil wars.[4] The farcical

---

[4] According to Lacy's modern editors, Maidment and Logan, the

elements are, however, of no less significance. It is reasonable to suppose that they were more responsible than the more serious topical material for keeping the play in the repertory a half century or more.[5] An examination of the other contributions made by Lacy would also suggest that the actor-playwright was chiefly interested in the slapstick involving Raggou—especially if, as has been plausibly suggested, Lacy himself played the part of the French cook.

Many of the scenes in *Old Troop* are devoted to Raggou's clever evasions as he is pursued on two accounts: one on a charge of plundering in the field, a crime of which the whole company is guilty but for which Raggou is to receive the blame; the other on a paternity charge when he is framed by his lieutenant after a *femme de guerre* appropriately named Doll Troop has preferred charges against the whole company. To follow Raggou as he employs a variety of evasive tactics is to be treated to an object lesson in the devices of farce.

The farcical action—which begins fairly late since most of the earlier scenes are devoted to the genre scenes of life in the field—starts with a fight, no doubt a ridiculous one, between Ferret-Farm and Raggou over the paternity charge. We then quickly shift to the other problem and see the French cook busy at his plundering. He wears a grotesque costume the chief features of which are its huge sleeves, one designed for horse feed and the other reserved for his own

---

actor-author had ample opportunity to become acquainted with the skirmishes he describes, since he had been "lieutenant and quartermaster under Colonel Lord Gerard, afterwards the Earl of Macclesfield." *The Dramatic Works of John Lacy, Comedian* (Edinburgh, 1875), p. xi.—Their acceptance of Langbaine's apparently precise date for Lacy's death in the introduction to this edition suggests that they had overcome their earlier confusion when, in their edition of the works of John Wilson, published two years earlier, they inform us at one point that Lacy died in 1667 and a little later quote without comment Davies' statement that Lacy died in 1684.

[5] Advertisements for performances at Drury Lane in July 1714 ran in the *Daily Courant*.

needs. We are reminded of Harpo's remarkable trenchcoat, which miraculously hides enough plunder to provision a whole theatrical company in the most recent Marx Brothers extravaganza.

In the closing scene of Act II Raggou imposes upon his helpless landlady. Having put her on the defensive by accusing her of delivering the pistol he left with her over to the enemy—he has actually stolen it from her himself—he makes her give up her last possession, a large cheese. He then sells her the cheese for a shilling, repossesses it, offers to sell it back again, and, when she refuses to be further imposed upon, sells it to a neighbor. By this time the problem of ownership has become so involved that the scene comes to a climax in a fight between landlady and neighbor and Raggou steals off to engage in more trickery.

Another variant of this familiar repetition motif occurs in the opening scene of the next act. Flea-Flint, a match for Raggou in rascally intentions but a decided inferior in carrying them out, has hit upon the notion of plundering to his own advantage but at Raggou's cost by dressing in a similar garb and talking in the broken English which is Raggou's trademark. Meanwhile, however, the same idea occurs to the French cook, who now appears dressed as Flea-Flint. Before this trick has been exhausted of all its possibilities, the other members of the company attempt to rid themselves of Raggou by still another fraudulent charge. They first place a treasonable letter in his pocket and then pretend to discover it. Raggou takes to his heels and the chase is on in earnest. His first pause, and the next opportunity for elaborate farce business, finds him acting as impresario in a puppet-show which he has purchased from a wandering Frenchman. When this ruse seems no longer effective, he sells his show to Flea-Flint, who is almost immediately detected and captured.

Still in flight as the last act begins, Raggou brings his farcical tricks to a climax in a contest of wits with his pursuers. In the dim light of early morning he comes upon some workmen about to set up and paint two new posts or statues. The painter adjourns to a nearby alehouse while he waits for the joiner to set up the second post. Hearing the watch in full cry at his heels Raggou adopts a ruse long familiar to farce players.

> RAGGOU *gets upon the post, and sits in the posture of the other post.*
>> *Enter* CONSTABLE *and* WATCH.

CON. Pox o' this outlandish French fellow for me!—I'm dry as a dog.

1 WATCH. So we are all; let's go and knock'em up at an alehouse, and eat and drink a little.

2 WATCH. With all our hearts.

>> *Enter* PAINTER.

Honest painter, canst tell where we may have a little ale?

PAINT. Ay, sure; two or three doors off you'll find 'em up, and a good fire, where you may toast your noses, boys.

CON. Thou didst not see an outlandish Frenchman this way?

PAINT. No, I saw no Frenchman.

>> *Exeunt* CONSTABLE *and* WATCH.

Why, what a devil!—this joiner has been here, and set up his post before I came. How time slips away at an alehouse!

RAG. Begar, would a good rope would slip away you too!

PAINT. Now to work.   *Whistles and paints him.*

RAG. He vill paint a me; vat sall me do?

> *As he stoops,* RAGGOU *throws a stone at him.*

PAINT. A pox o' these roguing prentices! Sirrah, I'll have you by the ears! A company of rogues; a man cannot work for you! If you serve me such another trick, I'll break all your windows.

Rag. De pox break all your neck!

Throws the pipkin at him as he stoops.

Paint. Why, you damn'd rogue, you have broke my head. 'Sheart, I'll complain to your master. Spoil'd all my colours, too! I'll not endure it; I'll be reveng'd, whatsoe'er it cost me. *Exit.*

Rag. A pox dis rogue!—he murder mine face wid his dam paint. Now de coast be clear, me vill take a de coat of Monsieur Jack Painter and go; for begar, dere be no stay in dis town for moy.

Enter Joiner *with his post.*

Hark! dere be something; me must be de post agen. A pox on dat!

He stands up for a post again.

Join. Why, how now?—what a devil! another post, and none of my work? 'Sheart, do you employ two men at once? I'll not be used thus; I'll be paid for my work, and then let the devil set up your posts. *Exit.*

With the coast finally clear Raggou seizes the joiner's tools and anything else he can lift and absconds. The scene ends with the painter and the joiner returning with their employer, only to find the offending post and their belongings gone.

Also early in this last act, within a matter of minutes after the last scene, we see Raggou in his final disguise "like an old woman." To make the pose more deceptive he has resorted to make-up. In one of those rare passages in this period telling us something about the use of devices to change an actor's appearance we find this interesting exchange:

Dol. . . . Who do you think that old woman is?

Capt. I know not.

Dol. 'Tis Raggou himself. Pray, fright him a little before you seal his pardon.

Capt. What a devil has he done to his face?

DOL. I know not. I believe he has clapt wax upon't.

In short, the game is up and in spite of clever ruse and frantic attempt, poor Raggou must earn his pardon by marrying Dol Troop.

The last act of *The Old Troop* contains two farcical scenes not involving Raggou and his evasive tactics but interesting in themselves in what they reveal of another range of farce devices: extravagant stage properties. The first involves a bear, enroute to Bristol Fair. The sole object of this scene is the amusement to be had from frightening an absurd hypocrite and Puritan, Captain Tubtext. The other is a ludicrous tourney between two men on hobbyhorses, "Queen Elizabeth's tilters, going to Bristol Fair." The hobbyhorse was evidently a familiar figure among the *commedia dell'arte* players of the day, but the context here suggests clearly enough a folk origin.[6] Both these last scenes approach the crude fun of the folk play or even children's games.

In the interest of brevity I shall allow the two plays already described at length to stand as examples of the structure of farce (structure in the first sense of the means of introducing the episodes, the real stuff of farce) in both short and long plays. Analysis of other pieces in the very full list of plays with farce in the century following the Restoration would reveal a great many variants in devices but no really significant new methods of introducing them.[7] It seems more profitable to turn directly to the briefer episodes, the *burle* or *lazzi* themselves.

Though the possibilities in the way of actual devices are

---

[6] There are references to hobby-horses in two epilogues written for revivals of Jonson's *Silent Woman* and *Everyman in His Humour*. The former, by Dryden, is clearly aimed at Fiorilli's troupe and their visit in the spring and summer of 1673; the latter, by Sackville, is more obscure, both in allusion and date, but may very well aim at the same event.

[7] Other examples of the way farcical *lazzi* could be strung together may be found in Chapter 8.

almost infinite, they can be reduced to at least a rough system. Among those motifs already outlined and illustrated I have mentioned repetition, disguise, and physical violence. To this division—the lack of logical neatness disqualifies any more pretentious term—may be added a motif peculiarly attractive to English audiences: the exaggerated or overdrawn character.

Perhaps it is necessary to justify the claim of farce here. After all, character is the basis of true comedy. Yet, if there is anything to the far from uncommon tendency to look upon farce as comedy gone to seed, there is sufficient justification for looking upon a certain type of exaggerated characterization as belonging in the less exalted province of farce. To illustrate we may take some of the characterizations of Ben Jonson or, even better, the followers of Jonson. When, as in the case of Shadwell's virtuoso, the satirical edge has been dulled by repetition and exaggeration, we are already drawing very near the line separating comedy and farce. And when, going still farther, we come to similar repetition in Durfey's imitation of Shadwell's imitation we have passed over the line.[8] Sganarelle or Jodelet, to range farther afield for illustration, may represent jealousy or avarice or boastfulness, but he also represents—Sganarelle or Jodelet, farceur.

Turning now to an elaboration of the motifs or devices listed, I find that the first, repetition, requires only a comparatively brief discussion and illustration. Examples of the device may be seen in the episodes from *Old Troop*. The cheese is confiscated, sold, reconfiscated, resold. Flea-Flint disguises as Raggou and, much to everyone's confusion, we have two Raggous, or would have if Raggou had not disguised as Flea-Flint so that the latter is multiplied. Finally,

---

[8] Sir Arthur Oldlove in Durfey's *Madam Fickle* (1676) is a crack-brained antiquary who dresses in Gustavus Adolphus's doublet and Pompey's breeches and who revels in a collection of such oddities as Sir Gawain's skull, Launcelot's sword, and a vial containing St. Jerome's tears.

with one more common variation of the device, Raggou buys the puppet show and manages to keep his own identity concealed; Flea-Flint buys it from him, expecting to be equally successful, but in his case the outcome is quite different.

At its most elementary level and under conditions where at least some improvisation is possible the device consists of the mere repetition of a gesture, a movement, an episode which has earned a laugh. By some principle which may roughly approximate a law of human reaction the response grows in intensity with each successive repetition. Since the result can only be gauged approximately, however, the number of times that a repetition will be greeted with the desired response must be left to the farceur's skill and judgment. Here as perhaps nowhere else we see the necessity of taking the living audience into account, for no playwright could possibly estimate ahead of time the range of possibilities.[9] Here we come face to face with the problem of improvisation, a subject which I shall take up more fully later on in this chapter.

Repetition is seen in still another form when characters are multiplied, usually by disguise, on more than one occasion by the use of identical twins. Of the numerous examples of this form of repetition perhaps the most familiar is in *The Comedy of Errors,* where Shakespeare elaborates upon Plautus by having not one but two pairs of twins and where most of the action depends upon the hilarious mis-

[9] In modern times the detailed accounts of the careers of our own great clowns show clearly enough how a farce is revised in accordance with audience response. For example, Felix Isman, in his biography of Weber and Fields, tells how a script would be revised after a Broadway tryout: "Julian Mitchell, Weber and Fields would wait for the opening night returns, tabulate the laughs, then prune the waste material accordingly. A week later the show would be fit and down to weight." *Weber and Fields* (New York, 1951), p. 123.—It has been plausibly suggested that an insuperable difficulty the clown faces in producing movies is his being deprived of a sounding board in the form of a live audience.

takes arising from their being so hopelessly confused. In the century covered here the farcical use of identical twins occurs more than once. Manning has twins in his *Generous Choice* (1700). In the last comedy he ever wrote, John Dryden, doubtless taking advantage of the tremendous following of Nokes and Leigh, then at the height of their careers, wrote his own *Amphitryon* (1690) around them.

Or, to take a more recent case involving identical appearance growing out of disguise, we see an inspired use of the repetition motif in the mirror sequence in *Duck Soup* when Groucho, pursuing his two zany brothers dressed at the moment exactly like him, comes upon one of them in an open doorway—after having been rendered cautious by plunging at his own image in a full-length mirror. The episode is played for all it is worth, coming to its final climax when one of those little variations which somehow add to a sequence of repetitions occurs: when Groucho has finally become almost fully satisfied that his foil is his image, the image is discovered to be carrying a bowler instead of the boater Groucho wears, and the chase is on again![10]

The last item, the introduction of a variant into the sequence of repetitions, suggests one other form the device often takes: the repetition with amusing variations, found, for example, in what Bergson calls the snow-ball device. A familiar variant of the type occurs in numerous comedies and farces when master beats valet, valet beats servant: two instances which readily come to mind appear in *The Conscious Lovers* and *The Rivals*.

One example will serve to show a more elaborate and sustained variant of the same general type. When Ravenscroft came to the last comic piece in his career, *The Anat-*

[10] I depend for this description upon my memory of a scene witnessed several years ago and therefore cannot guarantee the accuracy of every detail. Theodore Huff describes a scene from Chaplin's *Floorwalker* which he labels "ancestor" of the one from *Duck Soup*. He may well be right; I have never seen the Chaplin picture.

omist (1696), he took his plot from Hauteroche's *Crispin médecin,* but he improved on what he borrowed. In the second act he made full use of the scene in which poor Crispin, unable to find a better place to hide from the doctor, stretches out on the table, pretending to be the cadaver which the doctor has ordered. In this awkward position he is forced to listen to a learned discussion of all the incisions the doctor plans to make and is saved from the fate he expects momentarily only by the cleverness of the maidservant Beatrice. Ravenscroft, long trained in the production of lively farce, then proceeded to improve on his French source by repeating the scene with variations. In the next act a superannuated lover, Old Gerald, is caught in the same predicament and, at Beatrice's suggestion, adopts the same plan of concealment when the doctor enters. This time, however, the doctor is Crispin himself, disguised as the doctor and accompanied by his servant— actually his master, who has exchanged clothes with Crispin, thus introducing still another and thoroughly familiar form of the repetition with variation motive.[11] Now it is Crispin's turn to frighten the poor cadaver with a somewhat inaccurate but no less hilarious discourse on anatomy and surgery, all the while wielding an assortment of frightful looking knives and cleavers. This time Ravenscroft builds the scene up to a much higher pitch: Crispin makes his first incision—on the victim's waistcoat—and the cadaver bolts.[12]

What I have termed the disguise motif is so varied and complex that it proves difficult to fit under so specific a heading. It may range from the mere attempt to evade de-

[11] Documentation of this venerable device is almost supererogatory. To show its lineage I need only cite two illustrious examples: Aristophanes' *Frogs,* Shakespeare's *Taming of the Shrew.*

[12] Miss Lea describes a closely similar scene from Lachi's *Inimicizia tra i due vecchi con il finto Indovino* which may have been Hauteroche's model or may have come from a common source. *Italian Popular Comedy* (Oxford, 1934), p. 190.

tection by assuming another—or another's—appearance (a ruse as common in the romantic play as in farce), through a middle state where disguise is equally useful in forwarding intrigue and in getting laughs—*Charley's Aunt* is perhaps the classic modern example—to a point at which all pretense of verisimilitude is abandoned and the clown poses as a tree or a statue or other non-human object.

It is possible even to look upon the occasional transformation, whether real or mock, as a form of disguise. In those cases where magic enters and the transformation is assumed to be real, as in *The Devil to Pay* or *A Duke and No Duke*, there is actually no great amount of farce inherent in the transformation itself though other elements of farce in the play are greatly aided by its use. On the other hand, when the transformation is wholly in mockery and only the dupe assumes that his appearance has changed, as in *Albumazar* and its various adaptations or in the two *Cobler of Preston* plays based on Shakespeare's *Taming of the Shrew*, we have the very essence of farce.

Disguises of the first type, designed chiefly to aid the plot, are so numerous in the period and the farcical use made of them of such minor significance, that illustration would be superfluous. The second or middle stage, where the objective is both intrigue and laughter, requires some attention. One of the most common uses is suggested by the mention of *Charley's Aunt*. Several of the most popular clowns of the day resorted to the age-old trick of disguising as women. Perhaps the greatest farceur in the whole period made such frequent and successful use of female impersonation that he became known toward the end of his career as "Nurse" Nokes. Theatrical records show that Nokes played this type of role in at least five different plays, beginning with Payne's *Fatal Jealousie* (1672). By 1679 there was such demand for his services in similar roles that he may very well have appeared in female disguise in two different new plays within a month. One may wonder a little at the propriety of introducing a Lady Beardly into Durfey's *Virtuous Wife*; even more surprising is the comedian's appearance as the nurse in Otway's *Caius Marius*, from no less a play than *Romeo and Juliet*. Otway was evidently scornful of the playgoers who demanded such violations of taste, for he addresses them in his epilogue:

> And now for you who here come wrapt in cloaks,
> Only for love of Underhill and Nurse Noakes.

Nokes's fellow comedian Leigh also played the part of a silly old woman, Lady Addleplot in Durfey's *Love for Money* (1689), but he seems not to have made appearance in feminine attire so much a specialty.

It may be objected that the roles I have mentioned are not in the strictest sense of the word disguises but impersonations.[13] The distinction is, in this context, so slight as to be little more than academic. There are, in any event, adequate examples where true disguise is employed for nothing more than ludicrous purposes. Tony Leigh's disguising in his wife's night-clothes in *The London Cuckolds* only to be sent out to be beaten in the darkened garden is a case in point. And even more farcical use of this old device is to be found in the anonymous *She Ventures, and He Wins* (1695) in which several disguised characters appear. Two are wholly romantic "breeches" parts: Charlot and Juliana while they dress in men's attire have only the urge of romance as their motive. Squire Wouldbe, on the other hand, is a wholly ludicrous figure. When Wouldbe, played by Doggett, assumes feminine garb, it is at the suggestion of the young woman he is so vainly courting and it is only to begin a sequence of the wildest slapstick. Poor Wouldbe is frightened out of his few wits, ducked in a

---

[13] Lanson clearly suggests that the filling of female roles by comedians is an indication of farcical intent, as may be seen by his references to Hubert's playing Philaminte and Madame Jourdain. "Molière et la farce," *Revue de Paris*, III (May-June 1901), 131.

cistern, rolled in a tub of feathers, and finally, stripped of his ridiculous garments, dropped through a trapdoor and carted home in fear and ignominy by devils.

The comedians of the eighteenth century did not neglect the possibilities of getting laughs by adopting feminine attire. I may mention Pinkethman, whom Cibber considered a successor to Leigh, and his ridiculous disguise in *Love in a Chest* (1710); or his rivals in the Lincoln's Inn Fields troupe: Spiller, who played in feminine disguise in *The Perplexed Couple* (1715), and Griffin, who in the same year acted "Mother" Griffin in *Woman's Revenge*. Somewhat later, in 1733, Harper played Lady Termagant in *The Boarding School*, Coffey's farce drawn from Durfey's play mentioned above. Some idea of the farcical extravagance of this role may be gathered from *The Auditor's* report of a performance which proved more than Tom Cynick, the Auditor's highly critical companion, could bear.[14]

The farce player is not restricted in his use of disguise to a mere adoption of the clothing of another, even one of the opposite sex. In its more imaginative stages farce proves eminently unrestricted. At one time the clown may be a corpse, at another a devil, at still another an ape or a bear. In his highest flights into the ridiculously impossible he becomes a post or a tree or, discarding one dimension, a figure in a painting or tapestry.

In each of the two farcical pieces discussed at some length above we have at least one such wholly fantastic disguise or impersonation. In *Simpleton*, it will be recalled,

[14] *The Auditor*, No. 9 (February 1733). Among the group preceding Harper the elder Bullock should also be listed. We know that he played the bawd Mandrake in Farquhar's *Twin Rivals* (1702), though we can hardly call this a farcical role. From a somewhat later allusion we gather that he played a similar role in a far greater play. In Mrs. Davy's *Northern Heiress* (1716) Gamont, in trying to suggest to Welby the coarseness of the Yorkshire ladies, remarks: "It's impossible you should have any notion of 'em; for you never saw any thing like 'em, unless it were old Bullock, when he acts the Orange-Wench in *Sir Fopling Flutter*."

Doll has one of her admirers "play bellows" to avoid detection. In *The Old Troop* Raggou plays a figure on a post. In the brief droll the stage directions are too inadequate to give any detailed notion of how the trick was performed, but in the scene quoted from *The Old Troop* we have a clear picture of a sequence which a resourceful clown might use for several minutes of hilarious farce.

I have reverted to these two scenes for still another purpose than that of merely illustrating the fanciful or fantastic disguise. These two plays are wholly indigenous products of the English theatre and can therefore not plausibly be assigned to the influence of the Italians. As M. Lanson has just remarked, "La farce est un genre de drame ayant, bien que ces mots paraissent ambitieux, son esthétique, sa méthode d'invention." In applying this generalization to the particular item under discussion I maintain that the use of fantastic disguise is inherent in the very nature of farce, that without any influence from abroad the English would have employed much the same devices.[15]

One more example where a close parallel can be seen

[15] Merely to hint at the universality and the persistence of such a device I cite two widely separated examples. Professor Manly, in his full and scholarly notes in a modern edition of an old play, *The Merry Devil of Edmonton* (c. 1600), provides some plausible evidence that the play, which survives in only a very corrupt text, once contained a clever farcical scene of pursuit and escape. When Smug, the drunken smith, finds his pursuers closing in on him he scrambles up and sits motionless astride the sign of the inn, which happens to be the White Horse. His pursuers, seeing the mounted figure, decide they have mistaken the George across the street for the White Horse, dash across to the actual George, and, thoroughly puzzled by the two Georges, agree they have got even the villages of Edmonton and Enfield confused. When last seen they are on their way to Enfield looking for Edmonton. C. M. Gayley, *Representative English Comedies*, II (New York, 1913).—Far removed in time but wholly cognate in pattern are two scenes from Chaplin pictures cited by Huff. In *Shoulder Arms* Charlie develops a hilarious sequence from his disguising as a tree; in *The Circus* he makes similar but less extended use of the old device by posing as a figure in Noah's Ark.

but where there is clearly no influence in either direction is what may be termed the cradle *lazzo*. In that early English farce-comedy *The Second Shepherd's Play* a cradle is used to conceal the sheep which Mak has stolen, and the searchers are willing for a while at least to accept the sheep as a child. An even wilder scene of slapstick employing a cradle occurs in the Commonwealth droll *John Swabber*. The oafish husband after whom the droll is named almost catches his wife Parnel in the arms of her lover Cutbeard. Parnel has just enough warning to stuff the barber into the cradle where Swabber finds him. Obtuse as he is, even Swabber cannot avoid being suspicious of a year-old child with a beard, but Parnel quiets his suspicions with an old wives' tale of babies with beards and the credulous husband is content. He even begins to feed the marvelous infant, ladling food into the cradle from a "great Bowl of Batter" which Parnel had "mingled . . . but just now for pancakes." Farce as crude as this is, of course, largely confined to drolls. So far as I have been able to discover there is nothing quite of the same pattern until we get into the eighteenth-century fairs and provincial theatres of the lowest order. This same cradle scene occurs, for example, in the "opera" *Robin Hood* performed at Lee's and Harper's Booth at Bartholomew Fair in August 1730.

After everything has been said in favor of native motifs, however, there remains a considerable residue of influence deriving from the Italians. The highly stylized farce of the *commedia dell'arte* made very free use of the device of simulating inanimate or non-human figures, and some of the uses in English plays bear unmistakable signs of having been borrowed from this improvised comedy. In some cases the borrowing is quite direct. Mrs. Behn's *Emperor of the Moon* (1687), for example, is taken directly from a scenario by Fatouville published in 1684 and includes the several masked characters of the Italian-French play. Not only does Harlequin disguise at various times as an ambassador from the moon, a baker with his cart, an apothecary with his portable shop, or a woman with child, but he also appears at one point in the play as a figure in a tapestry, joining with the other characters in a *tableau vivant*. In other Italianate borrowings more or less direct, we get Pasquariel dressed as a monkey in Motteux's *Novelty* (1697), a live statue in *The Walking Statue* (1710), and the mummy and the crocodile of *Three Hours After Marriage* (1717). In time, however, most of the direct borrowing from the Italians was to occur in the pantomime and the native writers of farce learned to take what lay nearer at hand.

A few more examples will suffice to show how common the use of fantastic disguise, from whatever source, was in the period. The trick of having actors pose as statues or lay figures is employed in the tragi-comic *Wits Led by the Nose* (1677). Here two silly knights evade the pursuing watch by posing as statues in armor; the watch stop for rest, lean their staves against the supposed statues, and even throw wine on them.

A rather more ingenious use occurs in *The Fortune Hunters* (1689). Spruce, a gullible but jealous cuckold, returning home drunk at night almost surprises his wife in the arms of her gallant, Frank. The latter, taking advantage of the darkness and the cit's condition, hides beside the pump and, when Spruce drunkenly mistakes rival for pump and works Frank's arm up and down, the younger man "spirts" orange water in the cuckold's face and thus escapes detection.

One final illustration may be considered less fantastic but nonetheless interesting as it indicates also how closely farce may approach the play of children. Again trying to avoid his pursuers, the clown plays bench and is actually sat upon. In Mrs. Behn's *Roundheads* (1681) the trick fails and the young man is discovered, but in a later and far more farcical piece, *The Adventures of Half an Hour* (1716), the scene is played to the limit. Closely pursued by several bullies, Tagg and Aminadab kneel with heads against the wall in the darkened street and in this position suffer numerous indignities. After being stepped on and stumbled over they are obliged to bear the weight of Tagg's wife and her lover, who leisurely sit and plot an assignation until Tagg's groans frighten them away.

Since the ostensible object of disguise is almost always to prevent detection, this device suggests a related one: the liberal use in any age of certain traditional places of concealment. Continental drama seems to have favored the sack. Tabarin is reputed to have used the sack, and Molière used it, not only in the well-known *Fourberies de Scapin* but presumably also in one of the lost farces, *Gorgibus dans le sac.* Boileau may be credited with raising the sack to the level of a symbol, for everyone quotes the couplet in which he expresses his disapproval of the great comic dramatist for employing his talent to such base ends:

> Dans ce sac ridicule où Scapin s'enveloppe,
> Je ne reconnais pas l'auteur du Misanthrope.

The English used the sack too in their farces, chiefly in direct borrowings from *Scapin* but at least twice in plays which show little evidence of foreign borrowing: *Love in a Sack* (1715), a thoroughly farcical afterpiece, and *The Generous Free-Mason . . . with the Humours of Squire Noodle, and His Man Doodle* (1730), a Bartholomew-Fair droll.

English farceurs relied chiefly, however, on more traditional properties as places of concealment: chests, hampers, wash-baskets, and barrels. So many examples of the use of all these occur that it is hardly necessary to offer specific illustration. Much the same thing may be said of the numerous uses of rugs, of wells and cisterns, or of chimneys for concealment. The last items add another element, one to which I shall return later: the clown who hides in the well or the chimney is usually submitted to an additional humiliation of being drenched or covered with soot, all of which is effective in increasing the laughter at his expense.[16]

One final word on concealment. No other device has been quite so fully and universally used for laughs as darkness. Here again, however, the Italians took the lead in exploiting its possibilities. It is not by chance therefore that several of the English plays in which darkness is most extensively used—the Harlequin-Scaramouch scenes in Mountfort's *Faustus* (c. 1688), the Harlequin scenes in Mrs. Behn's *Rover II* (1681) and *Emperor of the Moon* (1687), Motteux's *Novelty* (1697)—are direct borrowings from the Italian comedians. In other cases the source is French—Caryll's *Sir Salomon* (c. 1669), from Molière; Farquhar's *Stage Coach* (c. 1704), from La Chapelle—but the possibility of Italian influence is very great. Here again, however, there is no suggestion of monopoly. In various plays of Shadwell, Durfey, Mrs. Behn, and even later dramatists who are known to have borrowed from native sources or depended upon their own invention, the use of darkness for farcical purposes is far from uncommon. Yet the award must go, finally, to the Italians, for it was out of the "Italian night scene" that eighteenth-century English pantomime, especially in its more farcical scenes, developed. To that story I shall return later.

[16] I note with some interest that one of the two examples of Spanish farce I have any familiarity with—there seem to be few translations of these pieces and I unfortunately do not know the language—contains one of these traditional sequences. In *The Talkers* (*Los Dos Habladores*), attributed to Cervantes, Roldan tries to avoid arrest by rolling up in a rug. Doña Beatriz, a voluble talker herself but no match for Roldan, gets revenge by having her servants beat the rug until the poor talker is forced to disclose himself. This human phonograph is, incidentally, a perfect example of Bergson's theory of mechanical inelasticity. Just after Roldan has got into the rolled-up rug, the constable enters and, not finding his man, goes off to another room briefly. Doña Beatriz takes advantage of the unaccustomed silence to begin complaining of the visitor's talking. At the very mention of talking, Roldan pops his head out of the rug and launches into another monologue! The translation appears in *The Colonnade*, xii (July-December 1916), 5-19.

So far I have made no attempt to discuss clothing except insofar as it is related to disguise. The fact is that in many cases the clown's garb may be looked upon as being more in the nature of stage property than as a means of disguise. For centuries the farce actor has placed heavy dependence for laughs upon his manner of dressing a part. In his urbane essay on the use—or rather the abuse—of certain venerable devices which repeatedly appear in tragedy, Addison speaks condescendingly of "the innumerable shifts that small wits put in practice to raise a laugh. Bullock in a short coat and Norris in a long one, seldom fail of this effect. In ordinary comedies, a broad and a narrow brimmed hat are different characters. Sometimes the wit of the scene lies in a shoulder-belt, and sometimes in a pair of whiskers. A lover running about the stage, with his head peeping out of a barrel, was thought a very good jest in King Charles the Second's time; and invented by one of the first wits of the age."[17]

Unfortunately we do not have the quantity of detailed information we should like on this subject of the comedian's dress. Aside from the brief hints of Addison concerning the way the elder Bullock and Dicky Norris were dressed— even here it would be helpful to know whether Addison refers to a specific performance or a general practice—we have few and scattered accounts of the manner of dressing a part. Wilkes gives us the details of Doggett's costume for Moneytrap in Vanbrugh's *Confederacy*, but it is clear enough in this case that the actor was more careful to emphasize character than merely to draw laughter.[18]

Some years earlier Downes, recounting his many experiences in the theatre, recalls the way Nokes dressed for Sir Arthur Addle in Caryll's *Sir Salomon*: "The French court wearing then excessive short lac'd coats: some scarlet, some blew, with broad wast belts; Mr. Nokes having at that time one shorter than the French fashion, to act Sir Arthur Addle

[17] *Spectator*, No. 44.
[18] A *General View of the Stage* (London, 1759), pp. 146-147.

in; the Duke of Monmouth gave Mr. Nokes his sword and belt from his side, and buckled it on himself, on purpose to ape the French: that Mr. Nokes lookt more like a drest up ape, than a Sir Arthur: which upon his first entrance on the stage, put the King and court to an excessive laughter; at which the French look'd very shaggrin, to see themselves ap'd by such a buffoon as Sir Arthur. . . .[19] Here once more we are dealing with a particular role and, moreover, are edging in the direction of burlesque; the laughter of Charles and his entourage is as much at the French as at the comedian.

Aside from such few scattered remarks as those just cited and an occasional hint in a stage direction we have little to suggest the specific practices of English farce players in the period. The hint from Addison may be sufficient reason for us to suppose that Norris, who was a very small man, made a practice of accentuating his own stature by wearing a long coat; but, if he did dress parts more or less uniformly, he is the exception to the rule. In striking contrast with Continental players,[20] the Italians especially, the English comedian did not adopt a uniform garb for all occasions. Harlequin and company did. What had been only a patched suit of the earliest Arlecchino had come on down to the late seventeenth century as a particolored garment hardly

[19] *Roscius Anglicanus* (ed. Summers, London [1937]), p. 29.

[20] That there was at least some use of fixed costume among the French players may be assumed from the descriptions and pictures we have of Gros Guillaume and the other players in the early Hotel de Bourgogne group. See Lancaster, *History*, Pt. I, vol. II, Chap. xi; Nicoll, *Masks, Mimes, and Miracles*, p. 249. We know also from the references in *Précieuses ridicules* to his paleness that Jodelet continued to play his roles *enfariné*. By the early eighteenth century, however, the practice of playing in fixed costume must have been confined to the Italians. Riccoboni is our witness: "At present [1738] no masqued actors appear on the French stage; they don't so much as wear false beards, except when it is absolutely necessary in playing the part of an old man; nor does any peculiar habit prevail in comedy, except that of Crispin, which is not very old. . . ." *Historical and Critical Account* (London, 1741), p. 142.

retaining a hint of its original form. In time it was to become the lozenge-patterned, tight-fitting costume which persists to this day. Scaramouche, Pierrot (heir to Pedrolino), Mezzetin—all had settled on a fixed costume.

The iconographic record has, incidentally, more than a little significance here. One of the reasons we know so little about the dress of the English comedian as compared to his Continental rival is that the record is so meager in the one case, so rich in the other. A primary reason for this comparative richness in the case of the Italians is this stability in costuming. The stylized grimaces and posture suggested by the repeated *lazzi*, added to a uniformity of costume even with a changing repertory, amounted to a constant posing which the artist could scarcely resist.[21]

In short, the Italian clown was a "mask," to use that equivocal term which was commonly employed in referring to comic roles and which may refer to the actual mask worn by the comedian or to the whole complex of personality and costume which made his identity clearly recognizable before he was half way out of the wings.[22]

The English were ready to accept the foreign "mask" in his mask. Cibber's story of Pinkethman's attempt to discard it in playing Harlequin in a revival of *The Emperor of the Moon* in 1702 indicates that they were insistent upon his keeping his face covered in these foreign importations.[23] With the adoption of the several Italian "masks" into the English pantomime, the masked face and the fixed character became traditional, but if the innovation made any appreciable impact upon English plays in the next few generations I have failed to discover it.

[21] Reproductions of some of the numerous sketches by Callot and others of the *commedia dell'arte* players in action are to be found in the volumes by Duchartre and Nicoll.

[22] Lanson, in his article on Molière and farce, struggles with the semantic difficulties of *masque*. See especially his notes on pp. 140 and 147.

[23] Cibber, *Apology*, I, 151-152.

In the very long run, to be sure, there was to be a change. Some of our own great farceurs have adopted costumes as fixed as those of Biancolelli and Fiorilli. Elie Faure speaks "of Chaplin's cane and hat, of his boots and tatters, as unchangeable as the mask and cothurnus of the Greek drama."[24] No less unchangeable have been the peculiar garb of Ed Wynn, the painted spectacles of Bobby Clark, the seedy refinement of the late W. C. Fields' Ascot hat and gloves. In this earlier day, however, the English comedian maintained his individuality, at least so far as costume is concerned.

A similar freedom from uniformity is manifest in the English farce actor's use of ridiculous props. Not notably refined in dialogue or action, the farces of the day show little of the addiction to the clysterpipe or the chamberpot which marks continental farce—if we may take any stock in the graphic records of Callot and other artists. As has already been suggested, the clown of this period was not above exploiting a physical peculiarity as we see from the numerous references to Norris's diminutive figure or to Spiller's one eye or to Hippisley's scarred face, but he did not commonly add to what nature had given him any artificial appendage comparable to Harlequin's *batte* or Chaplin's cane.

To insist upon the absence of fixed and uniform props is not, however, to banish all use of ridiculous props. Of these there were doubtless many. And, though the meager pictorial record and scanty stage directions leave us few specific details to judge from, we may assume that no opportunity to draw laughter was wasted when a little judiciousness in choosing a prop would turn the trick.

Of the numerous examples which could be cited we may concentrate on a few. Let us take, for an early example, two scenes from Orrery's farcical *Guzman* (1669) and *Mr. Anthony* (1671), in which Nokes and Angel clowned so

[24] *The Art of Cineplastics* (Boston, 1923), p. 58.

vigorously and successfully that Downes was still chuckling over them nearly forty years later. In the earlier play Guzman and Francisco, the clowns, fall out over their attempts to serenade their fair ladies and engage in a ridiculous combat in the dark. When two rivals appear and threaten them, "Guzman peeps between his own legs" and cowers before his new assailant when the latter points his own lost scabbard at him, Guzman taking it for a blunderbuss. Another duel scene between the same combatants ends, after much alternate swaggering and trembling by the cowards, with Guzman's taking flight "with two tucks in his tail." Orrery again uses Nokes and Angel in *Mr. Anthony* and repeats the duel scenes in even more extravagant terms. Angel, in the role of Cudden, is armed with a "Plymouth blade"— evidently a cudgel—[25] and Nokes, in the title role, is dressed in armor and equipped with bow and arrows.

Without attempting to cite all the numerous examples of similar uses of props we may let the above scenes suggest two lines of development. In one direction we have the absurd weapon used to induce fright and therefore horseplay. The pistol and the blunderbuss were used repeatedly and no doubt with similar effect in numerous farce scenes of the period. Along with firearms we might also include such cognate utensils as the surgeon's tools in *The Anatomist*. Though the stage directions are unfortunately lacking in specific details, we may safely assume, I think, that the clown provided himself with the most ridiculous and frightening assortment of surgical instruments he could obtain.[26]

[25] Downes's faulty memory caused him to substitute a blunderbuss for the cudgel. *Roscius Anglicanus*, p. 28.

[26] Some of the props employed during the period seem not unlike those used by prankish boys at Hallowe'en, as, for example, when Lacy introduced cowitch into the consultation scene of *The Dumb Lady* (1669), taken from *Le médecin malgré lui* and *L'amour médecin*, or when Tate introduced soap and bladder into *Cuckolds-Haven* (1685) so that Security (Tony Leigh) could

The more elaborate kind of stage properties, suggesting the machine play and anticipating the pantomime, are largely confined to continental borrowings. Plays of the *Faustus* and *Emperor of the Moon* type make full use of dishes which fly out of the hands, of tables which rise up to the ceiling, of statues which speak. Even the ingenious clock which Mrs. Behn used in the most wildly extravagant farce sequence in *Rover II* must have been borrowed, along with a Harlequin who jabbers Italian at intervals, from the Italian players. Since this particular scene represents an attempt to weld native and foreign farce it may be worth detailing briefly. Two thoroughly English clowns Fetherfool and Blunt (played by Nokes and Underhill) are, as usual, madly attempting to escape. Fetherfool is aided in his flight by Harlequin, who suggests that he hide in a clock, evidently one of the grandfather type but also evidently a stage clock, for the stage directions tell us that Harlequin "goes into the case, and shews him how to stand; then Fetherfool goes in, pulls off his periwig, his head out, turning for the minutes o' th' top: his hand out, and his fingers pointing to a figure." A few moments later Shift, one of the pursuers, wishes to find out the time and "lifts up the light to see, Feth. blows it out." Shift is made of sterner stuff than Fetherfool, it would seem, and instead of taking flight at this point draws his sword so that it is the latter who is obliged to flee.

With the crude and noisy action suggested by these last scenes we approach the basis of farce in all climes and ages. Divergent as they may be in the use of costume and props the farceurs of various theatrical traditions are in substantial agreement upon one point: the emphasis upon the grossly physical. True, we place the label of *farce* on such comparatively ethereal productions as *The Importance of Being Earnest* with perhaps no excessive strain on the term

---

frighten everyone by pretending a fit, foaming at the mouth and blowing up his stomach.

when we consider the wholly abandoned and delightful pursuit of the improbable in that play. But if *The Importance of Being Earnest* is farce it is also much more than farce. In many respects it is also very high comedy. No similar equivocation is present in the cases with which we have just been dealing.

Without attempting to reduce the emphasis on gross physical action to any all-embracing formula, I should like to call attention to two or three items which are basic even though not all-inclusive in the structure of farce. Though perhaps not all of the actions outlined here and to be touched upon in later chapters can be reduced to such a formula as M. Bergson's mechanical inelasticity, a case might be made for the gross indignities suffered by the farceur as covering a very wide range. The tumbling, the headlong flight, the beatings, all the physical discomfort the clown suffers is aimed at his dignity as a human being.

While it may not be necessary to go the whole way with the Hobbesian view that laughter is essentially scornful and triumphant, it must be admitted that there is a disposition to find enjoyment in the physical discomfort of the buffoon who has a pie thrown in his face or is knocked sprawling or is covered with soot. At the same time it is perhaps necessary to add that we are saved from any serious indictment of sadism by the fact that we are aware that no one is really being seriously injured.[27] Again, it seems to me that the animated cartoon of our present-day movies illustrates both points beautifully. The extremity of physical discomfort and indignity which Pluto and his companions are subjected to is completely matched by their resilience. Here, too, lies another advantage of the drawn figures over live actors. They may be repeatedly blown through the roof

[27] It is doubtful that Stephen Leacock meant to be taken seriously when he suggested that in our more primitive stages our enjoyment was complete only when the injury was real, even fatal. Eastmen has insisted, rightly I believe, that enjoyment is possible only when we are "in fun."

or wrapped around trees but they come out in the end none the worse for their experiences.

Perhaps enough has been offered already under other headings to show that the farce of the early eighteenth century made ample use of the fun to be had from physical discomfort or embarrassment. It might be well here merely to add some of the devices not mentioned so far which seem to be motivated solely by this purpose.

Among the most venerable of these is the mock-shaving trick, which goes back in English drama at least as far as the time of Shakespeare's birth. In Richard Edwards' *Damon and Pythias* (c. 1564) we have a scene in which the clever rogues Jack and Will treat dull-witted Grim the Collier to a painful shave while stealing his money. A similar and more elaborate use of the same trick is made in the farcical scenes in Marston's *Dutch Courtezan* and in the numerous adaptations made of these scenes.[28] A variant of the trick is introduced in the droll of *John Swabber* mentioned above. Here Swabber is afraid to trust himself under his rival's razor but allows Cutbeard to wash and powder him. Cutbeard changes from powder to soot and blackens Swabber's face while the barber's companions assist him in beguiling the vain ass into the belief that his natural beauty has been greatly enhanced. Other variations of the trick of blackening—sometimes flour or snuff is substituted for soot—an unsuspecting person's face appear in several other plays of the period.

In other cases the poor buffoon is frightened half to death by threats of bleeding or maiming, or of mistreatment by devils; he has water—or more offensive liquids—thrown on him or is ducked in a well; he is tossed in a blanket or at least treated to a noisy beating. In short, anything that suggests pain or discomfort may be made the stuff of farce.

Something ought perhaps to be said, in concluding this

[28] For an account of the adaptations, see L. Hughes and A. H. Scouten, "Some Theatrical Adaptations of a Picaresque Tale," The University of Texas *Studies in English*, 1945-1946, pp. 98-114.

chapter on the structure of farce, about another element which has always played an important role, the improvised or the accidental. Unfortunately for our purposes, farce did not seem sufficiently dignified or artistically creditable to draw the attention of commentators in our period—except of course when it was the object of condemnation. We are therefore left without any adequate record of the way in which farcical action was devised. Enough has been said of the lines of tradition to suggest that much or most of the devices employed were merely repeated by one generation of players after another. Our far more adequate knowledge of modern practice suggests, however, that there must have been greater room for innovation than the record shows. We know from recent studies of Chaplin, the Marx brothers, and other modern farceurs that improvisation—deliberate or even accidental—plays a large part in farce.

In the case of Chaplin we are told by Theodore Huff of "the reliance upon improvisation on the set instead of a written script."[29] But the all-time record for free improvisation seems to belong to the Marx brothers, according to the account by Kyle Crichton. His story of an evening with the Marxes on Broadway is worth quoting in full:

> The boys were making a shambles of *Cocoanuts*. They were romping and improvising; little was left of the show Broadway had seen on opening night. Audiences seemed to enjoy it, but there was apprehension in the ranks of management. Heywood Broun was annoyed backstage one night when he found George Kaufman [author of the original script] was ignoring his conversation.
>
> "What's the matter with you?" he asked testily.
> Kaufman held up an apologetic hand.
> "I may be wrong," he said, "but I thought I just heard one of the original lines."[30]

It is hardly possible that the eighteenth-century farceur

[29] *Charlie Chaplin*, p. 116.   [30] *The Marx Brothers*, p. 280.

could have treated an author's play in such high-handed fashion, but we have evidence in the form of contemporary comment to show that he could be too free with the text to suit a jealous playwright. The remark of Plotwell in *Three Hours after Marriage*, " 'Tis what the top players often do," may be an exaggeration of the satirical authors. Still there is adequate testimony that the practice of ad-libbing was far from uncommon, especially, to be sure, among the low comedians.

Comments on the practice are not numerous, but those we do have indicate something of its prevalence. Steele may serve as representative of the type of injured playwright who wants no liberties taken with his plays. At least twice in the *Tatler* he took occasion to complain of the ad-libbing actor. In No. 22 he adopts an ironic tone, praising the retiring Cave Underhill by seeming to dispraise him: "It must be confess'd, he has not the merit of some ingenious persons now on the stage, of adding to his authors; for the actors were so dull in the last age, that some of them have gone out of the world, without having ever spoke one word of their own in the theatre." In a later *Tatler*, No. 89, he drops the irony and descends somewhat more to particulars: "I was very well pleas'd this evening, to hear a gentleman express a very becoming indignation against a practice which I myself have been very much offended at. There is nothing (said he) more ridiculous, than for an actor to insert words of his own in the part he is to act, so that it is impossible to see the poet for the player: you'l have Pinkethman and Bullock helping out Beaumont and Fletcher."

The *Spectator* also contains references to ad-libbing. One relatively mild complaint seems to have been by John Hughes rather than Steele; in this essay, No. 539, the author remarks, in discussing a sermon he had recently heard, that the young clergyman was as wrong in taking liberties with the words borrowed from Tillotson "as Bullock and Penkethman when they mend a noble play of Shakespear or Jonson." But a little earlier, in No. 502, Steele himself lashes out in a tone not too often found in his essays: "The intolerable folly and confidence of players putting in words of their own, does in a great measure feed the absurd taste of the audience."

The repetition of the names of two specific offenders suggests that some actors were more disposed to interpolate their own words than others. Of course that is what we should expect and what seems to have been true. One of the first comedians in the period we find complaints about is Angel. Mrs. Behn, in her preface to *The Dutch Lover* (1673), complains that the actor who played Haunce in that play "spoke but little of what I intended for him, but supplied it with a great deal of idle stuff, which I was wholly unacquainted with until I had heard it first from him; so that Jack-pudding ever us'd to do; which though I knew before, I gave him yet the Part, because I knew him so acceptable to most o' th' lighter Periwigs about the town. . . ."

John Lacy too seems, at least on one occasion, to have taken liberties with the script though on the particular occasion he did not do so with impunity, for his impertinence brought down the wrath of King Charles on his head.[31] And Leigh, according to Cibber's account, got into similar difficulty with Charles' successor in much the same way. But the period in which Steele wrote may have been, after all, the one during which the practice flourished most freely. In addition to Bullock and Pinkethman, mentioned in the items above from both *Tatler* and *Spectator*, we find complaints against at least two of their fellow actors, Estcourt and Norris. Of the group, however, Pinkethman was not only the most popular actor but also the worst offender when it came to departing from the text. In addition to the comments by Steele and Hughes we have one in *A Comparison between the Two Stages*, in which he is referred to

[31] See Summers' notes to *Roscius Anglicanus*, p. 147.

as "a fellow that over-does every thing, and spoils many a part with his own stuff." In addition to these is a much fuller though unfortunately not perhaps so trustworthy account by Tom Davies in which he tells how Pinkethman simply stopped a performance of *The Beaux Stratagem* to carry on a discourse with his followers in the upper gallery while Wilks tried impatiently to get on with the business of the play.[32]

In time the influence of commentators like Steele may have had some effect in getting the worst abuses stopped, though we may gravely doubt that it was abolished entirely. I do not recall, however, seeing such frequent comment on ad-libbing among the followers of Pinkethman. Genest reproduces an amusing story concerning a clever interpolation by Hippisley,[33] but I do not find any evidence that the practice flourished as it had in the Queen Anne period. In fact, the last piece of evidence I have to offer is interesting in two ways, both because it suggests clearly that the practice had pretty effectively been stopped by mid-century and because in the case of one commentator at least it was not altogether disapproved of. The author of a treatise called *The Actor*, published in 1750, took occasion to describe the habit of improvising as it was practised by the Italian comedians. He seems to have had no high opinion of what the *commedia dell'arte* players actually produced under their much freer system of creation; yet he is willing to admire their obvious talents. His comment is most interesting when he turns from the Italians to the English:

This crime in actors, if it be one, is not peculiar to that nation. We have had instances of it among ourselves. Our celebrated Norris had introduc'd a thousand occasional pleasantries into every one of the ridiculous characters he was famous for playing; and wou'd seldom

[32] *Dramatic Miscellanies* (London, 1785), III, 88-90.
[33] IV, 253-254.

be prevail'd with to take much pains about acting a new part; he only made himself master of the heads and matter of it, and of the sense of the whole play; his own genius for drollery supply'd the rest; and if the author rav'd at the abuse, the audience never failed to be pleased with it.

We live, 'tis true, in an age of criticism in which nothing of this kind is suffer'd; but perhaps if some of the modern farces which have been cram'd down our throats had been play'd off in the same manner [i.e. improvised in the *commedia dell'arte* fashion], the delicacy of these gentlemen wou'd have been full as little shock'd as it has been at the representation of them as they were written.

It is indeed indisputable that the dramatic writings of a man of wit and genius, as they are studied and regular, are infinitely preferable to the impertinent additions that a player can be able to make to them extempore; but the imperfection of the human memory is one great obstacle to our seeing plays thus regularly compos'd, perform'd with all the advantages we cou'd wish.[34]

The other aspect of free improvisation I have mentioned, the accidental, must necessarily be treated only briefly—if for no other reason simply because of the meagerness of the record. Admittedly it is far less important than the deliberate kind of interpolation just discussed. Yet for our purpose here, in attempting to show the nature and the structure of farce, it is far from insignificant. Not only does the inclusion of a bit of stage business stumbled on by chance—when an actor accidentally falls into the orchestra pit, a piece of scenery topples on some one's head, or the like—demonstrate the looseness and flexibility of farce, it also shows clearly the close rapport between actors and audience, the dependence in farce scenes on a lively response from the house.

Two accounts of theatrical accidents will illustrate the

[34] pp. 214-215.

way in which an amusing piece of stage business may be chanced upon. In the first case the accident did not become permanently attached to the play, to be sure, but its failure to do so was not to be blamed on the audience or the principal comedians. In a letter attached to the Dublin edition of *Three Hours after Marriage*[35] we are given a detailed account of a prolonged and amusing series of mishaps which served to entertain the audience perhaps more than any of the prepared scenes did. On the fourth night of the run of *Three Hours* while Cibber as Plotwell, at the moment dressed as an Egyptian mummy, and Mrs. Hunt as Sarsnet the maid were on the stage, the famous clown Will Pinkethman came on. Since he was acting as Plotwell's rival Underplot he was trying to outdo the former in ingenious disguise and therefore appeared dressed as a crocodile. According to our informant, Pinkethman's entrance was greeted with a storm of applause to which the actor responded by strutting around the stage showing off his long tail. At that point the play almost came to a premature end. Pinkethman strutted perhaps a little more than usual and swinging his long tail about knocked poor Sarsnet head over heels so that "she disclosed more linnen than other habiliments, and, more skin and flesh than linnen: this began the first uproar in the audience." At that point "the crocodile Penketheman (whose face was a farce) rising from giving assistance to the fallen maid; unluckily, his back encountered the case for the mummy, which stood upright, open-mouth'd, to receive him, that case and crocodile fell back with such violent noise, that the body of the crocodile lay entirely inhum'd in the case of the mummy. . . ." So involved did the two clumsily attired actors become, it actually became necessary to call in the aid of the stage carpenters to extricate them. The ending of the account is,

[35] This story has, I confess, much of the "theatrical anecdote" about it. It is described, however, as being by "a person who is still alive, and tho' a woman, intimate with the poets of this century, and consequently with most of the theatrical persons worth notice."

though perhaps implausibly exaggerated, as amusing as what precedes. "This scene took more than half an hour in the action; with what roar of applause the reader must form his own imagination. Many of the audience next night, made an interruption of some minutes, to have the scene repeated, which so much alarmed poor Sarsnet, that she run off the stage extremely frighted, which provoked a peal of laughter from the spectators."

In the second case the bit of stage business happened on by chance did stay in the play. For this story we are indebted to Thomas Wilkes. In his *General View of the Stage* (1759) Wilkes comes inevitably on the subject which intrigued so many of his contemporaries: the amazing versatility of David Garrick. His attempts to illustrate this versatility bring up the story we are interested in. How, says Wilkes, can Garrick please equally well in such leading and serious roles as Lothario and Hamlet *and* "the mean Tobacco-boy" in the *Alchemist?*

> . . . yet in Abel Drugger he is as inimitable as in the other two. The stupid confusion which he shews at breaking the urinal, and his satisfaction at going out without its being taken notice of, are peculiar to himself. The introducing this incident was first owing entirely to accident. It happened to old Cibber, who was allowed to play this character well. He, while the other personages were employed, rather than stand idle, was fiddling about the table of the Alchymist; and by way of filling up time, took up the urinal, and held it to the light, when it by chance slipping through his fingers, broke to pieces; and he had presence of mind to put on an air of distress happy to the time and place; it told to admirable purpose. He played the part afterwards as usual; but the audience obliged him to restore the accidental addition; and it has been ever since retained by every other performer.[36]

[36] pp. 257-258. This interesting story has a possible flaw which goes a long way toward discrediting it; the records all seem to indi-

In the final analysis we are obliged to admit candidly that what remains of eighteenth-century farce by way of play-text and commentary is but an echo of what these pieces were really like on the stage in the hands of a great clown like Nokes or Pinkethman. The stage directions are especially inadequate witnesses of what the stage business —"by-play" was the term in the eighteenth century—was actually like. On only the rarest occasion does the text of the play indicate how dependent the playwright actually was upon the actor in farce. In *Rover II* (1680) for example, Mrs. Behn shows her willingness to let the actor provide his own devices when at one point in the play, she says merely "Harlequin meets him in the dark, and plays tricks with him." Or even more striking and suggestive is a unique stage direction at the end of Carey's *Hanging and Marriage* (1722). When the rustic hero of the play, Richard Stubble, played by Spiller, has succeeded in outwitting Betty's father and winning the girl, he leads the cast off to a bout of feasting. Carey's directions for this triumphal procession are highly interesting: Richard goes off "hugging Betty, and looking very arch, as Jemmy Spiller knows how."

Inadequate as the mere text of farce is, however, we may, with the assistance of the fuller and more useful commentary of contemporary theatre-goers, learn enough of the structure and devices of farce to observe the persistence of elements common in all ages.

---

cate that "old" Cibber usually played Subtle in this play; it was Theophilus who made something of a reputation as Abel Drugger. Professor Noyes repeats the story without questioning its authenticity, *Ben Jonson on the English Stage* (Cambridge, Mass., 1935), p. 135. An early pretended attack on Garrick, *An Essay on Acting* (1744), indicates that much was made of the urinal "by-play."

CHAPTER 3

FARCE AND THE AFTERPIECE

++

What a wretched pass is this wicked age come to, when Ben
Jonson and Shakespeare won't go down without these bagatelles
to recommend them, and nothing but farce and grimace will go
down?—TOM BROWN, *Amusements Serious and Comical*

++

IN SPEAKING of the Commonwealth droll *Simpleton*, I remarked that, while it served admirably to illustrate the
structure of untrammeled farce, it was not, because of the
peculiar circumstances of its production, a reliable example
of the way farce actually developed in the English theatre.
In order to study profitably any dramatic form we must
keep our eyes focused on the main stream of the drama
with all its currents and eddies. In the study of farce we
should pay particular attention to the circumstances of
theatrical production, for no other dramatic form is so
closely dependent upon the theatre itself. Since the main
stream of the drama disappeared underground in the 1640's,
only to emerge with the Restoration, it is dangerous to
generalize from what happened in that dark span.

Perhaps the first peculiarity of the Commonwealth droll
to strike the eye is its brevity. From the middle of the sixteenth century, with such plays as *Ralph Roister Doister*
and *Gammer Gurton's Needle*, there had been no place
for the short play of the sort which could be made up, as
Simpleton was, from the brief farcical episode two or three
times compounded. Farce, if it was to find a place at all,
could be used only as episodic relief, as comic filler—as
farce in its original sense of stuffing. Up to the time of the
Restoration there had been but this one period after 1642
when the tradition of five acts had been broken. It was in

time to be broken again and broken for good,[1] but meanwhile it persisted with the force that only an unexamined tradition based upon the most august authority can have. After all, had not Horace said that no self-respecting playwright need consider any number of acts other than five? Had not Plautus and, more especially, Terence thrown the weight of their example into the balance?[2]

To the modern student this easy acceptance of identical patterns for comedy and tragedy is hard to justify. Thorndike speaks of the five-act tradition as "a very foolish rule" and says, "There never was any real reason for dividing a play into five acts."[3] John B. Moore has been just as emphatic:

> Worse than all this [the stereotype of character and intrigue borrowed from Latin comedy] was the introduction into England of what appears to me to be the fallacy of the classical theory of comedy. The later Greek comic-writers and Plautus and Terence after them assumed that the extended form of drama was just as suitable for comedy as it had long been for tragedy. . . . The mistaken idea that a comic—a purely comic—play can be in any but exceptional cases sustained through five

[1] The history of our modern dramatic art form presents a striking contrast. Unhampered by tradition, the moving picture grew from a few flickering scenes recorded on crude film to the present-day spectacle of two hours and more. "At the beginning, every episode shown was brief—a matter of two or three or at the most five minutes. The first picture that ran an entire reel, approaching fifteen minutes, was considered a dangerous innovation. Very slowly the common average length of the current feature picture was developed and single reelers kept right on side by side with the longer features. (In comedy it should be noted that the long feature was very slow to develop. Chaplin appeared in *Tillie's Punctured Romance*, but scurried back to one-reelers, and this remained the dominant form for many years. . . .)" Seldes, *The Movies Come from America* (New York and London, 1937), p. 103.

[2] For a detailed study of these matters see Professor T. W. Baldwin's *Shakspere's Five-Act Structure* (Urbana, 1947).

[3] *English Comedy* (New York, 1929), p. 416.

acts is the burden that Plautian comedy laid upon the English drama to counterbalance the "good Turns" that it, also, did for that drama.[4]

If there is any significant number of cavilers against the five-act tradition in the period covered here, I have not had the fortune to discover them. At the very end of the period two voices were raised in mild protest. In his essay on dramatic rules prefacing Book V of *Tom Jones*, Fielding hints of his dissatisfaction with some of the dogmas then rigidly in force, such as those concerning the dramatic unities. He also questions the tradition under discussion here: "Hath any commentator well accounted for the limitation which an ancient writer hath set to the drama, which he will have contain neither more nor less than five acts."

Two years later Samuel Johnson is a little more explicit in one of his *Ramblers*:

By what accident the number of acts was limited to five, I know not that any author has informed us, but certainly it is not determined by any necessity arising either from the nature of action or the propriety of exhibition. An act is only the representation of such a part of the business of the play as proceeds in an unbroken tenor without any intermediate pause. Nothing is more evident than that of every real, and, by consequence, of every dramatick action, the intervals may be more or fewer than five; and indeed the rule is upon the English stage every day broken in effect, without any other mischief than that which arises from an absurd endeavour to observe it in appearance. (No. 156.)

These objections come relatively late in our story, a full generation and more after the tradition in its most rigid form had broken down. For over a century after Lyly it had been strictly adhered to. It must be recognized that

[4] *The Comic and the Realistic in English Drama* (Chicago, 1925), pp. 109-111.

one strong reason for its persistence—aside from the mere weight of custom and tradition—was that it had caused no hardship to the English playwright, that it was, in fact, a convenience. Since English writers had never been unduly concerned about keeping their genres separated, they had no misgivings about mixing them all in one package. As John Palmer has put it, "The Englishman . . . point-blank refuses to be departmental." What may seem to us a foolish tradition was scarcely examined critically by the earlier playwright since he saw nothing incongruous about filling up his play with a miscellany of effects until he had the required number of acts.[5]

To return for a moment to *Simpleton*, we find its theatrical context as striking as its brevity; in fact, the one grows out of the other. In more normal times in the English theatre, when the traditional requirement of five acts could not so readily be set aside, the sort of play *Simpleton* represents could scarcely have appeared. But the Commonwealth period was far from being a normal one. Like bear baiting and Sunday sports, the theatre had come under the Puritan ban. In short, the highly novel form represented by the Commonwealth droll grew out of a novel set of circumstances in the theatre itself. And what is true of this particular period is applicable to the whole range of theatrical history. The story of the development of farce, more especially of *the farce*, the distinct dramatic genre, is in many ways actually the story of the theatrical bill. And since that story has never been adequately told for the period under survey here, it will be the object of this chapter to relate it in some detail.

To provide contrast and to gain perspective, however, it

[5] A casual statement made by an Elizabethan playwright takes on added significance in this context. Marston says, in a prefatory note on his *Dutch Courtezan* (c. 1604), "The difference betwixt the love of a curtezan, & a wife, is the full scope of the play, which intermixed with the deceits of a wittie citie jester, fils up the comedie."

might be well to look first at the parallel and yet strikingly different story of the French theatre. Seventeenth-century France had inherited a tradition of farce writing and acting that was wholly unlike anything that England had ever known. The *sociétés joyeuses* of the Middle Ages had composed and acted farces by the hundreds. The vast majority of these have been lost or were never published but enough are available to give us a reasonably clear idea of their nature. The best known of them, *Pathelin*, is perhaps above the common level of medieval farce, yet with its emphasis on coarse and lively scenes of physical action and its division into really discrete episodes it serves to illustrate the type.

With the disappearance of the *sociétés joyeuses* the farceur fell into disrepute among the educated but was never without an audience among the lower classes. His place in the early seventeenth-century professional theatre is a little hard to ascertain in the absence of that wealth of documentary evidence with which the latter half abounds, but however hostile the Parisian theatre of Richelieu may have been he was not homeless so long as the theatres at the fairs and at various other places outside the pale of respectability remained open. Turlupin, Gros Guillaume, and Gaultier-Garguille kept the older and coarser genre alive at the Hôtel de Bourgogne, while Tabarin and his associates on the Pont-Neuf played to audiences with even less refined tastes.

In the more regular theatres farce had shown signs of being eclipsed as the century progressed but by the time Molière had successfully established his hold on Parisian audiences, not far past the mid-century mark, it was well on its way toward becoming a permanent fixture in the theatrical bill. We are told, for example, that the Illustre Théâtre on its first appearance before Louis XIV had asked and readily been granted permission to play the sort of farce with which Molière had been regaling provincial audiences.[6]

[6] Lanson, following La Grange, tells the story: "Lorsque ces

The combination of a monarch who loved to laugh and a playwright and actor who owed much of his success to farce seems to have been a happy one for the genre.

Nor did Molière neglect farce writing and acting once his triumph in Paris seemed assured. The most casual examination of his own published works will reveal almost a preponderance of farce. The descriptions we have of his acting—and these not all by enemies—reveal a consummate skill in the form. His associates in the theatre were, some of them at least, possibly more addicted to farce than he. With Jodelet in his own troupe, he had the company of an actor who has been called the greatest of farceurs and a link with Turlupin and his fellow clowns. Nor must it be forgotten that for a considerable time Molière shared a theatre with Biancolelli and Fiorilli, past masters of Italian farce.

Molière provided strong support for the farce afterpiece in the French theatre, but he was not without aid from other playwrights of the day. Though we do not have a full record of theatrical bills before 1680, when the Comédie Française was formed, we can learn a great deal from examining the list of plays published between 1650 and 1680. Professor Lancaster points out that it was Boisrobert who in 1655 set the fashion of publishing one-act plays with his *Amant ridicule*, a farce which had served as part of a long bill of divertissements.[7] Following Boisrobert's lead many playwrights began to publish shorter pieces with the result that in a little while the number of plays in one or three

---

comédiens paraissent au Louvre devant le roi, le 24 octobre 1658, après avoir joué Nicomède, Molière demande à Sa Majesté la permission de jouer 'un de ces petits divertissements qui lui avaient acquis la réputation et dont il régalait les provinces'; et il donne le Docteur amoureux. C'est une farce, mais, la farce n'étant plus à la mode Molière n'ose se servir du mot, et emploie le terme plus relevé de divertissement." "Molière et la farce," pp. 138-139.

[7] For a full account of the return of French farce to something approaching acceptance, see Pt. III, Vol. I, Chaps. II and III of Professor Lancaster's *History*.

acts greatly outnumbered those in five. In the period 1659-1662 twenty-four of thirty-seven plays issued were in one act and several of the remainder in three. Or, to take a later sample, in the first decade after the Comédie Française had established its monopoly, the tradition had become so firmly established that twenty-three of forty comic plays published were in one act, only twelve in five. Not all these one-act pieces were invariably farcical but the majority evidently were.

From 1680 on we no longer have to resort to conjecture as to what the theatrical bill was like; we have a daily record of plays and receipts. By this time in the French theatre the custom of double-billing had become fixed. Only when the main play was new, unusually long, or unusually expensive to produce was one piece considered enough for an evening's offering. At least half the time the company would perform a full-length play followed by a short afterpiece. Other combinations were more rarely offered. And while the afterpiece was not always or necessarily farcical, it was more likely to be so than otherwise.

So firmly had the afterpiece become entrenched in the Parisian theatre by 1680 that it was considered hazardous to venture an evening's production without one. As early as 1681 we find Hauteroche testifying to its indispensability when he writes to La Grange, "Mon cousin, vous ne pouvez pas douter que nous n'ayons esté obligés de cesser de théâtre aujourd'hui. Vous sçavez que de représenter une pièce sérieuse sans une petite pièce, c'est absolument chasser le peuple; vous n'ignorez pas aussi, que nous ne pouvons donner aucune comédie, tous les comiques estant à Fontainebleau."[8]

This insistence of the audience on having an afterpiece grew with the years until in time it was decided to stop venturing a new production without the assistance of an

[8] J. F. Privitera, *Charles Chevillet de Champmeslé* (Baltimore, 1938), p. 32.

established *petite pièce*. According to a review in the *Gentleman's Magazine* for September 1754, the *Dictionnaire portatif des théâtres* credits La Motte with establishing a new tradition:

> Till the exhibition of this tragedy [La Motte's *Romulus*, first performed 28 January 1722] it had been customary to play new pieces without an entertainment, and to add a pantomime or a farce after the 8th or 9th night; so that when the entertainment was added, the success of the piece was thought to be on the decline, though custom had made the addition necessary, when the play wanted no support: To prevent this disadvantage, La Motte caused an entertainment to be played after his piece the first night; and his example has been followed by all succeeding authors in France, who wished a custom established which they had not courage to begin, lest the town should believe their performance wanted on the first night that aid, which others did not call in till the 9th.

The history of the theatrical bill in the English theatre shows striking differences as well as some interesting parallels. On the one hand there is no actual connection between the two; that is, each follows its own independent course. On the other hand either account will demonstrate fully the dependence of the lighter kinds of entertainment upon the exigencies of theatrical production. When there is any grave danger that omitting the frills from an evening's bill will "chasser le peuple," the frills are retained; when under favorable conditions, such as those provided by a theatrical monopoly, there is no dearth of spectators, the frills may very well be cut—unless, as both the above sketch of the French afterpiece has shown and the following details on the English theatrical bill will show, the custom of offering an afterpiece long antedates the monopoly or other favorable circumstances.

To speak of English farce only in connection with "entertainments" in the theatrical bill is, however, to plunge into the midst of the century of activities covered here, since the remarks immediately preceding apply chiefly to the later stages of the development of English farce as a distinct genre. In order to complete the parallel—and the contrast—with the French situation, it might be well to look briefly at the status of farce in the earlier English drama.

Though no separate genre similar to the French farce appeared in England until late in the seventeenth century, and therefore no special term was required to label it, there was admittedly an abundance of farce in earlier English drama. As in France, the medieval cycles which grew out of liturgical drama provided a great deal of comic relief to the scriptural pageant. To select only two examples from many, there are the episode of Noah's difficulty in getting his wife to leave her gossips and board the ark and, even better, the adventures of the sheep-stealing Mak, both Towneley plays. In these little plays may also be seen the beginnings of English comedy, as distinguished from farce, for they contain some elements of satire and, particularly in the second piece, a by no means crude or primitive characterization. Still there are enough of the elements of pure fun, ridiculous disguise, farcically impossible situations, beatings, and other forms of slapstick to justify our classifying them as farces.

With the breaking up of the dramatic cycles and the rise of independent plays, farce continued to be used as comic relief in longer and more serious productions. Completely farcical pieces are so rare, in fact, that their appearance in the work of John Heywood, to give an almost unique example, has provided a nice problem for the historians of the drama.[9] Such plays as the lively little farce

[9] Fifty years ago the late Karl Young pointed out Heywood's indebtedness to French farce and his independence of the main current of strictly English drama in "The Influence of French Farce

Johan Johan were unquestionably waifs whose origins are to be sought in France, where the specific genre had both a name and a following.

Other brief and largely farcical plays, such as *Thersites, Jack Juggler,* and *Tom Tyler,* indicate the possible existence of a large body of similar pieces which have not survived.[10] Nor do we know as much as we need to about the circumstances of production. The Plautian source of *Jack Juggler* suggests a school play; native pieces like *Tom Tyler* may have been performed at various seasonal festivities or by strollers at almost any time. This last is a jig and may conceivably have served as an afterpiece, though the practice of adding a jig afterpiece seems not to have been established before the last decade of the sixteenth century.

While the earliest five-act plays, *Ralph Roister Doister* and *Gammer Gurton's Needle,* were very largely farcical, the rapid development of the five-act structure in the professional theatre soon reduced farce to a wholly ancillary status. There is a great deal of incidental farce even at the height of the Elizabethan period but virtually all of it is in the form of excrescent comic relief. In at least a few plays—*Dr. Faustus, The Comedy of Errors, The Two Angry Women of Abington, Albumazar,* to name some better known ones—the farcical materials are quite or nearly as important as the romance and intrigue. More commonly, however, there are only incidental farcical episodes, as in Greene's mixtures of history and romance, Marston's tragicomic *Dutch Courtezan,* or the highly popular *Merry Devill*

upon the Plays of John Heywood," *Modern Philology,* II (1904), 97-124. More recently an Australian scholar, Ian Maxwell, has issued a study, *French Farce & John Heywood* (Melbourne, 1946), which is admittedly no more than an expansion of the earlier article.

[10] The studies of medieval English drama by various scholars reveal a surprising paucity of extant farces or evidence of farce playing. The seasonal mumming in the folk plays, as analyzed by E. K. Chambers, seems to have been far stricter in its adherence to conventional patterns than might have been expected.

of Edmonton and *Mucedorus,* favorites of the provinces, to select only a few of many possible examples.

The sole exception to all this is the Elizabethan jig, which made its appearance between 1590 and 1642. From the studies of Chambers, Rollins, and Baskervill we know that there was a practice of tacking brief pieces on to the end of plays, especially in such popular theatres—as distinguished from the so-called "private" houses—as the Fortune and the Red Bull. From the comparatively few pieces of this sort which have been preserved, however, I do not believe the jig can be described as being more than vaguely cognate with farce. It was usually no more than quasi-dramatic, resembling more nearly the older ballad or the modern song-and-dance turn.[11] Some use was made of jigs in the Commonwealth drolls but it seems hardly to have been extensive; of the thirty-eight drolls in the collection called *The Wits* only two are clearly derived from jigs. The evidence provided by items printed after 1642 is scarcely admissible in any event, for the very obvious reason that theatrical conditions were so strikingly different from those of any other period before or since. Similar and even stronger objections apply to the *Singspiele der englischen Komödianten,* the repertory of English strollers in Germany.[12] The exigencies arising from performances before

[11] Professor Rollins defines the jig as "a miniature comedy or farce, written in ballad-measure, which, at the end of a play, was *sung and danced on the stage to ballad tunes* [emphasis supplied]." *A Pepysian Garland* (Cambridge, 1922), p. xiv.—The interdiction of 1612 also suggests the nature of these pieces. It provides "that all actors of everye playehouse . . . utterlye abolishe all jigges rymes and daunces after their playes. . . ." Quoted by C. R. Baskervill, *The Elizabethan Jig* (Chicago, 1929), p. 116. See also pp. 115, 120-121.

[12] In his *Commonwealth and Restoration Stage,* Leslie Hotson reproduces, opposite p. 174, a Frankfort playbill which he assigns somewhat tentatively to an English troupe playing there in 1656. According to this bill the main play was *Die Standhaffte Mutter der Machabaeer,* but a note informs us that "Nach der Action soll ein lustiges neues Nach-Spiel beschliessen."

foreign audiences naturally led to the use of crude and acrobatic forms of drama.[13] Quite naturally also the English troupes on the Continent turned for their basic materials to English drama and song, but what they produced did not necessarily resemble closely what they borrowed from.

In the absence of any certain knowledge of short farces in the pre-Commonwealth period, then, we are forced to conclude that the first to appear, after the second quarter of the sixteenth century, were the drolls of the dramatic interregnum. Conditions brought about by the proscription of regular plays led inevitably to the creation of short farces, where any dramatic production was at all possible. The few troupes that dared to flaunt the law were necessarily small and highly mobile with few or no properties and almost none of the ordinary means of publicity.[14] Under such conditions they found it impossible to produce the elaborate five-act play of the ante-bellum period but depended instead upon a repertory of drolls.

Fortunately, we have in the Marsh and Kirkman's *Wits* (1662 and 1673) a quite adequate sample of the Commonwealth repertory. Largely drawn from farcical scenes in earlier full-length pieces, these plays are typically nothing more than brief and coarse scenes taken from earlier plays. Most interesting to the student of farce are the lively little prose farces *Simpleton,* analyzed in the preceding chapter, and *John Swabber,* the jigs *Simpkin* and *The Black Man,*

[13] For a modern instance we may turn to Theodore Huff: "During the run of 'Casey's Court Circus' Chaplin gradually gave up his ambition of becoming a dramatic actor and concentrated on comedy. Once, while playing in the Channel Islands, he found that his jokes were not getting over because, as he soon discovered, the natives knew little English. He resorted to pantomime and got the desired laughs. From this he learned the power of pantomime which became the major element in his art." *Charlie Chaplin,* p. 15.

[14] On the means employed in publicizing performances during the Commonwealth period, see H. E. Rollins, "A Contribution to the History of the English Commonwealth Drama," *Studies in Philology,* XVIII (1921), 267-333.

and among those from well-known plays, *The Cheater Cheated* from Marston's *Dutch Courtezan.*

It seems clear that the continued or even growing opposition to the players, especially after 1647, had made the production of full-length plays quite impossible. Since the hunger for dramatic spectacle remained, however, the more daring actors made a precarious living by supplying contraband materials. After the ban was lifted at the Restoration, the makers and actors of drolls quickly surrendered in the face of the powerful opposition of the patent theatres or carried their slender repertories and meager props off to the fairs or the provinces, where we shall see them again in a later chapter.

With the removal of the proscription against drama, after the return of Charles II, the English theatre reverted almost wholly to the practices of a happier day before the triumph of the Puritans and began producing the usual five-act play as a full theatrical bill. If, as frequently was the case, there was farcical material in the plays revived from the older repertory it was allowed to stand. In fact it was often added to, as can be seen by comparing the revised versions of Restoration plays taken from the earlier native drama. A good example of the practice of revision may be found in *The Cutter of Coleman Street*, from Cowley's *Guardian*, or, somewhat later, any of the plays taken by Durfey from Fletcher.

Davenant, playwright and theatre manager, has expressed what may be taken as the conventional attitude toward the admixture of farce—even increased amounts of farce—with non-farcical or even non-comic material:

> Pure wit, like ingots wrought without allay,
> Will serve for hoard, but not for common pay.
> Th'allay's coarse metal makes the finer last;
> Which else would in the peoples' handling waste.

So country jigs and farces mixt among
Heroic scenes make plays continue long.
Prologue to the revived *Witts* (1667)

In short, the Restoration audience had no horror of farce. On the contrary they were even more receptive to it than their predecessors had been; moreover, like the English audience of an earlier day and quite unlike the French of their own day, they had no objections to finding the various genres mixed. The protest of Dryden, expressed in his *Of Dramatick Poesie* (1668), must be put down as too refined and too Gallic for his day:

There is no theatre in the world has any thing so absurd as the English tragi-comedy; 'tis a drama of our own invention, and the fashion of it is enough to proclaim it so; here a course of mirth, there another of sadness and passion, a third of honour, and fourth of Bedlam. The French affords you as much variety on the same day, but they do it not so unseasonably, or *mal à propos*, as we: our poets present you the play and the farce together; and our stages still retain somewhat of the original civility of the Red Bull: *Atque ursum et pugiles media inter carmina poscunt.*

If, by a somewhat strained inference, we may suppose that Dryden was calling for the introduction of theatrical bills of the French type with a comic or tragic main piece and a farcical afterpiece, we must assume that he was to remain disappointed. No such bills were to appear for more than a generation. What records we have indicate that the Restoration audience was content with a five-act play as the main, virtually the whole, bill. To this rule there are a few notable exceptions.

In the summer of 1663 Davenant produced his *Play-House to be Lett*, a medley on the pattern of Quinault's *Comédie sans comédie* (1657). *The Play-House to be Lett* is a hastily and loosely contrived hodge-podge of several parts of Davenant's own earlier plays and two new pieces, a translation of Molière's *Sganarelle ou le cocu imaginaire* serving for a second act and a burlesque of the Anthony and Cleopatra story as the fifth. Though Davenant's innovation seems to have been popular enough to enjoy occasional revival it did not result in any immediate imitations. It will, in fact, be necessary to wait until the very end of the century and the beginning of the next to find the medley gaining any favor.

A second exception is possibly more extensive. From Pepys and Evelyn we learn of some use of entr'acte and afterpiece material such as that described in the passage quoted from Pepys in the first chapter. Even this is hardly more than quasi-dramatic, consisting rather more of music and dancing than of any dialogue material, though there is more than a suggestion of pantomime.

Unfortunately Pepys ceases to provide us with a detailed account of theatrical performances after 1669 and he has no comparable successor; our other diarist hardly approaches him in either his fascination for the theatre or his fullness in reporting details. Hence our knowledge of theatrical bills beyond the time of Pepys' account is meager though we do have some scattered items, perhaps enough to suggest that until well along toward the close of the century nothing comparable to the French bill appeared.

The last specific exception runs quite counter to this statement, however, and is as remarkable for its uniqueness as for anything else. I refer to the production, almost at the very middle of the Restoration period, of a typical French bill. In 1676 Otway brought out a translation of Racine's *Berenice,* and realizing that an English audience would find a single French tragedy devoid of incident—it had become customary by this time to throw parts of two or three French plays together to make an English one—he added a farcical afterpiece, a translation of Molière's *Four-beries de Scapin.*

Just what the English audience thought of so striking an innovation we do not know. Clearly it established no precedent: there is no record, so far as I have been able to discover, of a similar double bill until after the turn of the century. In view of what was to happen around 1700 when two companies were in desperate competition, it may not be too far-fetched to suppose that a similar custom of adding attractions might have grown up twenty years earlier as the two companies then performing found their audiences growing slimmer and slimmer, particularly with the mounting strife over the Popish plot and the bickering over Charles' successor. With the union of the companies in 1682, however, the possibility of such an outcome disappeared, and the farce afterpiece found no place in the bill. As late as 1692 Dryden is still obliged to look to the Continent for an illustration of the practice of double-billing. In *A Discourse Concerning the Original and Progress of Satire* he tells, following Dacier, of the revival of interest in the older forms of satire among the Romans. Until Andronicus came along, the story runs, the Romans had allowed their earlier satirical pieces to fall into disuse. "But not long after, they took them up again, and then they joined them to their comedies; playing them at the end of every drama, as the French continue at this day to act their farces, in the nature of a separate entertainment from their tragedies."

Though there was no movement towards developing a distinct afterpiece until the very end of the century, the last quarter did see the beginnings of a breakup of the monopoly of the five-act play. With the single exception of the unique afterpiece by Otway, in which he retained Molière's three-act arrangement, there is no play between 1660 and 1680 in less than five acts. Even Davenant's *Play-House,* which can scarcely be called a *regular* five-act play, does manage to fill up the required number. On the other hand, during the period of a little better than a dozen years from the formation of the united company in 1682 to its dissolution in 1695 there are seven plays in three acts. As often as not, these are of about the same actual length as the more conventional play, but they do represent a change, slight though it may be.

The movement toward change in the theatrical bill before the secession of Betterton and company in 1695 is, however, glacial by comparison with what happens in the years following that event, particularly in the decade 1695-1705. These years are easily the most significant in the whole range of English dramatic history in the development of the afterpiece and, consequently, the development of English farce as a distinct genre, for they saw the farce afterpiece established in the English theatre as it had long been known in France. The significant difference between the two theatres is clearly discernible at this point, for while the afterpiece in France was developed through convention, by the persistence of a fondness for a native dramatic genre plus the neo-classical insistence on keeping genres separate, it was developed in England through competition, from the struggle of the rival companies to outbid each other for audiences at a time when there simply were not enough spectators to fill two houses week after week.

In order to study this significant development in the English theatre closely, it will now be necessary to plunge into a detailed examination of the fortunes of the rival companies and their specific offerings.

The theatrical union of 1682 had been brought about, by royal intervention, when it became apparent that the company of Hart and Mohun had fallen into an advanced state of decline and when it had become even more apparent that the audiences, distracted by civil strife, had grown too thin to support two companies adequately. The separation of 1695 did not, however, come about because of any new prosperity in the theatre. It was the result of a bitter war between the veteran actors supporting Betterton and their notorious manager Christopher Rich.[15] The restoration of competition was to have grave and far-reaching results.

Immediately after the seceders had set up their company in the newly refurbished house in Lincoln's Inn Fields, they began to thrive. Most of the spectators flocked to see them while the patentees' makeshift company at Drury Lane played to slender houses. Before the end of the century, however, fortunes began to change. There were quarrels among the strong individualists in the company at Lincoln's Inn Fields. There was slow but steady progress among the younger actors still under Rich. In time, something like a balance had been restored, and an almost suicidal competition began.[16] In order to gain the upper hand first one and then the other company began to employ added attractions, and soon bills of variety became the rule. Though these added inducements to patronage ran at first to nondramatic or quasidramatic items such as song and dance, acrobatic feats, and "night scenes" (i.e., pantomimes), the typical bill from about 1704 on had begun to turn into a regular play plus an afterpiece, usually a farce.

Meanwhile, during the decade of transition at the turn of the century, variety throve while profits dropped lower and lower, expenditures on extravaganza and "foreign mon-

---

[15] Professor Nicoll reproduces some of the documents revealing the issues in this quarrel, "Documents Illustrative of the History of the Stage," Sec. VIII, *History*. See also Hotson and Barker.

[16] It is difficult to find precise information on the theatrical fortunes of the day. Much of the comment, especially in the prologues and epilogues of the plays produced by the rival companies, suggests that times were hard in the theatre. Hotson has some interesting facts and figures in his *Commonwealth and Restoration Stage*, especially pp. 308-310. These indicate that by the turn of the century the patentees' company, playing at Drury Lane and Dorset Garden, had begun at least to play a respectable number of plays each season until 1702 but underwent "a sharp falling off" after that.

sters" cutting ever deeper as the seasons passed. A glance at
some of the now more plentiful newspaper bills or at the
dozens of references in prefaces and prologues to the growing expense and declining merit of the theatre will show
the state of affairs.

Quite typical is a comment made by Tom Brown in the
fall of 1699. In a letter dated 12 September, Brown in-
dulges in mock sorrow over the close of Bartholomew Fair.
He goes on to say that the fair will not be missed so long
as Drury Lane and Lincoln's Inn Fields continue producing the kind of bills they have been offering, with Clinch
of Barnet, rope walkers, and the like, particularly the dancers imported from France. Things have come to such a
pass, says Brown, that the theatres themselves are rapidly
approaching self destruction, so that Jeremy Collier's wildest hopes may become a reality without the intervention of
the government or the church. He looks for the time when
both Drury Lane and Lincoln's Inn Fields will be taken
over by "the strong Kentish man . . . , as he has already
done of that in Dorset Garden."[17]

Any suspicion that Brown was merely indulging in his
usual fondness for hyperbole, in the manner of Ward and
others of the new school of muckraking journalism, is dis-
pelled by a glance through the prefaces, prologues, and
epilogues of current plays. Frequently the dramatists of the
two houses indulge in mutual recrimination, it is true, but
the only reasonable conclusion to be drawn from all they
have to say is that things were in a bad way indeed. But

---

[17] *The Compleat Works of Mr. Thomas Brown*, p. 247. No attempt can be made here to give an adequate sample of the concern,
even the hostility, of critics of theatrical affairs during this trying
period; even a list would run to dozens of titles. For a few of the
most accessible items, see Hotson's quotations from *The Country
Gentleman's Vade Mecum* (1699); Lowe's reproduction of Wright's
Historia Histrionica (1699) in his edition of Cibber's *Apology;*
A Comparison between the Two Stages (1702), edited by S. B.
Wells; or Downes' *Roscius Anglicanus* (1708), edited by Montague Summers.

instead of devoting space to lengthy quotation of typical comments, let us take a bill or two as reproduced in the newspapers. At the end of the 1699-1700 season, for example, this advertisement appeared in the *Flying Post*, 2-4 July:

> At the Request, and for the Entertainment of several Persons of Quality, at the New Theatre in Lincoln's-Inn-Fields, tomorrow, being Friday, the 5th of this Instant July, will be acted, The Comical History of Don Quixote, both parts being made into one by the Author. With a new Entry by the little Boy, being his last time of Danceing before he goes to France: Also Mrs Elford's new Entry, never performed but once; and Miss Evans's Jigg and Irish Dance: With several new Comical Dances, composed and performed by Monsieur L'Sac and others. Together with a new Pastoral Dialogue, by Mr Gorge, and Mrs Haynes; and variety of other Singing. It being for the Benefit of a Gentleman in great distress; and for the Relief of his Wife and Three Children.[18]

A few seasons later the quality of the "entertainments" had, if anything, deteriorated, and this kind of bill was printed in the *Daily Courant* for 18 June 1703:

> Love's Last Shift, or The Fool in Fashion, being the last time of Acting it this Season. With an Entertainment of Flute Musick by Mr. Bannister and his Son. And also a new Piece of Instrumental Musick on the Stage by the best Hands. And the Famous Mr. Claxton and his Son will perform The Highland, and The Whip of Dunboyne. And the Famous Mr. Clynch being now in Town, will for this once, at the desire of several Persons of Quality, perform his Imitation of an Organ with 3 Voices, the Double Curtel, and the Bells, the Huntsman with his Horn and Pack of Dogs; All of which he per-

[18] Reproduced by Alfred Jackson, "Play Notices from the Burney Newspapers," *PMLA*, xlviii (1933), 815-849.

forms with his Mouth on the open Stage, being what no Man besides himself could ever yet attain to.[19]

Along with the singing and other forms of variety appeared the first pantomimes or, to give them the title then current, "Italian night scenes," of which more will be said in the next chapter.

The craze for bills of variety created a greater demand than ever for farce and prepared the way for the separate farce afterpiece. The transition was gradual but by no means slow. Following a precedent already established, the two companies first coupled the shorter farces, which were beginning to appear, with song and dance, or produced loose medleys similar to Motteux's *Novelty* or the much earlier *Play-House to be Lett*. A bill of 30 April 1703, for example, calls for

The Cheats of Scapin. The Comical Rivals, or The School-Boy. "Being the last time of Acting till after *May-Fair*. . . . With several Italian Sonatas by Signior *Gasperini* and others. And the *Devonshire Girl*, being now upon her Return to the City of Exeter, will perform three several Dances, particularly her last New Entry in Imitation of *Madamoiselle Subligni*, and the *Whip of Dunboyn by* Mr. Claxton *her* Master, being the last time of their Performance till Winter. And at the desire of several Persons of Quality (hearing that Mr. *Pinkethman* hath hired the two famous French Girls lately arriv'd from the Emperor's Court), They will perform several Dances on the Rope upon the Stage, being improv'd to that Degree, far exceeding all others in that Art. And their *Father* presents you with the *Newest Humours of Harlequin,* as perform'd by him before the Grand Signior at *Constantinople.* Also the Famous Mr. Evans

[19] This and the following bill are from Avery and Scouten, "A Tentative Calendar of Daily Theatrical Performances in London, 1700-1701 to 1704-1705," *PMLA,* LXIII (1948), 114-180.

lately arriv'd from *Vienna*, will show you Wonders of another kind, Vaulting on the Manag'd Horse, being the greatest Master of that kind in the World. To begin at Five so that all may be done by Nine a Clock.

Then, in the following season of 1703-04, come the first bills with a regular play followed by a single afterpiece. The record is too spotty to insure our knowing which of the several brief farces introduced about this time and destined to stay in the repertory was actually the first to be offered in this manner. Vanbrugh's adaptation of Dancourt's farce-comedy *Maison de campagne* had been produced as early as 1698 and became a regular afterpiece, but there seems to be scant reason to suppose that it was the first to be offered. Cibber's *School-Boy*, the first play in the two-act form which had become almost a requirement for afterpieces by Garrick's day, appeared early in February of this season along with Mrs. Centlivre's equally farcical *Love's Contrivances*. Perhaps as strong a candidate as any is Farquhar's *Stage Coach*, produced at Lincoln's Inn Fields 2 February 1704 after *The Countrey Wit*. There is even some reason to believe that *The Stage Coach* had appeared somewhat earlier. W. J. Lawrence conjectured that it had originally been offered in 1701 as an afterpiece to *Sir Harry Wildair* but offered no real evidence to support his belief. Then, pushing his conjecture to the limit, he suggested that "it was the ultimate vogue of *The Stage Coach* which brought about the firm establishment of the principle of the afterpiece early in the eighteenth century." But he has attached far more importance to the piece than it can possibly have.[20]

[20] "The Mystery of 'The Stage Coach,'" *Modern Language Review*, XXVII (1932), 392-397. Lawrence is disposed to move *The Stage Coach* up several years on the basis of three bits of evidence: (1) a reference to "Stage-coach fare" in the prologue to *The Inconstant*, 1702; (2) a reference to an earlier performance in the epilogue to the farce printed in the London edition of 1705; (3) the phrase "last new farce"—rather than "never acted"—in the bill for the first known performance. Now I have no explanation for the

The use—in 1704, not 1701—of Farquhar's play as an afterpiece had some significance no doubt but no more than that of half a dozen other plays. The absence of any one of them could not have altered the course that events in the theatre were taking.

The decade 1695-1705 has, as I have said, great importance in the history of farce, since out of the strong competition marking those years came eventually the regular use of the farce afterpiece. During this time the bill had been expanded, first to include any catch-penny, crowd-pulling device from song and pantomime to juggling and rope-dancing. Eventually, however, there seems to have been every indication that the solution of the "entertainment" problem would be to settle upon a more consistently dramatic form, the farce.

The next decade, up to the opening of John Rich's new Lincoln's Inn Fields theatre in December 1714, is hardly less significant. The far more detailed record provided by newspaper playbills provides us with a much fuller account of the shifting fortunes of the farce afterpiece during these years. And this account, when studied in connection with the numerous changes in theatrical companies, demonstrates the intimate tie-up between the English farce afterpiece and the fortunes of the theatre.

The practice of giving a single afterpiece after a full-length play, probably introduced sometime during the 1703-04 season, was continued in the two seasons following. In 1704-05, the first season of competition between Drury Lane and the new theatre in the Haymarket which Vanbrugh and his associates opened in April 1705, there

---

reference in the prologue to *The Inconstant*; it may refer to Farquhar's farce but that it does seems far from inevitable. The reference to an earlier performance in the epilogue printed in 1705 is highly inconclusive; it hardly warrants our pushing the date back so far as April 1701, where Lawrence places it. The phrase "last new farce" in the bill does not indicate a first performance, true enough, but it indicates pretty clearly that the first performance was *recent*.

were some twenty afterpieces at Drury Lane. As yet they were likely to be merely comic scenes from older plays, such as Cibber's *School-Boy*, derived from his own *Womans Wit* (1696) and destined to become a fixture in the repertory. It will be noted that in the early stage the practice of hastily concocting afterpieces by merely excerpting scenes closely parallels that which brought the Commonwealth drolls into existence. The Haymarket gave somewhat fewer afterpieces than Drury Lane; only a performance of *The Stage Coach* was an unmistakable farce; the rest of its bills were filled with such plays as *Europe's Revels*, Congreve's *Judgment of Paris*, and the like.

One full season as manager was enough for Vanbrugh, and in the summer of 1706 he approached Swiney with a proposal to rent him the new theatre at what would seem a very low figure, five pounds a day. Whether Vanbrugh knew it or not, Swiney was not a free agent but had been acting all along for Christopher Rich. And Rich was delighted at the proposal, as it would leave him in command of both London theatres. He agreed therefore to let Swiney take the Haymarket and his pick of the company at Drury Lane. Rich was content with singers and dancers, hoping to thrive on the newly aroused interest in opera. During this season of 1706-07 he produced a great many operas, as compared with former years, and relatively few plays; of course, he had only the remains of his former group of actors. There were not more than a half dozen performances of afterpieces, all of them running to song and show. Swiney's company, composed of the pick of the two former troupes, ran a full season of plays, with almost no afterpieces; both *The Stage Coach* and *The Cuckold in Conceit* were acted twice.

The next season is slightly more complex. Sir Thomas Skipwith, one of the sharers in the patent, had previously assigned his large share to a Mr. Brett, no doubt despairing of ever realizing any profit from Drury Lane while Rich

remained in power. Brett proceeded to assert his newly
acquired authority—with no apparent interference from
Rich, who saw that Brett's political connections might be
turned to advantage—and used his influence to force a union
of the two acting companies early in January. The actors
were to perform at Drury Lane while poor Swiney at the
Haymarket had to be content with opera only. Operating
under this arrangement, which virtually ended competition, the two companies finished the season without a
single afterpiece, so far as the records show.

During the season of 1708-09 the Haymarket continued
to give operas only, performing on Wednesdays and Satur-
days. The united players at Drury Lane also continued to
give a full season of plays, but their good luck soon ran out.
It is unfortunate that we do not have a more specific account of the events and their dates, but it seems clear that
something like this happened. Skipwith, seeing that he had
made an error in so casually giving up a share that could
be profitable, now reclaimed it from Brett, who gave up in
disgust. As a result, Rich then found himself in the position he had schemed for all along: he was in command of
a monopoly over plays. And he proceeded to resume at
once the ruinous practices which had led to the secession
of 1695, cutting salaries, making heavy inroads into benefit
receipts—anything calculated to vex his actors and make
them feel insecure.

There was a rather full run of plays this season, but unfortunately production was suspended from 26 October to
14 December on the death of Prince George. There were
no afterpieces this season until the very end, six being
offered in May and June. The company must certainly
have been trying to hold full houses as long as possible—
both because of losses from bad luck and because of the
manager's rapaciousness. Sometime toward the end of the
season the actors petitioned formally for redress, with the
result that Rich was ordered to cease and desist from his

mistreatment of the company and later, when he ignored the order, to stop acting altogether.[21]

Fortunately, the actors, who had come fairly close to petitioning themselves out of their jobs, had the foresight to arrange their affairs ahead of time with Swiney. He now came forward and asked permission to recruit a company from the unemployed Drury Lane actors and resume production at the Haymarket, where a fair run began in September 1709.

Meanwhile Rich bided his time and, fully expecting the ban to be lifted, made preparations to start at Drury Lane. When it became clear that the authorities were through with Rich for good, Collier, another sharer in the patent, sought and obtained permission to resume production at the idle theatre. On 23 November the new Drury Lane company, with a small group of actors not hired by Swiney and the few properties Rich had been unable to make off with,[22] began a regular season's run.

Now, with two companies in regular competition once more, the farce afterpiece was restored to something like the importance it seemed destined to attain five years earlier. The Haymarket company, much the stronger of the two, but handicapped by a poor theatre and by an obligation to perform at least some operas, performed over thirty afterpieces, two of the most popular being *The Stage Coach* (eight times) and *Higgins Variety*[23] (nine times). The

[21] Lowe, in his edition of Cibber's *Apology* (II, 78, n. 1) gives the very interesting rejoinder by Rich, prepared by Rich's treasurer, Zachary Baggs, dated 8 July 1709.

[22] See *Tatler* No. 99 for Steele's amusing mock-heroic account of Collier's taking forcible possession of Drury Lane. Divito, Steele's usual title for Christopher Rich, was routed but he managed to get off with most of the props.

[23] *Higgins Variety* was the name given the performances of a Dutch contortionist. The bills appear in the *Daily Courant* and a description—by a quite unedified spectator, Addison—in *Tatler*, No. 108. It is quite possible that Higgins was aimed at by an order of the Lord Chamberlain of 24 December 1709, cited by Aitken, in

Drury Lane company produced just under thirty, a new farce, *The Walking Statue* by Aaron Hill, the director of the company, being the main attraction (twenty times).

To digress for a moment from the story of theatrical fortunes, I should like to call attention to an interesting bill offered during this 1709-10 season. On 20 April the Haymarket offered two plays by Charles Johnson, a tragedy called *The Force of Friendship* and a farce, *Love in a Chest*. Neither play is worth much attention in itself but the combination is remarkable, for these two had originally been parts of one tragicomedy. The English were tardily coming around to the French view toward mixed genres.[24]

The preface Johnson wrote for the pair of dramas is almost as noteworthy as their history of composition and production. He gives a very dim view of the present state of taste,

> When we see no Audience now can bear the Fatigue of the two Hours good Sense tho' Shakspear or Oatway endeavor to keep 'em awake, without the promis'd Relief of the Stage-Coach, or some such solid Afterlude, a few Lines indeed are now and then forced down their Throats by the help of this Gewgaw, 'tis tack'd to the Tragedy or rather the Tragedy to it, for 'tis the Money Bill; the Actors may design it as a Desert, but they generally find the Palates of their Guests so vitiated that they make a Meal of Whipt Cream, and neglect the more substantial

---

Spectator, 1, 128, n. 2. It forbade added attractions "not necessary to the due performance of the play, 'such as ladder-dancing, antic postures,' &c., without leave being first had." *Higgins Variety* had started on 7 December and was evidently enjoying a good run, but it ran for only three days, 27-29 December, after the order was issued and then was dropped for good.

[24] See Professor Hooker's very interesting article, "Charles Johnson's 'The Force of Friendship' and 'Love in a Chest': a Note on Tragicomedy and Licensing in 1710," *Studies in Philology,* xxxiv (1937), 407-411, based on a study of the prompt copy of the plots as originally joined in one play.

Food which was design'd for their Nourishment; methinks those Gentlemen who have the Management of
the Theatres shou'd agree to banish everything that cou'd
be thought the least below the Dignity of the Stage, but
this I fear we can hardly hope to see while there are two
Houses open—since as the General Taste now is, that
which does not outmonster the other must starve; here
are no publick Stipends for the Player or Poet, they must
submit to the Taste of the Town, nay they are oblig'd
(while they are divided) servilely to emulate one another
in that Submission, nor can we think of seeing any thing
hereafter but Bombast and Farce in the Room of Nervous
Sense and Sterling Wit. . . .

He develops the theme of union at some length, calling
attention to the scarcity of good actors, aggravated by the
splitting up into two companies. With so few good actors
available, the only wise course is to join forces once more:
"There is no other way to Banish Posture-Makers, Foreign
Monsters, Tub Scenes, &c from the Theatre. . . ."[25]

Again change seemed the only thing permanent in theatrical affairs, and the next season began under a new arrangement. One season as manager had been enough to
convince Collier that the Drury Lane company as it was
then constituted was no mint and he therefore decided to
exert his political influence to improve things for himself.
He took over the Haymarket and devoted it once more
entirely to opera. Thus he forced Swiney and the again
united acting company back to Drury Lane and added two
further provisions: a requirement that no plays be acted on
Wednesdays, while the opera was running, and another that
he be paid £200 a year to run the opera. Once more competition was ended and again farce afterpieces were slighted.
There was not a single afterpiece until the season was al-

[25] Old Cibber, looking back to this period in 1740, heartily agrees
with the sentiments of Johnson. See *Apology*, II, 139-140, 179-185.

most over. The first record we have of one is for 30 April. Then for the rest of the season, which ran till the last of August, there are ten, *The Walking Statue* getting most of the attention, *The Stage Coach* being performed three times.

The season of 1710-11 may serve as a pattern for the three to follow, that is, up to the opening of the new Lincoln's Inn Fields theatre in 1714. The Haymarket can be safely ignored as it was now settled as the official opera house and offered plays only rarely. The Drury Lane company, with a monopoly over plays, began to prosper and continued to do so until the next decade, when new troubles arose. Afterpieces had evidently been well enough established by this time to continue being used in spite of the disappearance of competition, but they figured most prominently at the beginning and the end of the season when houses were slimmer than at the height of activities. And even during these three seasons they steadily declined in numbers and might conceivably have disappeared entirely had it not been for the opening of a new theatre. In 1711-12 there were thirty-seven performances of farce afterpieces, in 1712-13 only seventeen, and in 1713-14 the number had dropped to twelve. In this last season there was only one in January, none in February or March.

Then came the 1714-15 season and, on 18 December, the opening of John Rich's new theatre. Without attending to any other details, we can note the effect for a season or two of the restoration of competition, so far as mere numbers of farce afterpieces are concerned. By the end of December 1714 Drury Lane had produced exactly two, but by the end of the season the total had reached forty-five. The new company, starting after mid-December, gave forty-six farce afterpieces and a great variety of "entertainments of dancing" before the close of the season. In short, we are back to the status of the farce in 1705.

In 1715-16, the first full season of competition for several years, Drury Lane produced around a hundred afterpieces, most of them short farces though some were "night Scenes" or musical pieces. Lincoln's Inn Fields had sixty-four farce afterpieces and the usual quantity of "entertainments." It had begun to appear that the farce afterpiece was well on its way to becoming a fixture in the bill. And so it was. The victory was not, however, to be so easy, for another decade was to bring a new enemy in the form of pantomime, which for a time, between 1724 and 1728, seemed on the point of driving the short farce out of existence once more.

The story of pantomime and of the other rivals of farce is significant enough to deserve treatment in a separate chapter. It will be sufficient here to close this story of the theatrical bill, so far as the farce afterpiece is concerned, by glancing at a few critical seasons in the remainder of the period.

The impact of pantomime can readily be seen by comparing the bills of the last season analyzed with those of a decade later when pantomime was flourishing. The two companies in their first full season of rivalry in 1715-16 had produced a total of over 225 afterpieces of one kind or another, well over half being short farces. A good many of these, especially at Lincoln's Inn Fields, were mere "entertainments of dancing," musical offerings, and so on, but there was only the merest beginning of pantomime, in six or eight "Italian night scenes" at the new theatre.

From this extreme, in which dialogue-farce is clearly in command, we move forward a decade and get this pattern: In the season of 1726-27 there were eleven performances of farce afterpieces at the two theatres, Lincoln's Inn Fields offering one lone farce, *The Country House*; meanwhile there were just under 150 performances of pantomimes. There were no new farces: there had been no new ones for five years. There were no great numbers of new pantomimes either, but that was simply because Rich and his rivals needed only one new success each season. During this particular season *The Rape of Proserpine,* at Rich's theatre, was the current sensation.

The fortunes of the two companies provide similar extremes. These may best be shown by letters of Steele and his fellow managers at Drury Lane on two widely separate occasions. At the end of the 1716-17 season we find Steele writing "Dear Prue" a glowing account of the successes of the Drury Lane company and of the imminent collapse of the rival company. Less than ten years later, in December 1724, his co-managers are writing him an agonizing letter telling of *their* imminent collapse and of the flourishing condition of Rich and company.

Both the above letters have a single basis: the great vogue of pantomime, throughout the mid-twenties especially. Until the triumph of *The Beggar's Opera,* with its train of ballad operas and farces and the appearance of several new companies in London, there were times in which the short farce, so popular around 1715-16, seemed doomed to perish from neglect and pantomime to replace it as incidental theatrical entertainment.

The closing seasons of the 1720's, after the triumph of Gay's ballad opera in 1728, saw still another reversal of fortunes, and the farce afterpiece quickly recovered. Having been threatened with near extinction, it now returned to its former flourishing state. Of the two principal causes for this remarkable convalescence one has just been suggested. The unprecedented success of *The Beggar's Opera* introduced a new vogue to rival that of the pantomime. Though Gay's play was itself neither farce nor afterpiece, its fortunes had a very direct bearing on the revival of many an old farce—with songs added, to be sure—and the creation of many a new one. A second cause, the burgeoning of theatrical activity in London, is somewhat less direct but no less effective. Potter's Little Haymarket had opened as early as 1720 but for the first years of its existence it had offered only foreign bills by visiting Frenchmen or, after

1727, the productions, largely acrobatic, of Mme. Violante and her company. From about 1728-29, however, the Little Haymarket came into more direct competition with the other theatres and began offering the usual bills of plays with "entertainments," both pantomime and farce. With the opening of Goodman's Fields in the East End in 1729 and Rich's new Covent Garden house three years later, theatrical business began to flourish in a way London had not seen in just short of a century.

In these propitious times farce also flourished. Pantomime shared in the theatrical prosperity of the 1730's, though its early popularity when it had been very much the fad was now considerably reduced. The newer companies at the Little Haymarket and Goodman's Fields gave fewer of these more expensive productions than their more established rivals at the patent theatres. The Little Haymarket went in for still another genre when, especially during Henry Fielding's management, it produced numerous burlesque afterpieces. But burlesque never proved to be so dangerous a rival of farce as pantomime had been.

A few samples of the remaining seasons up to mid-eighteenth century will show how well established the farce afterpiece had become. In 1733-34, for instance, there were six theatres running. Much of the time not all six were operating simultaneously, but there were occasions, especially at the height of the holiday seasons, when the London theatre-goer had all six to choose among. This season saw over 500 productions of afterpieces of one kind or another of which only about half were pantomimes. The season of 1736-37, the last season of free competition before the Licensing Act closed down all but the two patent houses, produced somewhat fewer than 500 afterpieces, and again pantomimes and plays were about on equal terms though this time the latter ran somewhat more than usual toward burlesques—it was after all the vogue of the burlesque which proved chiefly instrumental in bringing about the ban on the non-licensed theatres—and to sentimental or allegorical pieces like Dodsley's *Toy-Shop* or *King and Miller*.

The last dozen years of the period under survey find the farce afterpiece firmly established on the London stage and farce itself largely restricted to the afterpiece except for the occasional revival of a full-length play with farcical scenes. Pantomime seemed for a time to be on the wane, in part at least because of the war against raised prices for these more extravagant productions. Appearances proved deceiving, however, and pantomime was to enjoy greater popularity in the decade following the mid-century, so much so that Professor Stone has called the 1750's the "decade of pantomime,"[26] a label which would be more appropriate for the 1720's. In any event, pantomime remained a formidable rival of farce for generations but it never again regained its early ascendancy.

Perhaps as clear a picture of the typical playbill as one can find is to be found in an interesting document reproduced by Miss Rosenfeld. A troupe of London actors making plans for a summer campaign in Kent in 1739 announced their entire repertory at the beginning of the season, so that anyone desiring a particular play or bill could make his wishes known to the manager. The list contains the titles of twenty-seven tragedies, thirty-nine comedies, and the following twenty "farces": *Cheats of Scapin, Contrivances, Country House, Damon and Phillida, Devil to Pay, Flora, Honest Yorkshireman, Intriguing Chambermaid, King and Miller, Lottery, Mock Doctor, Stage Coach, School-Boy, Lover's Opera, Sir John Cockle, Toy-Shop, Tanner of York, Virgin Unmask'd, What D'ye Call It,* and *Wedding.*[27]

It will be observed that the majority of the pieces listed are actually farcical. A few are short sentimental comedies;

[26] "The God of His Idolatry," *Joseph Quincy Adams Memorial Studies* (Washington, D.C., 1948), p. 117.
[27] *Strolling Players* (Cambridge, 1939), p. 232.

one is chiefly burlesque; at least one is what we may call, for want of a better term, *petite comédie*. While the list may run slightly too much toward the farcical, and while it applies to a troupe on tour and therefore unable to produce its quota of pantomimes, it will serve as an approximate pattern for decades to come. On occasion there will be a shift in taste or fashion which will increase the number of sentimental pieces or raise the quality of the afterpiece to genuine comedy—just as in the 1730's the influence of Fielding brought about the vogue of the burlesque or in the 1750's Foote was to popularize the short satirical piece. At no time, however, did genuine farce relinquish the lead.

CHAPTER 4

RIVAL ENTERTAINMENTS: PANTOMIME, BURLESQUE, SATIRE, SENTIMENT

++

> Here you've a Dragon, Windmill, and a Devil,
> A Doctor, Conjurer, all wond'rous civil;
> A Harlequin, and Puppets, Ghosts, and Fiends,
> And Raree-Show to gain some Actors Ends:
> So perfectly polie is grown this town,
> No Play, without a windmill, will go down.
>   —*The British Stage* (1724)

++

CHIEF among the forms competing with the short farce for the position of afterpiece—or, to use the eighteenth-century term, "entertainment"—was the pantomime, which for a time threatened to drive the farce out of existence. The English pantomime was perhaps as much ally as rival, but it was looked upon as a dangerous competitor, as indeed it was. In the long run the success of pantomime served to strengthen the position of the farce afterpiece by helping to insure a bill with added attractions, but during the earlier stages of its history its influence looked anything but benign.

Like the farce afterpiece, the pantomime grew out of the period of cutthroat competition following the breakup of the united company in 1695. Part of that story has been covered in the preceding chapter, but the history of the part taken by pantomime in this struggle calls for a somewhat more detailed account.

The early history of English pantomime is even more obscure than that of farce, not only because of the low esteem with which it was looked upon by the critics but also because the scenari describing the action were not printed. Earlier than the end of the seventeenth century we find only hints of pantomimic action, chiefly in connection with dancing, in the theatre. Some of the "entertainments" recorded by Pepys, such as the Polichinelli dance following *The Sullen Lovers* on 2 May 1668, clearly involved pantomime. A good bit more ambitious and extensive were some of the scenes hinted at in stage directions of plays borrowed more or less directly from the Italians: Ravenscroft's *Scaramouch* (1677), Mrs. Behn's *Emperor of the Moon* (1687), the latter play having sometimes been referred to as "pantomimic farce."[1] It will soon become clear, in fact, that the chief influence of the *commedia dell'arte* on the English theatre is to be found in pantomimes much more than in plays.

With the deadly rivalry between the two companies at the turn of the century we begin to get the first signs of pantomimes. These appear at the start to be no more than "Scaramouch dances" of a type known much earlier, but it is not long before "Italian night scenes" enter. In the absence of scenari we must depend upon the necessarily meager description of newspaper playbills or the comments of an occasional critic.

One of the earliest and most circumstantial of these latter is to be found in *A Comparison between the Two Stages* (1702). When Ramble proposes to his companions that they shift their discussion to the vogue of singing and dancing in the theatre, they fall to with a will, one trying to outdo the other in condemnation. However biased their comments may be, they still provide us with some interest-

---

[1] Summers quotes the phrase from Lowe, with approval (*Behn*, III, 387). There are partially pantomimic scenes borrowed from the Italian comedians in Mountfort's *Faustus* (1688) and Motteux's *Novelty* (1697). Professor Nicoll suggests that the operatic version of *Midsummer Night's Dream*, called *The Fairy Queen* (1692), anticipated pantomime, *History*, I, 161. The description given by Downes lends support to this conjecture.

ing particulars. After a vigorous assault on Italian opera, which was just then making its first big campaign in the English theatre, they turn to the dancers recently imported from France:

> CRIT. Oh what a charming sight 'twas to see Madam— what a pox d'ee call her?—the high German Buttock— swim it along the stage between her two Gipsie daughters: they skated along the ice so cleaverly, you might ha' sworn they were of right Dutch extraction.
>
> SULL. And the Sieur Allard—.
>
> CRI. Ay, the Sieur with a pox to him—and the two Monsieurs his sons—rogues that show at Paris for a groat a piece and here they were entertainment for the court and his late Majesty.
>
> RAMB. Oh—Harlequin and Scaramouch.
>
> CRI. Ay; What a rout here was with a night piece of Harlequin and Scaramouch? with the guittar and the bladder! What jumping over tables and joint-stools! What ridiculous postures and grimaces! and what an exquisite trick 'twas to straddle before the audience, making a thousand damn'd French faces, and seeming in labour with a monstrous birth, at last my counterfeit male lady is delivered of her two puppies Harlequin and Scaramouch.
>
> SULL. And yet the Town was so fond of this, that these rascals brought the greatest houses that ever were known: 'Sdeath I am scandaliz'd at these little things; I am asham'd to own my self of a country where the spirit of poetry is dwindled into vile farce and foppery.
>
> RAMB. But what have you to say to Madam Ragonde and her eight daughters? I assure you I think Nivelong a very humorous dancer.[2]

With the help of the now comparatively full record of theatrical events and persons we are able to determine with

[2] p. 28.

some accuracy what this critical blast was all about. From other commentators of the day, from the newspaper bills (the date here, 1702, is highly important in the annals of journalism; this is the year in which the first English daily, the *Daily Courant*, began), and from the records of the French stage we can identify the persons named and hazard a good guess as to the nature of the performances. "Nivelong" was Louis Nivellon, "un des meilleurs danseurs pantomimes qui aient paru aux foires," as Campardon describes him. He was dancing at Drury Lane in mid-August of this year, along with the philoprogenitive Mme. Ragonde.[3]

The Harlequin and Scaramouch are a little less certain since the actors are not named. John Weaver, the dancing master, recalled a "night scene of the Sieur Alard and his two sons, performed on the stage in Drury-Lane about seven or eight and twenty years ago. . . ."[4] The specific performance described by Critic is more likely to have been by an even more interesting pair whom Weaver also recalls and who were in the newspaper bills a few days after Nivellon and his company. The bill in the *Daily Courant* for Saturday, 22 August, reads, after the announcement of the main play and a list of "entertainments" much like a modern vaudeville bill, "And Monsieur Serene and another person lately arrived in England will perform a night scene by a Harlequin and Scaramouch, after the Italian manner."[5]

"Monsieur Serene" was, without much question, the French actor-dancer Sorin, who had signed a contract with Betterton six years earlier at Lincoln's Inn Fields[6] and had appeared the following summer in Motteux's *Novelty*. "An-

---

[3] *Les Spectacles de la foire* (Paris, 1877), II, 175. From the hint in Ramble's last speech and the fact that Campardon lists no Mme. Ragonde, I assume that this was a farcical impersonation by Nivellon.

[4] *The History of the Mimes and Pantomimes* (1728).

[5] The entries from the *Daily Courant* for 1702-1705 may be found in the articles by Alfred Jackson (see Bibliography).

[6] Nicoll, *History*, I, 384.

other person" suggests an unmanageable latitude, but here again there seems to be little doubt as to the identity of Sorin's companion. Behind the vague phrase is almost certainly Richard Baxter, the other half of the international team of Sorin and Baxter which was to endure for at least twenty years in the French and English theatres.[7]

There is no uncertainty about the bills announcing the pair a little over a year later. The *Daily Courant* for 7 October 1703 announces "a night scene between Scaramouch and Harlequin, to be perform'd by the famous Monsieur Surrein and Mr Baxter, who make but a short stay in England." Their short stay lasted till at least 29 October, when the patrons of the theatre were warned that Sorin and Baxter were to give a last performance. From an intervening bill, that for 12 October, we get something more detailed as to the nature of their performance, which is described as "a comical entertainment in a tavern between Scaramouch, Harlequin, and Punchanello." This piece seems pretty certainly to have been the first production of John Weaver, *The Tavern Bilkers*, which he places first in the list of English pantomimes in his *History of Mimes and Pantomimes* and which he admits, regretfully, to have been based upon the Italian comedians.

One is tempted to find a connection between these early pantomimic scenes performed by foreign visitors and the

---

[7] Detailed accounts of this interesting pair appear in the *Mémoires* (Paris, 1743) of the brothers Parfaict and the works of Bonnassies and Campardon. For some years they were in the troupe of Madame Baron, daughter-in-law of the famous actor. Much of the time they lent their own names to the company, as she was under the shadow of the law because of the debts her husband had left her. When she was finally forced out of control about 1718, Baxter and Sorin are said to have retired to the provinces. They returned in 1721 for one last and unsuccessful attempt at the fairs, and then they disappear from the records after that. The problem of tracing them is complicated a little by some curious orthography. In England Sorin's name is spelled Surrein, Surin, Surene, and Serene; in France Baxter becomes Bastee.

spectacles produced at the Parisian fairs of St. Germaine and St. Laurent in these same years, but the possibility of getting beyond mere conjecture is remote. The nature of the productions of the *forains* is if anything more obscure than that of the shows at Drury Lane. It is a matter of record, however, that they took over some of the devices and eventually even some of the plays of the Italian comedians when the latter were dispersed in 1697. Lancaster says that from "1701-8 the *forains* gave crude plays, or detached scenes, many in the manner of the Théâtre Italien or directly derived from it, some borrowed with modifications from the French repertory."[8] What is intriguing—and baffling—here is the kind of modifications used. Certainly the *forains* must have learned much about pantomiming from the Italians. And the long series of subterfuges employed to get around the ban on dialogue must have included various kinds of miming.[9] As early as 1699 d'Argenson had forbidden "*tous particuliers de représenter aucune comédie ni farce.*" Clearly the actors at the fairs had not obeyed, for in 1706 the police were obliged to repeat the ban on "*spectacles où il y ait des dialogues.*" Campardon, in quoting various reports of visits made by the police after complaints had been lodged against the *forains*, gives us some idea of the ingenious use made of monologues, intermittent dialogue, and mixtures of speech and pantomime.[10] Repeated decisions from 1707 to 1710 favoring the Comédie Française finally drove the actors into playing *à la muette*—that is, into pantomime supplemented by *cartons* or *écriteaux*, speeches copied on strips of paper to be held up

[8] *Sunset* (Baltimore, 1945), p. 316.
[9] Lancaster informs us that certain scenes of the play on the fall of Troy printed in 1705 are entirely pantomimic. *Sunset*, p. 313.
[10] Campardon reproduces so many of these depositions that specific reference is hardly necessary; the fullest are given in the entries for the impresarios of the various booths at the fairs, such as Mme. Baron. See also the Parfaict *Mémoires*, pp. 108-109.

before the audience, much in the manner of our modern teleprompter—and, very shortly afterwards, to *vaudevilles*, which anticipate the English ballad opera by several years.

All of these events to which dates can be attached are after the events of 1702-03 at Drury Lane. We cannot even be sure that the visiting actors were as yet connected with the fairs, though I suspect they were. The Alards had been producing some kind of spectacle there at least as early as 1700, but the first record we have of the appearance of Sorin and Baxter is in 1707.

For the decade following 1705 the story of English pantomime is largely a blank. The reasons for so large a gap after what might have seemed a promising beginning have already been set forth in the preceding chapter: with the ending of competition between two companies on approximately equal footing after the union of 1705 there was little call for "entertainments" before John Rich reestablished competition late in 1714.

There are scattered examples of pantomime suggested here and there in this period, usually by way of a revival of earlier pantomimic pieces. Mrs. Behn's *Emperor of the Moon*, for instance, enjoyed a revival of sorts. In focussing attention on the activities of foreign visitors from 1700 to 1705, I have passed over a curious and interesting story involving this play. It will be recalled that Sorin and possibly Baxter made their first appearance in a "night scene after the Italian manner" in August 1702 and that, if this is the actual performance referred to in *A Comparison between the Two Theatres*, their playing brought "the greatest houses that ever were known." With such encouragement the Drury Lane company could hardly resist trying their luck in pantomime. Consequently, on 18 September, some weeks before the regular production of plays was to start, they tried an experiment. The *Daily Courant* gives this interesting bill for the occasion:

At the Desire of some Persons of Quality, this present Friday being the 18th of September, at the Theatre Royal in Drury Lane will be presented a Comedy called, The Emperor of the Moon; wherein Mr Penkethman acts the part of Harlequin without a Masque, for the Entertainment of an African Prince lately arrived here, being Nephew to the King of Bauday of that country. With several entertainments of singing and dancing and the last new Epilogue never spoken but once by Mr Penkethman.

Pinkethman's venture was not destined to meet with success. Years later Cibber remembered the event as disastrous:

Penkethman could not take to himself the Shame of the Character without being concealed—he was no more Harlequin—his Humour was quite disconcerted! his Conscience could not with the same Effronterie declare against Nature without the cover of that unchanging Face, which he was sure would never blush for it! no! it was quite another case![11]

In any event *The Emperor of the Moon* remained a staple in the repertory as one of the few stock pieces providing an opportunity for pantomimic farce. Pinkethman was still playing Harlequin at Drury Lane in March 1709, presumably with mask. The records tell us that Estcourt, another popular clown of the day, was the Scaramouch. When Collier founded a new company at Drury Lane the following November, after Rich had been stopped by a court order and the regular company had gone over to Swiney at the Haymarket, *The Emperor of the Moon* was performed at Drury Lane with Jemmy Spiller, in time to become a popular farceur, as Harlequin and "with a new Italian night scene." Precisely what was new about the scene I am unable to say. I call attention to it to indicate

[11] *Apology*, I, 151-152.

the persistence, especially when any competition seemed to call for it, of the search for novelty, this time apparently pantomimic novelty.[12]

In the period just before 1715 pantomime remained dormant with only a few signs of reawakening. There are "Harlequins" in the bills of late May 1714 at Drury Lane, though the record is too meager to suggest what the performances were like. Then in the following November and December there are more performances of *The Emperor of the Moon.* For these performances Pinkethman—we are safe, I believe, in assuming that he was the Harlequin in these productions—doubtless complied with the wishes of his audience by wearing a mask. At any rate the Theatre Collection at Harvard contains a manuscript wardrobe bill for 27 October signed by Wilks, Cibber, and Booth and listing, along with other items, one "ffor 2 Harlekene Masques 0:10:0."

The revival of free competition with the opening of John Rich's new theatre in Lincoln's Inn Fields in December 1714 had, it will be recalled, the immediate and striking result of restoring vigorous life to the almost moribund farce afterpiece. In less than a decade this same event was to have an even more sweeping effect upon pantomime, which had never quite managed to establish itself in the English theatre.

For the first seven or eight years after the renewal of competition the actual events concerning the revival of pantomimes are obscure, or, to adopt another point of view, the responsibilities of the rival companies in establishing this enemy to regular drama have not always been accurately assessed. Too often the blame has been placed entirely on John Rich and his company. Percy Fitzgerald, for example, has left a misleading account of what took place:

[12] Aitken reproduces an order of the Lord Chamberlain for 24 December 1709, indicating a renewal of interest in variety. The order forbade "representation on the stage not necessary to the due performance of the play, 'such as ladder dancing, antic postures, &c.' without leave being first had." *Spectator*, I, 129, n. 2.

It was in this year, 1717, that Rich devised this new species of entertainment; and it is curious that for a period of nearly forty years he was to hold possession of the town, and cause successive generations of managers—Cibber, Fleetwood, and Garrick—the most serious inconvenience, owing to this superior attraction. "Harlequin Sorcerer" was the first of these successes.

The other house, for all their classical professions, had to follow suit. . . .[13]

This account has the great advantage, so ardently sought after in a history, of fixing responsibility by identifying the culprit, but the facts are somewhat at odds with it. That Rich did begin fairly early in his career as entrepreneur to use pantomimic entertainments is a matter of record. The tastes in theatrical fare he had inherited from his father were by no means exalted. He soon found it necessary, moreover, to resort to any measures which promised to help at the box office. The newspaper bills show him using a variety of combinations: tragedy or comedy with farce, farce with farce, and a strong mixture of "Entertainments of dancing." During one season, that of 1718-19, he turned his theatre over to a troupe of visiting Frenchmen.

Meanwhile Drury Lane did not allow Rich's challenge— feeble as it was—to go unanswered. Cibber gives an account which will prove on examination to be disingenuous but nonetheless interesting:

I have upon several occasions already observ'd, that when one company is too hard for another, the lower in reputation has always been forced to exhibit some new-fangled foppery to draw the multitude after them: of these ex-

---

[13] *A New History of the English Stage* (London, 1882), I, 419-420. The reference to *Harlequin Sorcerer* is misleading. If, as I assume, the reference is to Theobald's pantomime of that name, first produced in January 1725, it was neither the first nor the first to succeed.

pedients, singing and dancing had formerly been the most effectual; but, at the time I am speaking of, our English musick had been so discountenanced since the taste of Italian operas prevail'd, that it was to no purpose to pretend to it. Dancing therefore was now the only weight in the opposite scale, and as the new theatre sometimes found their account in it, it could not be safe for us wholly to neglect it. To give even dancing therefore some improvement, and to make it something more than motion without meaning, the fable of Mars and Venus was form'd into a connected presentation of dances in character, wherein the passions were so happily expressed, and the whole story so intelligbly told by a mute narration of gesture only, that even thinking spectators allow'd it both a pleasing and a rational entertainment. . . .[14]

John Weaver was responsible for concocting this pleasing and rational entertainment which the Drury Lane company had substituted for the new-fangled foppery introduced by their rivals under Rich. His story of the beginnings of English pantomime has, as the reference to it above in connection with the "night scenes" of 1702-03 shows, its own peculiar bias but it uses somewhat more facts and somewhat less rhetoric than the later and better known account just quoted. If we examine Weaver's list of early pantomimes we find that in the period between 1716 and 1723, when the first big success, the Drury Lane *Doctor Faustus*, was presented, there are eight pantomimes at Drury Lane to only five at Lincoln's Inn Fields. And to judge by titles, which is about all Weaver provides us, the Drury Lane offerings were no less "monstrous medlies," than those presented by Rich.

Though Weaver's account is not completely accurate, it does suggest a reasonably even distribution of responsi-

[14] *Apology*, II, 179-180.

bility, and this verdict is borne out by the newspaper records and by certain other documents recently made available. The actual competition in pantomime began well before the spring of 1717 when *Mars and Venus* first appeared. John Rich began the war, but his more successful rivals were not slow in counterattacking. In the first few months after the opening of the Lincoln's Inn Fields house Rich presented an "Italian night scene" and an "Entertainment of music" called *The Beau Demolished* (3 March 1715). At least three other bills this season at Lincoln's Inn Fields suggest pantomime. In 1715-16 there are still more. In addition to four pieces which have the unmistakable "Italian night scene" label there are numerous "Entertainments of dancing," some of which involve Harlequin and Punch. Then in 1716-17 there are still more "Italian night scenes" and, by April, a full-fledged pantomime, *The Cheats, or the Tavern Bilkers*, which looks very much like Weaver's old *Tavern Bilkers* of 1702.

Meanwhile the other house was beginning to show an interest in pantomime. Unlike Rich, they could hardly plead hard times as their excuse. Twenty-five years later Cibber looks back to this time and recalls that he and his fellow sharers had begun to prosper as they had never prospered before. By the end of the 1716-17 season we find Steele writing his wife jubilantly: "I write this from Richmond, where I have been since yesterday morning at a Lodging near Wilks, who I believe, will bring matters to bear so that there will be no Play-House but Ours, allowing Rich, who is almost broke, a Sallary while there is but one House. I am in hopes one way or other let the Courtiers do as unthankfully as they please, I shall pick up a Comfortable fortune."[15]

[15] *Correspondence of Richard Steele*, p. 353. Miss Blanchard in a note on this letter cites a story in the *Weekly Packet* of the following 28 September-8 October rumoring that Rich had assigned his patent to Keene and Bullock, Jr.

Yet with all their prosperity the managers of Drury Lane were not so scornful of the new entertainments as they sometimes publicly professed to be. Earlier, in No. 2 of his *Town-Talk* (23 December 1715), we find Steele writing about projected reforms in the theatre. The ones he specifies have to do largely with the encouragement of writers, but no doubt other reforms were intended or a promise of them even implied. Significantly he admits that the project had been set aside on the opening of a new house "against them," but now they are ready to start their improvements.

If the reforms did include dispensing with song and dance and other entertainments, as seems to me to be implied,[16] Steele is being disingenuous here, or he has an exceedingly short memory. For just a month before this he was corresponding with the Earl of Stair, then acting as minister to Paris, over having the latter hire a certain "Mr. Baxter and his companion." Stair's response leaves no doubt as to the identity of the pair mentioned. They were Baxter and Sorin, the Harlequin and Scaramouch of the "Italian Night Scenes" of 1703-05. The letter is interesting enough to quote in full:

I received y^r commands some time ago concerning Mr Baxter and his companion, they took some days to consider wt answer they should make, it is yt they are engaged to a woman here for ye fair of St Germain wch begins ye 2nd of February. Baxter has 5000 livres from her, so ye time being so short they are unwilling to make ye journey into England; when the fair is over you may command y^m but I suppose y^t wont answer to y^r view wch was to have em for ye winter.

I'm sorry my negociation has no better success, but I

---

[16] Six years before, in *Tatler* No. 12, Steele had taken Divito (Christopher Rich) severely to task because "he having no understanding in this polite way, brought in upon us, to get in his money, ladder-dancers, rope-dancers, jugglers, and mountebanks, to strut in the place of Shakespeare's heroes, and Jonson's humorists."

hope y^t wont rebut you from employing mee whenever you think I can be usefull to you. I'll give you my word [no one] can be wth more sincere value and esteem y^n I am, Sir,

Y^r very obedient and very humble servant
Stair[17]

In spite of Stair's apologies, Steele seems to have found that the later arrangement suggested would "answer." The Fair of St. Germain, for which Baxter and Sorin were under contract to Madame Baron, now Madame Beaune, would ordinarily run till Palm Sunday, which was on 25 March this year. On 3 April 1716, two days after Easter, the Drury Lane company was able to announce that on the very next day they would present, after *The Relapse*, "an Italian Night Scene, perform'd by Mons. Sorin, and Mr. Baxter, lately arriv'd from Paris."[18]

On the next day, Wednesday, 4 April, the bill called for *The Country Wife* instead and added "an Italian Farce call'd The Whimsical Death of Harlequin. The Parts of Scaramouch and Harlequin to be perform'd by Mons. Sorin, and Mr. Baxter, lately arriv'd from Paris: who have variety of Entertainments of that Kind, and make but a short stay in England."

During their stay, which lasted through 14 May, these two performed some four or five of their boasted variety of pieces, perhaps the most notable being one called *La Guinguette: or, Harlequin turn'd Tapster*, which was doubtless the Abbé Pellegrin's *Arlequin à la guinguette*, accounted for as in their repertory by Campardon and described by the Parfaict brothers in their *Dictionnaire*.[19] Though it was

---

[17] *Correspondence of Richard Steele*, p. 109.
[18] This item and the following are from the *Daily Courant*.
[19] The Parfaicts describe this piece as a "Divertissement en trois entrées, par ecriteaux, de M. l'Abbé Pellegrin, représenté au jeu de Bel-Air, sur le Théâtre des Sieurs Baxter & Saurin a l'ouverture de la Foire S. Laurent, 1711." "Tavern" scenes were evidently held in

probably necessary to adapt it somewhat to the English theatre, it was pretty certainly played as a pantomime since it was already being played at the fairs *à la muette.*

But even if the pieces performed by Baxter and Sorin in the spring of 1716 were only partially pantomimic, audiences at Drury Lane had not long to wait for the real thing, for in March of the following season the company began the run of John Weaver's *Mars and Venus* mentioned above. Steele and company were giving Rich tit for tat.

Pantomimes continued to appear on occasion in the bills for both theatres during the next five or six seasons, with Rich offering a good many more than his Drury Lane rivals—sufficient indication that Weaver's memory was none too reliable—but with neither company showing any disposition to neglect the "entertainment" portion of the bill. Then at the height of the 1723-24 season both companies introduced tremendously popular pantomimes based on the old Doctor Faustus story: the age of pantomime had arrived.

It has sometimes been customary to suppose that Rich's company again took the lead and that Drury Lane followed in mere self-defense,[20] but the facts are just the opposite. John Thurmond prepared an elaborate pantomime on the old legend and had it produced at Drury Lane on 26 November. It was successful enough to catch the attention of Rich, who soon had his pantomime composers and stage carpenters busy on the same story. In less than a month, on 20 December, the new company brought out

---

high esteem by these pantomimic actors who shuttled back and forth across the channel. We have already seen a *Tavern Bilkers* at Drury Lane as early as 1702. I have no way of knowing whether there is any connection between these pieces, or whether either had any connection with the *Guinguette angloise* performed at the French fairs in 1729 and 1731 by a troupe of actors of whom some were playing in pantomimes at Drury Lane in 1726. (See n. 21 below.)

[20] See, for example, H. B. Wheatley, *Hogarth's London* (London, 1909), p. 350.

The Necromancer: or, Harlequin Doctor Faustus, with the manager no doubt occupying the title role under his stage name of Lun.

These pieces created a sensation and were performed for many nights, much to the detriment of more legitimate dramatic forms and to the chagrin of "people of taste." The literature of the period is filled with the sharpest criticisms of both the major theatres for their pandering to the fondness for novelty. When we add the older Haymarket Theatre with its steady run of operas and the new Little Haymarket, which was offering French plays during most of these seasons, and which would descend even lower by 1726-27 and offer nothing but tumbling and dancing, we do have a pretty dismal picture indeed for lovers of refined tragedy and comedy—to say nothing of ambitious composers in these genres. Nor was the short farcical afterpiece in much better situation. From a high point of over one hundred performances in 1715-16 the short farce had dropped in ten years to a mere dozen performances, these appearing usually toward the end of the season when the size of the audience had declined to an extent where it was no longer profitable to offer the more expensive pantomime.

With the 1723-24 season the fortunes of the two major theatres began to turn. For some years Rich had found hard sailing at Lincoln's Inn Fields. We have seen Steele's letter of June 1716 telling of Rich's verging on bankruptcy. Four years later, according to an undocumented statement by Fitzgerald, the company was said to be dissolved and the house seized in execution for debt. Actually the company continued to produce, but for at least a few more seasons, right up to 1723-24, it labored under severe difficulties. Then came several months of crowded houses and the tables were quickly turned.[21] We can now match Steele's

[21] Though Rich's pantomime, *The Necromancer,* became a great drawing card, the fortunes of Lincoln's Inn Fields had already begun to turn the preceding spring when, in February, Rich had produced Fenton's *Mariamne.* Ironically, Fenton's play had been turned down by Cibber; it had phenomenal success under Rich.

exulting letter of 1716 with a desperate plea from his co-managers in December 1724:

> We have long wish'd for your coming to Town; but, are now oblig'd to desire you to make all possible speed to us. Our audiences decrease daily, and those low Entertainments which you & we so heartily despise, draw the Numbers, while we act only to the Few who are blessed with common Sense. Though the Operas are allow'd to be much worse than they were formerly, yet they draw much better Audiences, and some persons of distinction, not to be nam'd have Encourag'd a set of *French Comedians* to come over by *Subscription*, who are to act next Wednesday at the Little Theatre in the Haymarket. Thus, while there are three Playhouses exhibiting nonsense of different kinds against us, 'tis impossible we shou'd subsist much longer. Both the Courts have forsaken us. All we can do is, to make the best of a losing Game, and part from the whole upon the best Terms we can. No person living, but ourselves, is sensible of the low state we are reduced to, Therefore, we need not observe to you, how very needful it is to keep the secret.
>
> There are several persons of Fortune, that, we have reason to believe, wou'd be glad to purchase our Interests, and put it upon the Foot of the Opera by fixing the Direction into an *Academy*, which is, we think, the only way to support & perpetuate the English Theatre. We have nothing more to add but our hearty wishes for your Health, and quick arrival among us, and in the Mean time to begg y^r speedy answer.
>
> We are, Sir,
>
> > Your most Obedient, Humble servants,
> > Robert Wilks, B. Booth, C. Cibber
>
> London, Dec. 12, 1724[22]

[22] *The Correspondence of Richard Steele*, pp. 184-185. The writer of *A Letter to My Lord . . . on the Present Diversions of the Town*, 1725, defends Steele while condemning Wilks, Booth, and

I find it impossible to resist commenting on the statement about "low Entertainments which you & we so heartily despise," for here is an excellent illustration of rationalization.[23] We have just seen that even during prosperous times the Drury Lane managers could not resist the comparatively insignificant demand for "low Entertainments." We know also that they had unwittingly wrought their own destruction by taking the lead in the Faustus affair. And if we look once more at the theatrical calendar we will see that this particular demonstration of contempt for pantomime is the merest sour grapes.

In the early part of the season during which this letter was written, their pantomime artist John Thurmond had hit upon what must have seemed a clever idea for a new pantomime. The notorious Jack Sheppard had provided a major news sensation by his last series of escapades in the fall, culminating in his being hanged on 16 November. In less than two weeks Thurmond was ready with his new pantomime, *Harlequin Jack Sheppard,* based upon the desperado's last hours in Newgate and at Tyburn. It was produced on 28 November. Unfortunately for Thurmond and his patrons, on the very same night Rich began an enormously successful revival of the old Beaumont and Fletcher *Prophetess.* So successful was this piece that for a solid month and more the receipts at Lincoln's Inn Fields tripled

---

Cibber. The three professionals, he thinks, have been deceiving Steele.

[23] One thing upon which Rich and his rivals seem to have been able to agree was the method of justifying these entertainments. In addition to Cibber's remarks, in his *Apology* and elsewhere, we have Booth's (or at least what the younger Cibber puts into Booth's mouth) in *The Lives and Characters,* 1753, p. 68. Rich spoke for himself, in the dedication of *The Rape of Proserpine,* 1727, defending, as Booth and Cibber had done, the production of "Entertainments" on the grounds of economic necessity. He goes so far as to promise, "for my own Part, that whenever the Publick Taste shall be disposed to return to the Works of the Drama, no one shall rejoice more sincerely than my self."

and even quadrupled. Thurmond's novel pantomime was lost in the rush and was quietly withdrawn after a brief week's run. At this point, the actor-managers sent out their distress signal to Steele—and their pious condemnation of "low Entertainments."[24]

To complete the story of the disastrous turn of fortune for Steele and his partners, by the time *The Prophetess* had completed its run Lewis Theobald had a new pantomime, *Harlequin Sorcerer*, ready for a run of well over a month, and Rich was on easy street.

The triumph of pantomime over farce, though almost devastatingly complete, was not destined to be permanent, as the story of the farce afterpiece told in the last chapter has indicated. With the revival of interest in plays, largely stimulated by the amazing success of *The Beggar's Opera*, the farce afterpiece enjoyed a full recovery, and, from the close of the 1720's on to mid-century and beyond, the two rival forms competed on fairly even terms. True, the bitterest criticism continued to be levelled at pantomime rather than at farce, but it would be hard to demonstrate that these assaults had any appreciable effects upon its popularity.

There was a so-called "war on pantomimes" around 1744-45, but the title is more than a little misleading. The opposition to pantomime was actually caused by the insistence of the managers—especially Fleetwood of Drury Lane—on raising admission prices sharply when presenting a new pantomime. The audiences soon began to complain, with considerable justice it appears, that the managers were using the excuse of added expense for pantomimes to get all prices raised. For some months there was trouble, growing in time into actual rioting in the theatre and producing several pamphlets against rapacious managers. Even Horace Walpole, who prided himself on his obvious superiority to

---

[24] *The Laureate* (1740), p. 86, lashes Cibber for his hypocrisy in sneering at pantomimes while taking the lead in producing them.

the mob of theatre-goers, found himself suddenly projected into the midst of the fray one evening at Drury Lane. In a letter to his friend Mann he tells us of one of the battles in the war then at its height. There had been a particularly warm exchange of pleasantries in the theatre that night when some of Fleetwood's professional bullies were engaged by the young bucks in the pit. Then, when an actor appeared on the stage to make a few remarks in extenuation of the conduct of Fleetwood, Walpole momentarily lost his self-possession and shouted, "He is an impudent rascal!" This one impetuous outburst was enough, however, to place him in a most embarrassing position as leader of a mob.[25] The rebels were eventually appeased, however, and pantomime was able not only to survive but to become a permanent fixture in the British theatre.

Enough and more about the rivalry between pantomime and farce in filling the demand for "entertainments." I want to turn back now to an earlier point, the statement that pantomime was also a relative—an ambitious younger brother—of farce in that the typical pantomime production contained a good bit of farce.

In his account of English pantomimes up to 1728 John Weaver suggests that the pattern for the successful pantomime was the result of a compromise. His own ambition all along had been to follow the ancients, as he clearly demonstrates by lengthy quotations from Lucian's "Of Pantomimes" with its high praise of the art of the mime. Weaver manages eventually to pay the art the highest possible compliment when he connects it with Aristotle: "It is plain, from Lucian and others, they pursued the rules of Aristotle, and the old poets, by confining each representation to a certain action with a just observation of the manners and passions which that action naturally produced."[26]

[25] Letter to Mann, 26 November 1744.
[26] Machine, in Fielding's *Tumble-Down Dick* (1736), sounds even more impressive: "Aristotle, in his book concerning entertain-

By the time Weaver had written his history, however, it was quite clear that pantomime in the English theatre was not destined to stay at all times on so high a level, that some compromise must be made with the less exigent taste of the rabble—in short, that pantomime, like the earlier English masque, must satisfy both high and low tastes at once by paralleling the "serious and the grotesque."[27] Weaver's treatise ends with a description of this two-part division, the serious part being described as genteel and natural, the grotesque as going beyond nature, "as Harlequin, Scaramouch, Pierrot, etc."

Unfortunately for our purpose it is just this latter part which is most inadequately accounted for in the few surviving printed scenari. The usual practice was to publish only the "vocal parts" of the serious plot, with just enough stage directions to give some idea of the nature of the whole piece. We may take for purposes of illustration any of several highly successful pantomimes Lewis Theobald composed for Rich. *Perseus and Andromeda*, which first appeared at Lincoln's Inn Fields 2 January 1730, will serve as well as any. Most of the twenty-four pages of the text are devoted to two episodes from the familiar myth, the slaying of the Medusa and the rescue of Andromeda. In both, but especially in the first, there is every indication of an elaborate machine production, with various odd creatures generated from the blood of the slain Medusa and so on. These two episodes are matched by two comic ones, but whether or not they constitute a sort of antimasque it is impossible to tell from the meager stage directions. These

---

ments, has laid it down as a principal rule, that Harlequin is always to escape."

[27] There were several attempts in this period to combine the old and the new in the form of masques. In the spring of 1716, for example, Rich produced a "dramatick masque" called *Presumptuous Love*, said to be based on Lucian, and a "comick masque" called *Pyramus and Thisbe*, based on *Midsummer Night's Dream*.

run to little more than, "Here the comic part begins, in which is sung the following recitative and air. Enter Harlequin, shewing actions of despair,[28] and to him a magician." Or, still more meager, "The actions of Harlequin continued."

An examination of several other texts of popular pantomimes of the 1730's and 1740's reveals this same paucity of detail, particularly for the grotesque parts. What the sparse directions clearly indicate is farcical action but what the exact nature of this action was it is impossible to tell.

A few of the scenari, especially among the earlier ones, are more informative. Take, for example, a piece which appeared at Drury Lane in the same year as Theobald's *Perseus*. The title reads *Cephalus and Procris, a dramatick masque: with a pantomime interlude call'd, Harlequin Grand Volgi*. We have the usual combination of the serious and the grotesque in alternate scenes, but here the latter are more fully described. The action runs, in part, like this: Harlequin sees Columbine, his mistress, in the balcony of her brother's house in Venice. He sends her a letter by pigeon, is shot onto the balcony from a mortar, carries on a running war with the stupid Pierrot, servant to the Venetian who has kept his sister virtually captive. A little later Pierrot is almost drowned when caught on a large mill-wheel and turned round and round. Other machine elements in the piece involve magical transformations as Harlequin turns into a rose tree and the like. From this it seems clear that the grotesque element was designed more to produce surprises than laughs.[29] So intent on spectacular

---

[28] Harlequin's "actions of despair" suggest a *"scène du désespoir"* which occurs in Fatouville's *Arlequin empéreur dans la lune*, reproduced in Gherardi's collection. Gherardi considered the scene "une des plus plaisantes qu'on ait jamais joué sur le théâtre Italien."

[29] A German visitor, Christlob Mylius, seeing an English pantomime in 1753, carried home the impression of something "absolutely beautiful." See J. A. Kelly, *German Visitors to English Theaters in the Eighteenth Century* (Princeton, 1936), pp. 25-26.

flights did the managers, especially Rich, become that the performers must often have been in peril of their very lives. Chetwood tells us of several accidents, of which some ended fatally for the luckless performers.[30]

Going back farther to the 1720's, we find in some of the "books of the entertainments," such as those based on the Faustus story, a still more satisfactory account of the farce turns. John Thurmond's last pantomime, *The Miser; or, Wagner and Abericock: a grotesque entertainment*, performed at Drury Lane during the closing days of December 1726 by an interesting combination of English comedians and French *forains*,[31] provides a more detailed picture of farce in pantomime than most of the later, more sensational pieces. Like all the Faust-pantomimes of the time it runs a great deal to magical transformations and magical escapes, but at least two sequences employ the most venerable of farce devices. In one the miser's daughter, at the moment jealous of her lover Harlequin, gets the help of poor Peirot (*sic*). She "prevails upon him to personate Harlequin, to counterplot him. The Spirit changes Peirot into a Harlequin. The return of Harlequin, and their variety of actions

[30] "Another accident . . . fell out in *Dr. Faustus*, a pantomime entertainment in Lincoln's-Inn-Fields Theatre, where a machine in the working broke, threw the mock Pierrot down headlong with such force, that the poor man broke a plank on the stage with his fall, and expired: Another was so sorely maimed, that he did not survive many days; and a third, one of the softer sex, broke her thigh. But to prevent such accidents for the future those persons are represented by inanimate figures, so that if they broke a neck, a leg, or an arm, there needs no surgeon." *General History of the Stage* (1749), p. 139.

[31] Along with regular members of the company, like Theophilus Cibber and John Harper, appeared Roger, Rainton, and Houghton, all of whom we find recorded in the Parfaict *Mémoires* as appearing at the Parisian fairs. On 16 August 1729 Roger and Renton [at another point this is given as Rinton] danced in something called *La Noce Angloise*. On 28 June 1731 Roger, Rinton, and Houghton, "*trois excellens danseurs pantomimes, nouvellement arrivés de Londres*," performed in a *Guinguette angloise*.

and attitudes, Harlequin mistaking Peirot for his shadow, is the conclusion of the scene." Though most of the scene is left to our imagination we see clearly enough here the outlines of the familiar identical-twin or mirror-image device of farce.

A second scene uses a trick which is to be found in the Commonwealth drolls or earlier. Peirot, carrying a bag of money to his master, is waylaid by Harlequin's servant, called simply "Clown" and played by the plump comedian Harper, dressed as a "lady of the town." "A scene of courtship passes between 'em; during which, Harlequin in the habit of a nurse takes an opportunity of changing the bag. Peirot and the Clown part amorously. On hearing a child cry, Peirot examines his bag, and finds an infant in it, and runs off frightened, etc."[32]

It would actually be possible merely by reading contemporary comment on pantomime to arrive at a fair notion of its devices—both the marvels and the farce—if no scenari had been preserved. In the eyes of most of the more serious commentators of the time the devotion to pantomimes exhibited by the public and the willingness of the theatrical managers to exploit that devotion were nothing short of disgraceful. Every theatrical season brought out at least some protest. In some seasons, especially those around 1724-28, pantomime all but monopolized the attention of critics of the stage, just as it seemed about to monopolize the attention of most spectators. Some of these comments are decidedly interesting for what they reveal about the nature of pantomime.

Particularly in the earliest seasons the very novelty of these stage entertainments called for detailed comment.

[32] This trick of exchanging one bundle for another, usually an unwanted child for valuables, goes back at least as far as Middleton's *Chaste Maid in Cheapside* and appears in Thomas Jordan's Commonwealth droll *The Cheater Cheated*. A variant appears in one of Chaplin's most famous movies, "The Kid."

One of the very first attacks, the one in *A Comparison between the Two Stages* (1702) was, as noted, fairly detailed. Among the farcical devices specified were certain props, "the guittar and the bladder"; a great deal of violent or fantastic action, "jumping over tables and joint-stools . . . ridiculous postures and grimaces . . . a monstrous birth"; and grotesque disguise, such as a "counterfeit male lady."

The successful runs of the two Faustus pantomimes at Drury Lane and Lincoln's Inn Fields brought out the most detailed criticisms. Two of these, *The Dancing Devils* and *The British Stage*, both issued in 1724, are devoted in part to mock plays supposedly in imitation of the pantomimes they jeer at. These satires provide more details than many of the printed scenari do. Equally helpful are the burlesques of pantomime, such as James Ralph's *Fashionable Lady; or Harlequin's Opera* (1730), Fielding's *Tumble-Down Dick* (1736), or the anonymous *Harlequin Student: or the Fall of Pantomime* (1741), in which the typical plots of pantomimes are revealed in the process of ridiculing current favorites. Without rehearsing detailed sequences, I may sum up the typical plot by quoting Thomas Wilkes' description:

> Harlequin is generally supposed to be some being under the power of enchantment, in love with, and beloved by Colombine; but crossed in all his designs by Pantaloon her father, his man Pierrot, and the Squire who courts her. Harlequin's only wit consists in his activity, displayed in escaping from them either by assuming another form, turning a bed-chamber into a garden, a tavern into a church, or hunting his pursuers with spirits. After a number of pursuits, crossings, turnings, and transformations, some god or superior being interposes in favour of the enchanter Harlequin, makes him friends with his pursuers, and gives him Colombine for a wife.[33]

[33] *General View*, pp. 77-78.

Three items in this description written just past the mid-century need to be emphasized: the amount of attention devoted to "machine" and scenic effects; the persistence of devices basic to farce, all in a context of the familiar chase; and the inevitability of the *commedia dell'arte* masks.

Farce had a less formidable rival in the burlesque. Like the pantomime it too was in part relative and ally, so much so that it is often difficult to distinguish between the two forms. It might be well to return to this problem of the confusion in terminology by which burlesque and farce have often been treated as identical. The confusion stems partly from a close similarity in method: both genres make use of the extravagant, the exaggerated, even the grotesque. Like farce, burlesque is fond of exploiting the physical; like farce, it employs some of the same devices: disguise, repetition, noisy horseplay. Yet if we consider the burlesque writer's intent we see how far apart the two forms are, much farther than farce and pantomime. For the latter two are aimed at mere entertainment; burlesque, on the other hand, frequently overreaches itself in its desire to criticize. The first essential of burlesque is *imitation*; the second is *ridicule*. That is, the burlesque writer is aiming at something he dislikes. By comparing that something with something else—in the best burlesque there can be metaphor rising even to the poetic—which is grotesquely ridiculous he hopes to condemn, even to annihilate it. What Canon Collins has said of Aristophanes will, I think, serve to underline my point about intention:

> It is difficult to compare it [the "old" comedy of Greece] to any form of modern literature, dramatic or other. It perhaps most resembled what we call burlesque; it had also very much in it of broad farce and comic opera, and something also (in the hits at fashions and follies of the day with which it abounded) of the modern pantomime. But it was something more, and more important to the

Athenian public, than any or all of these could have been. Almost always more or less political, and sometimes intensely personal, and always with some purpose more or less important underlying its wildest vagaries and coarsest buffooneries, it supplied the place of the political journal, the literary review, the popular caricature, and the party pamphlet, of our own times.[34]

Burlesque does in some stages approach much nearer farce, particularly when the point of critical comparison has been worn out or lost. That is, when an audience is no longer concerned over the issues raised or no longer able to recognize what the issues are, the two forms may in practice coalesce. To turn for a moment to Aristophanes for an example, our own reception of the noisy buffoonery in *The Clouds* will vary with our intimacy with the context in which the play originated. If our knowledge of the times is great enough we may approach the feelings of the first audiences who saw *The Clouds* and with them be able to see the real point in such apparent foolishness as Socrates' being suspended in a basket, in the joke about dividing the lands, in the remedy suggested by Strepsiades' burning the thinking shop. When some of the same materials reappear in an eighteenth-century English farce there is a strong likelihood that the point of criticism has been lost and what was imitation with the intent to ridicule has become mere ludicrous clowning. I am not at the moment referring to a hypothetical case but to a three-act farce of 1704 by John Corey called *The Metamorphosis*, derived chiefly from Tomkis' old pre-Commonwealth play *Albumazar* but making use also of some of the items from *The Clouds*. I assume that Corey did not expect his audience to recognize either original since he professed to have taken the materials from Molière.

Whatever the basis of the confusion between farce and

---

[34] William Lucas Collins, *Aristophanes* (London, 1872), pp. 2-3.

burlesque, it persists today, to an extent that is sometimes baffling. The dramatic works of Henry Fielding seem to me to constitute a particularly bad focus of irritation. It is hard to see how any useful purpose can be served by lumping together indiscriminately his farces, his adaptations of Molière, his mock tragedies, and his political burlesques all as farces; yet the practice has been common and shows no signs of diminishing.

Though the burlesque was eventually to compete with pantomime and farce, it began as a distinct form long before the vogue of afterpieces had arrived. The grandfather of eighteenth-century burlesques was *The Rehearsal* (1671), a play so popular and so durable that it not only remained in the repertory itself for a century but also served as model for numerous others.[35] Of these imitations the burlesques "in the manner of a rehearsal" by Fielding and Sheridan are only the most successful. *The Rehearsal* itself, usually referred to in the Restoration period as farce, was neither a farce nor a mere brief appendage to a playbill but a full-length five-act burlesque; and so it remained throughout its career, in spite of the numerous alterations it underwent when changing times called for changing satirical allusions in the text.

The heyday of the burlesque afterpiece came in the 1730's, but there were scattered examples in the two decades preceding. The most important name in these years is that of John Gay, wit and companion of wits, whose satiric talents led him to use the mocking forms of the burlesque. Gay's first effort in dramatic writing resulted in a one-act "tragi-comical farce" called *The Mohocks*, which was published in 1712 without ever having been acted, though Gay supplied a prologue indicating that he had hoped for theatrical production:

[35] For predecessors and successors of *The Rehearsal* see D. F. Smith, *Plays about the Theatre in England* (New York, 1936).

This farce, if the kind players had thought fit,
With action had supplied the want of wit.

The Mohocks is a mixture of lively action approaching farce and realistic scenes satirizing the young bucks whose practice of roaming the dark streets of London terrorizing the more sober populace gained them a lasting notoriety. Only in the mock-solemnity of the rites of the society of Mohocks does the play become true burlesque. The rest is given over to noisy action and a portrayal of the activities of the Mohocks among tavernkeepers, whores, and the pitifully inadequate watch—all foreshadowing the author's famous picture of low life in *The Beggar's Opera*.

Three years later Gay produced a "tragi-comi-pastoral farce," *The What D'ye Call It*, a more successful piece in the theatre and a closer approach to pure burlesque. Again we have a mixture, as the playful title and the long mocking preface suggest, of several genres. The play's popularity—it enjoyed at least scattered performances for over fifty years—must have come mainly from the bold and comparatively fresh handling of the love intrigue, but there is fun too in the mock theatricals of the play-within-the-play. Here Gay is in the tradition of *The Rehearsal*, a manner to be carried on in *Tom Thumb* and *The Critic*, in his mocking imitation of declamatory tragedy.[36]

There are burlesque qualities in later pieces by Gay, in the ill-fated *Three Hours after Marriage* (1717), written with Pope and Arbuthnot, and in the phenomenally successful *Beggar's Opera* (1728). There is even more burlesque in *The Rehearsal at Goatham*, which borrows from Cervantes to jeer at English elections, but this piece was never produced in the theatre and was not even published

[36] In *A Complete Key to the Last New Farce, the What D'ye Call It* (1715), which has been ascribed to Griffin and Theobald, both attached to the Lincoln's Inn Fields company, the author of the burlesque is taken to task for his temerity in mocking "the beauties of Shak., Otway, & Dryden."

until years after the author's death. In summary, the only burlesque by Gay that had any real merit as an afterpiece— *Three Hours* and *The Beggar's Opera* were main pieces— was *The What D'ye Call It*.

Besides Gay's burlesques there were only a scattered few produced at the theatres before 1730.[37] In the spring of 1719 Lincoln's Inn Fields ridiculed Italian opera in a three-act piece called *Harlequin-Hydaspes*, but this was evidently an almost complete failure. Nine years later Cooke and Mottley had their *Penelope*, a vigorous but not very adept travesty of Homer, produced at the Little Haymarket with only slightly greater success than *Harlequin-Hydaspes*.

It was not until Fielding's second and more successful venture in writing for the theatre, in the 1730-31 season, that burlesque came into its own, and then only for a period of six or seven years. During this time it proved a formidable rival to the other entertainments in the after-piece spot on the bill, but, it will be recalled, this was at a time when four or five theatres were in regular competition, all presenting double bills. The demand for entertainments was so great that no single form could establish a monopoly.

Fielding produced half a dozen burlesques between 1730 and 1737, several of them highly successful, and his lead was followed by other writers, though none quite matched his success. It is hardly necessary here to devote any considerable space to an analysis of Fielding's burlesques. I have already called attention to the far too common practice of applying the misleading label of farce to these pieces.

[37] The Jacobite rebellion of 1715 produced several burlesques, as did the South Sea Bubble of 1720. Most of these pieces, commonly labelled farces, were clearly not intended for the stage or, if written for production, were considered poor theatrical risks. In at least one, John Philips' *Earl of Marr Marr'd; with the Humours of Jockey, the Highlander* (1715), a three-act burlesque labelled "tragi-comical farce," a provincial theatre produced what the London theatres may well have rejected, according to Sybil Rosenfeld, *Strolling Players* (Cambridge, 1939), pp. 50-51.

The most casual examination of them should make it clear that, while they all used the grotesque devices of laughter-producing buffoonery, they are actually far removed from mere farce. Fielding himself added to the confusion by calling his first burlesque *The Author's Farce*, but his label is as ironically meant as the *tragedy* he applied to *Tom Thumb*. The prologue to *The Author's Farce* sets the tone:

No tears, no terror plead in his behalf;
The aim of farce is but to make you laugh.
Beneath the tragic or the comic name,
Farces and puppet-shows ne'er miss of fame.
Since then, in borrowed dress, they've pleased the town,
Condemn them not; appearing in their own.

The piece itself, particularly the "puppet-show" called "The Pleasures of the Town," which forms the third act, is devoted chiefly to an assault on what Fielding considered the depraved taste of both audiences and producers. When, at the rehearsal of this piece, the Player objects that it is beneath the dignity of the theatre, the Master of the Show replies, "That may be, so is all farce, and yet you see a farce brings in more company to a house than the best play that ever was writ—For this age would allow Tom Durfey a better poet than Congreve or Wycherley. . . ." Among the characters who serve as targets in this burlesque puppet-show Sir Farcical Comic and Monsieur Pantomime are prominent. Fielding himself produced farces—two or three of his adaptations of French farce were to have as persistent and as ardent an acclaim as *Tom Thumb*, the best of his burlesques—but in *The Author's Farce* at least he is assailing farce, not actually producing it, as his title suggests.

In his later burlesques Fielding turns his attention more and more to politics, with results fatal to his career in the theatre, but he never failed to find some space in his burlesques for attacking debased entertainments. Still, and most significant in our particular context, he spent more and more of his satirical talents deriding John Rich and pantomime. In the long run, then, he proved as much a supporter of farce as an enemy, not so much by his own work as farce-writer, though this is by no means negligible, as by his vigorous campaign against the more sensational competitor pantomime.

Fielding's work in the burlesque was so successful that he helped create a vogue in that form in the 1730's, though it should be added immediately that his earlier followers, producing chiefly full-length plays, had no great success. On the same night that *The Author's Farce* first appeared at the Little Haymarket, the Drury Lane company produced a burlesque by Gabriel Odingsells called *Bays's Opera*. Odingsells' prologue gives a clear idea of his attitude and objective:

> In vain with sense, or musick, we begin;
> Crowds will be ready to explode the scene,
> Unless it ends with jig and Harlequin.

In other words, *Bays's Opera* is similar in method and intent to *The Author's Farce*, but Odingsells did not share Fielding's good fortune in the theatre. His piece failed, he contends in his preface, largely because his ironic purpose was misunderstood and the satire was taken in a personal way he had never intended.

Not to be outdistanced by the theatres in the West End, the Goodmans Fields company came out three days later with *The Fashionable Lady; or Harlequin's Opera* by James Ralph, native of Philadelphia, friend of Benjamin Franklin, and friend and collaborator-to-be of Fielding. *The Fashionable Lady* is another of those burlesques that attacked by satirical allegory the popular entertainments of the day, chiefly pantomime, though Ralph sweeps even ballad opera into his net. The success of this piece was somewhat greater than that of *Bays's Opera*, but it produced no sensation and doubtless had no great effect upon the entertainments it attacked.

There are other burlesques in this period but only one writer, Henry Carey, ever approached Fielding in producing successes. Carey's good fortune may be laid in part to his taking himself less seriously than Odingsells and Ralph. His most popular burlesques, *The Tragedy of Chrononhotonthologos: Being the Most Tragical Tragedy that ever was Tragediz'd by any Company of Tragedians* (1734), *The Dragon of Wantley* (1737), and, a sequel to the latter, *Margery: or, a Worse Plague than the Dragon* (1738), were not full-length plays but afterpieces poking good-natured fun at the sober doings of tragedy and opera. Although they are real burlesques, they actually approach farce in intent, and they stayed in the repertory as rivals to farce, though perhaps not very formidable ones.

In addition to pantomime and burlesque there were miscellaneous other dramatic forms introduced as afterpiece entertainments though, since none proved so dangerous a rival as these, especially pantomime, it is perhaps unnecessary to take more than casual account of them.

Closely allied to the burlesque was the dramatic satire using allegory or other forms of fantasy. Perhaps most popular of this type is the "Aesop" play, which involves a series of judgments in the manner of Lucian on current follies. An early example is the *Aesop* (1696-97) of Vanbrugh, taken from Boursault. A later one is the first play of David Garrick, *Lethe: or Esop in the Shades* (1740). Here again is a satirical play and not merely a farce—though all too often labelled as farce—but, unlike Vanbrugh's play, *Lethe* was an afterpiece and a highly successful one.

Hardly less popular was a type of afterpiece-play developed principally by Robert Dodsley, which may best be described as the sentimental or moralizing afterpiece. Such brief plays as *The Toy-Shop* (1735) and *The King and the Miller of Mansfield* (1737) were successful enough to encourage Dodsley to try further experiments in substituting a kind of morality for mere entertainment. He even went so far as to attempt a moralizing pantomime, but his *Rex and Pontifex, Being an attempt to introduce upon the stage a new species of pantomime* failed to reach the stage though it was published in his *Trifles* (1745). Other attempts in the moralizing vein, such as the anonymous *Henry and Emma, or the Nut-Brown Maid* (1749),[38] failed to attain the popularity of Dodsley's afterpieces.[39]

Still another form, almost negligible in effect, is the pastoral or, as it is sometimes called, the pastoral ballad opera. Of this type Colley Cibber's *Damon and Phillida* (1729), altered from his pastoral *Love in a Riddle*, will serve as an example of some success; the anonymous *Judgment of Paris* (1730) of the rival Lincoln's Inn Fields company was of the same general type but much less successful.

In many cases the afterpieces were nothing less than *petite comédies*. As Wilkes puts it, "We have indeed a

[38] Only the songs were printed, but the MS is preserved in the Larpent collection. From it we learn that this play was, like *The London Merchant*, based upon the old ballad.

[39] I despair of classifying the plays of Samuel Johnson of Cheshire, who began his strange career on the London stage at the Little Haymarket in March 1729, in *Hurlothrumbo*. At the time his pieces were frequently called farces, perhaps as a desperate resort. They seem to me to be the productions of a crazy man, which Johnson unquestionably was. Their popularity was due, it appears, to the current craze for novelty plus a suspicion that they were somehow profound, so that to scorn them might turn out to be socially dangerous. As a matter of fact, Watson Nicholson in *The Struggle For a Free Stage in London*, reproduces, p. 24, a notice from *Fog's Weekly Journal* for August 1731, telling how Johnson and his troupe were forbidden to act until the authorities could figure out whether "the silly character of Lord Flame in Johnson's *Cheshire Comics* is meant as a Satyr upon anybody." Of Johnson's unprinted plays preserved in the Larpent collection, the brief afterpiece called *Sir John Falstaff in Masquerade* (1741) is reasonably coherent and clearly satirical; it is not at all farcical. Among the many commentaries on Johnson at this time one of the most interesting occurs in John Lloyd's poem *The Play, a Satire* (1730).

species of drama, which, though it takes the place of farce, cannot properly be called so, because it answers all the ends of comedy, commixing use with entertainment. Such is Garrick's fine piece of Lethe, Foote's Englishman at Paris, and his Englishman returned from Paris."[40] There are, in fact, so many plays of this type that it is hardly possible even to list them all here. Some are only a step or two removed from farce; others are quite different in purpose and method. Fielding's Lottery (1732) will serve to illustrate the first type; a decade or two later the plays by Foote mentioned by Wilkes would serve equally well. The opposite extreme can perhaps best be exemplified by the interesting but obscure plays of Thomas Odell, who tried to adapt the two- and three-act form to the needs of realistic comedy. Unfortunately for him, his attempts, represented by The Chimera (1721), The Patron (1729), and The Smugglers (1729), met with no success, possibly because they were much too critical of contemporary manners.

Between these poles are numerous short plays, some merely shortened versions of older successes, some attempts to exploit a current fad. When, for example, it became clear from Gay's overwhelming triumph in 1728 that coarse genre pieces depicting low life were going to have a vogue, a number of imitations appeared in the afterpiece form, such as Ryan's one-act Cobler's Opera (1728) and Coffey's Beggar's Wedding (1729).[41]

Many comedy-afterpieces were quite successful and therefore offered keen competition to farce and pantomime. Yet the circumstances would suggest the strategic advantage of the latter forms. Once an audience has spent two hours and a half watching tragedy or high comedy, it usually requires

[40] General View, p. 64.

[41] In the supplement to Appendix C, History, ii, 434, Professor Nicoll describes this piece as "a ballad-opera version of T. Jevon, The Devil of a Wife (1686)." Evidently he has confused two of Coffey's plays, for the description fits the far better known Devil to Pay, not The Beggar's Wedding.

the diversion offered by one of the lighter kinds of entertainment. As Luigi Riccoboni has put it, "Les petites pièces d'un acte qui occupent aujourd'hui la place de la farce, & que l'on donne à la suite d'un tragédie, ou d'un comédie, ne remplissent point l'intention pour laquelle les farces ont été introduites sur la scène: au lieu de delasser l'esprit, elle le fatiguent par une nouvelle attention."[42]

[42] *Observations sur la comédie, et sur le génie de Molière* (Paris, 1736), pp. 95-96.

CHAPTER 5

SOURCES AND INFLUENCES

✦✦

> Dances you have and various here to night,
> But they are English all, all English quite.
> Throughout, English songs, farce English too,
> That's French sence,
> All non sence without any more ado.
> —Prologue to *The Devil of a Wife.*

✦✦

IN TRACING the sources of farce in this period it is expedient to call attention once more to the distinction made in Chapter 2 between mere farce turns or *lazzi* on the one hand and the intrigues which provide a framework for the shorter episodes on the other. In the first case we are dealing with materials so basic, and often so primitive, that it is sometimes impossible to discover a source. Or, to put the same idea into different terms, it is difficult to resist the temptation to see only one kind of influence and to exclude others. Since the devices of disguise, repetition, and the like are universal and ageless, it would be possible to make a strong case for the persistence of the native tradition of clowning and rule out all foreign influences. The same traits of universality and agelessness make it possible to detect parallels between the various national traditions and therefore easy to claim influences.

But farce in the theatre does not consist merely of the primary turns. It would be hard to imagine an audience so unsophisticated in its demands as to be content with anything so elementary. In a repertory theatre where comparatively sophisticated preferences must be met night after night, such an easy solution is clearly impossible. After all, the differences between the full-length play requiring from two to three hours and the short farce running only a half hour or so are not polar. Convention demands some plot, some continuity, for each. It is usually in the plots of the farce repertory that a more nearly proximate kind of source can be detected and the various influences, native and foreign, traced.

The results of such an attempt will lead to the conclusion that, especially in the earlier half of the period, the native influence is paramount. Still the influence of the Continental theatre, especially that of France, is far from negligible. At times, in fact, it is at least as great as the native tradition. The Italians had somewhat less influence than the French on the farcical play—as distinguished from the pantomime—though they too made a considerable impress on English farce, both directly and through French mediation. Other Continental influences, such as that of the Spanish, are negligible and, where they exist at all, largely indirect.[1]

Of these various influences the native one, despite its importance, requires perhaps the least discussion. After all, farce itself was not new to the stage in 1660 even though the name was.[2] The long established practice of adding comic filler to long and even basically serious plays had

---

[1] See Nicoll, *History*, I, 191-192. Calling attention to the absence of any exhaustive study of Spanish influence, Professor Nicoll describes the influence as "no slight one." As the titles he cites suggest, however, the influence was chiefly felt in comedies of intrigue, not in farce. In his edition of Lord Orrery's plays, Professor Clark reproduces Nahum Tate's congratulatory epistle on *Guzman*, in which Tate praises the author for adding English humor to what "appears to have been a Spanish design, and therefore naturally grave." Langbaine and others considered the play to be founded on the Spanish, but Clark thinks Orrery "invented the whole flimsy structure." I, 437.

[2] For an account of the introduction of the term into the English language, see my article "The Early Career of *Farce* in the Theatrical Vocabulary," The University of Texas *Studies in English*, 1940, pp. 82-95.

provided an extended apprenticeship in farce for the English actor and playwright.

In order to demonstrate the persistence of the native tradition, it will be sufficient to trace one salient feature, the stress on grossness of character and physical action. Students of English culture in the eighteenth century are fond of speculating on the possible cause of this typically John Bullish feature of English comedy. The climate, the tradition of independence, especially among the lower classes, even the vast quantities of roast beef consumed—all have been advanced to explain this peculiarly English exuberance of character, both in real life and on the stage. Whatever its source, the fact seems undeniable. The great clowns of Shakespeare, for example, are often gross enough to be called farcical, even in such plays as *Much Ado*, where romance and sophistication and melodrama seem the paramount features of the play. In Jonson's plays, similarly, the "humours" tradition encourages the creation of characters who approach farce. And, as was indicated in Chapter 2, Jonson's successors, Shadwell and Durfey especially, carry over into farce in many of their characters.

Dryden points out, in his prologue to *The Assignation* (1672), this persistent demand for "Fooles out of the common road":

> Th' unnatural strain'd buffoon is onely taking:
> No fop can please you now of Gods own making
> Pardon our poet if he speaks his mind,
> You come to plays with your own follies lin'd:
> Small fooles fall on you, like small showers, in vain:
> Your own oyl'd coates keep out all common raine.

As Professor Wilcox has indicated, Dryden himself had already demonstrated how strong the native tradition of characterization can be by making over Molière's *L'Etourdi* into a thoroughly English piece.[3] As another English play-

[3] *The Relation of Molière to Restoration Comedy* (New York, 1938), p. 37.

wright of the time, John Crowne, put it, "All foreign coin must be melted down, and receive a new stamp, if not an addition of metal, before it will pass current in England, and be judged sterling. . . ." That Crowne's remarks are not intended to be applicable only to serious plays, of which he chanced to be speaking when he made this generalization, can be demonstrated by an examination of his own *Countrey Wit* (1676). The play is presumably based upon Molière's *Sicilien* but it contains, in Sir Mannerly Shallow and his servant Booby, as grossly English a pair of rustic clowns as the most patently native play can boast.[4]

But it is not necessary to trace in detail the persistence of the farce "character," the native buffoon. The type, so quickly reestablished on the stage after the Restoration, flourished throughout the period and beyond, not only in pieces which were clearly borrowed from earlier plays but also in such more or less original farces as *The Journey to Bristol* (1731), *The Honest Yorkshireman* (1735), and *The Lucky Discovery* (1738). Needless to say, the English booby was always at home in the "drolls" of the London fairs and the provinces. We shall meet him again in the next chapter as Hodge and Squire Noodle and the Pindar of Wakefield.

It would be superfluous, not to say impossible, to account for all the specific borrowings from earlier English drama. The works of Shakespeare, of Fletcher, of Jonson, of Marston—all are levied upon time and again. And to these must be added the names of minor figures, like Shirley, Brome, and Tomkis. Occasionally a play or scenes from a play were borrowed repeatedly as in the case of

[4] That there is more than chance dependence on native materials in this play is indicated by Crowne's inclusion of an old droll sequence: Booby, coming to the aid of his master in a street fight, hands the bag containing all of Sir Mannerly's funds to a beggar woman to hold; she substitutes another package, containing her illegitimate child, and poor Booby soon finds himself under arrest for kidnapping.

Shakespeare's *Taming of the Shrew* or Marston's *Dutch Courtezan*. In some cases also it is clear enough that the source is native, even though no particular play can be suggested as having provided the material. Such plays as *The Devil of a Wife* (1686), which in turn provided the materials for the most popular of all farce afterpieces, *The Devil to Pay* (1731), or *The Country Wake* (1696), the basis for an almost equally popular afterpiece, *Hob* (1711), are as English as roast beef or plum pudding. In short, no amount of interest in the foreign fad of the moment could permanently alter the tastes of an English audience.

Among foreign influences that of the *commedia dell'arte* was somewhat less than has sometimes been claimed for it. I refer here to the *direct* influence of the Italians on the dialogue of English farce. I do not deny them their rightful place in pantomime, where their influence was overwhelming; nor do I wish to ignore an indirect influence through the works of Molière and his successors.[5]

There has sometimes been an unfortunate tendency to see the influence of the *commedia dell'arte* where only accidental parallels exist. W. S. Clark, for example, in his introduction to Orrery's *Guzman* (1669), finds evidence of its influence in the emphasis on posturing and grimacing. I have no doubt that the Italians were given to over-acting, since there is considerable evidence, from pictures and from commentators, that they were. Still it seems unnecessary to send two such notorious clowns as Nokes and Angel, who played the leading comic roles in Orrery's play, to school to the Italians to learn posturing and grimacing.

An even more strained connection appears in E. M.

[5] Dozens of students of the French theatre have commented on the influence of the Italians. In addition to contributions by such writers as Lanson and Lancaster, there are monographs addressed to the specific subject, such as Moland's *Molière et la comédie italienne* (Paris, 1867) and Schwartz's *Commedia dell'arte and Its Influence on French Comedy in the Seventeenth Century* (Paris, 1933).

Gagey's *Ballad Opera*. In a comment on a passage in Drury's *Mad Captain* (1733), where Sergeant Sly gulls two cits, Snip and Pinch, into accepting a guinea each and then has them impressed into service on the grounds that they have accepted the king's money, Gagey suggests an indebtedness to a play in Gherardi in which a similar trick occurs. Again it seems unnecessary to go so far afield when the same ruse can be found much nearer home. Farquhar in his much more famous *Recruiting Officer* (1706) has used the same device, although he—or Drury—could quite easily have taken it from the life about him. It has a plausible air and is certainly no worse than some of the other means used in recruiting for military service.

Quite aside from the fact that the Italian improvised comedy was sufficiently different in style from the sort English audiences were accustomed to, there are two or three adequate reasons for its comparatively minor influence on English farce. The main one is that composers of farce had only limited opportunities to become acquainted with Italian comedy. Those who had the benefit of residence in Paris, or in various Italian cities, could of course have seen regular performances. The troupe in which Fiorilli and Biancolelli were the leading attractions performed regularly in Paris from early in this period until its banishment in 1697.[6]

For those whose fortunes confined them to England no such opportunity offered. True, there were several visits of foreign troupes, but in the early decades of our period these were often by French companies, evidently playing a typically French repertory.[7] The total number of visits paid by

[6] For Fiorilli, Biancolelli, and the other Italians see the various works of Rasi, Campardon, et al.

[7] W. J. Lawrence, Miss Boswell, and other English scholars give a number of details concerning both French and Italian visitors, but their concern is chiefly with dates and persons. It may be possible, however, to arrive at some idea of what French travelling troupes commonly played in England by examining the works of Liebrecht

commedia dell'arte troupes between 1660 and 1700 seems
to have been not more than four or five. Tiberio Fiorilli
and his confreres made an extended visit in the summer
of 1673 and possibly two in 1675. There is ample evidence
of their activities in the Treasury Books and in the comments of John Evelyn, who saw them during both summers, and of Andrew Marvell, who registered his irritation
with the frivolity of Charles and his court in a letter dated
24 June 1675 and in his poem, "The Statue at Charing-
Crosse." Rasi corroborates the two visits in 1675 when he
tells us that one member of the troupe, Marc Antonio Romagnesi, lost his wife "a Londra il 1675 in uno dei due
viaggi che la compagnia fece in Inghilterra col permesso
dell corte di Francia."[8] It is possible, though unlikely, that
Fiorilli also performed in London in the summers of 1674
and 1683. Charles II did try to secure the services of the
Parisian troupe at the later date, but Fiorilli's past experience with the English king had made him suspicious. As
with his own actors, Charles was generous in his promises
but slow to pay. Another Italian troupe spent some months
in London during the winter of 1678-79. This was not the
company long settled in Paris but another one directly from
Italy and under the patronage of the Duke of Modena.[9]

We must add to the infrequency and the brevity of these
visits by the Italian players a few more significant facts.
For one thing, they played not in the public theatres but
in the King's quarters, though the difference is perhaps not

---

and Fransen. These deal with activities in Belgium and Holland,
but in at least a few cases we find that the troupes covered visited
England and presumably offered their usual repertory.

[8] III, 394. See also, in addition to the works of Lawrence and
Miss Boswell, the various entries in Nicoll, *History*, I, and *Masques,
Mimes, and Miracles* (London, 1931).

[9] See A. L. Bader, "The Modena Troupe in England," *Modern
Language Notes*, L (1935), 367-369. It seems likely that the troupe
noted by Fransen as appearing in Nimeguen on 10 March 1679 was
the Modena company heading home.

so great as it would appear. Charles virtually turned the
royal banqueting hall into a public theatre, much to the disgust of Marvell and to the chagrin of the patent companies.
A still greater barrier to the would-be borrower was the
language itself. The Italians of these earlier troupes were
apparently still using their own language, though in a very
few years they were to begin interpolating speeches and
eventually whole scenes in French. While a good share of
the upper classes who made up much of the London audiences must have been reasonably skilled in French, comparatively few of them knew Italian. Duffett in a new prologue written for the Drury Lane company's revival of
Everyman out of His Humour in July 1675 took occasion
to jeer at those who went to watch the Italians without
knowing the language.

> As thick-scul'd zealots, who from Churches fly,
> Think doleful nonsense good that makes them cry;
> Y'are pleas'd and laugh because—you know not why.
> There ign'rant crouds round travel'd gallants sit,
> As am'rous youths round vizards in our pit,
> And by their motions judg the farces wit.
> If they but grin, a jest is understood.
> All laugh outright and cry—I'gad that's good;
> When will our damn'd dull silly rogues do so?
> Y'are very complaisant, I fain would know
> Where lies the wit and pow'r of (*il ohe*).

The greatest handicap of all was the lack of a printed
text from which a translator or adapter could work at his
own pace. The Italians were above all else *improvvisatore*
and proud of their ability to play an impressive repertory
without benefit of script. They were not only proud of their
independence of a written text; they were jealous of it—
as Gherardi was to learn when he attempted to publish the
French scenes in his *Théâtre Italien*.[10] So there could have

[10] For Gherardi's interesting account of the struggle he had with

been little chance for the most alert and fortunately circumstanced English writer to copy from the Italians.

A survey of the years between the Restoration and the time when the Italians were driven from Paris reveals few visible effects on the English farce repertory directly traceable to the *commedia dell'arte* players. Aside from a "Pugenello" dance here and a "Scaramouche" costume there, an allusion to "Scaramouche's Academy in Paris" in this play and an attack on the visiting "Italian merry-andrews" in that prologue, we have only two full-length plays and some scattered scenes.[11] The plays are Cokain's *Trapolin* (1658), later reworked by Tate as *The Duke and No Duke* (1684), and Mrs. Behn's *Emperor of the Moon* (1686). *Trapolin* was, according to its author, patterned after a performance he had seen in Italy; Mrs. Behn's play is evidently based on a play by Fatouville published in 1684.[12]

In addition to the full-length plays there are various

---

other members of the troupe after his first attempt at publication, see his preface, or, as he prefers to call it, "*Avertissement qu'il faut lire.*"

[11] There are several interesting allusions to the Italians in plays and prologues. One is the passage in Wycherley's *Gentleman Dancing-Master* (1672) where M. Paris speaks of his experiences in France: "I didde go to the Italian Academy at Paris thrice a week to learn to play de fool of Signior Scaramouche." Such a passage, to be sure, proves nothing beyond what we already know: that it was common for members of the upper classes to resort to Paris or even to spend some time there, as Wycherley himself did. Presumably, however, only the more affected or giddy Englishman would frequent the theatre of Fiorilli three nights a week.

[12] Nicoll, *History*, I, 262, seems to be following Langbaine, for he repeats the latter's erroneous version of the title. Summers, *Behn*, III, 387, states that she "of course used the edition of 1684," but he does not demonstrate that he has grounds for being so positive. From Lancaster, IV, 615, n. 15, and 628, I gather that it would be impossible for a modern scholar to check the 1684 edition against the English version. There are indications that Summers checked the latter against the version given by Gherardi. From such a comparison it is clear that Mrs. Behn follows the French-Italian play only approximately.

scenes drawn or freely imitated from the Italians. Ravens-croft seems to have added some scenes taken from a *commedia dell'arte* scenario concerning Harlequin in the role of student when in 1677 he found that his latest novelty concocted from Molière had been forestalled by Otway's *Cheats of Scapin*.[13] Mrs. Behn anticipated her own whole-sale borrowing from Fatouville's play by including some Italianate scenes—possibly with some improvised dialogue in Italian though the stage directions are too obscure to indicate clearly what was intended—in her hodgepodge of leftovers from Killigrew called *The Second Part of the Rover* (1681). And Mountfort managed to work some *commedia dell'arte* scenes into his farcical rendering of *Faustus* (1688). And finally there is the last act of Mot-teux's *Novelty* (1697), a somewhat compressed piece called *Natural Magick*, which the author describes as being "after the Italian manner."[14]

With the banishment of the Italians from Paris by Louis in 1697 their influence began, ironically, to be disseminated more widely than ever before. By this time Evaristo Gher-ardi had, in defiance of his fellow actors, seen the first edi-tion of his *Théâtre Italien*, containing the French scenes of numerous *commedia dell'arte* pieces, through the press. Later editions in Paris and Amsterdam helped broadcast

---

[13] I follow here not Nicoll, who credits the Italians with "im-mediate inspiration" for the play (*History*, I, 255), but E. T. Nor-ris, whose unpublished Johns Hopkins dissertation on the plays of Ravenscroft, completed in 1932, contains a wealth of material on that author.

[14] Motteux's preface has some interesting information on the cool reception of his Italianate materials, which obliged him to cut the piece down. "I have seen most of the things that were misliked, much applauded when acted by Harlequin and Scaramouch. But it must be own'd, that many fooleries pleas'd when grac'd by those incomparable mimics which may not suit with the genius of our stage." It seems not to have taken long for the English audience to grow fond of such materials, for within a comparatively short while they were applauding them *when they were presented in pantomime*.

these scenes, even in England, where some evidence of their influence can be seen, though they can hardly be said to have proliferated there.

With the withdrawal of Louis' favor from the Italians, some of their functions and even some of their actors were taken over by the *forains*, who, as we saw in the preceding chapter, had some influence on the English theatre, especially in pantomime.

The number of farces in the eighteenth century repertory taken directly from Italian sources is even smaller than that for the Restoration period, even though many more farces were performed. So far as I can discover, the only piece from the Italian destined to find a secure place among farce afterpieces was Aaron Hill's *Walking Statue; or, the Devil in the Wine Cellar*, first performed in 1710 at Drury Lane and later in various other London and provincial theatres. A part, if not all, of this farce may well have been derived from an Italian scenario that was later, in 1726, to appear in English as *The Most knowing, Least Understanding: or, Harlequin's Metamorphosis*.

If we accept the testimony of the unknown author of *A Complete Key to the New Farce, call'd Three Hours after Marriage*, Gay and his collaborators took the play from an Italian piece, though in making the charge he contradicts himself. Here is his confused but interesting account: "The character of Dr. Lubomirski is copied from a farce (or Spanish comedy as Gay will have it) call'd the *Anatomist or Sham-Doctor*, but spoil'd rather than improv'd." Yet at another point he says, " 'Tis high time to conclude, and I heartily beg the reader's pardon for reciting so much of this trumpery, which is all stole from a farce, in the Theatre Italien, call'd, The Mummies of Egypt." A comparison of the three plays involved reveals no real basis for either of the charges. All that *Three Hours* has in common with *The Anatomist* is a doctor; all with the Gherardi play, a mummy.

With the triumph of pantomime after 1723 the tenuous connection between English farce and the *commedia dell' arte* repertory is completely broken. From now on all borrowing is done by the writers of pantomimes. This is true in spite of the increased accessibility of printed scenari, for by this time the Gherardi collection had gained at least limited recognition in England and, with the visits of a troupe of *forains* in 1718-20 and the reestablished Italian comedians in 1726-27, more Italian plays and scenari were published.[15] In short, the *commedia dell'arte* exerted a profound influence on pantomime, for which its broad style of posture and grimace, its frequent use of magic transformations, and its fixed and striking costume in the "mask" tradition were admirably fitted, but its influence upon English farce in dialogue was slight as compared to that of the native tradition on the one hand and French models on the other.

There are several reasons for the greater influence of French farce in this period. For one thing, there is the enormous and persistent popularity of Molière, who was himself no stranger to farce and whose plays were much closer in spirit to English comedy than to that of the Italians. In fact the English composer of farce copied more *lazzi* devised by the Italians through Molière than he took directly from the Italians, for Molière had lived on intimate terms with the Italians for some years, having shared a theatre with them. It is to be expected that he would not only borrow numerous farcical patterns from them but would ultimately serve as a transmitter of these patterns

[15] For the various translations of plays and scenari of visiting troupes published, see Professor Avery's "Foreign Performers in the London Theatres in the Early Eighteenth Century," *Philological Quarterly*, xvi (1937), 105-123. There were several attacks on the Italian visitors in the contemporary press, e.g., in *The English Stage Italianiz'd* (1727) and in *The Speculatist* for 26 November 1726,

to his successors in farce, Dancourt, Regnard, Hauteroche, and others, and to his many English debtors as well.

The circumstances under which the farce afterpiece arose also made a heavy dependence on borrowed materials inevitable. When, especially at the turn of the century and again after 1714, a sudden demand for short plays to make up a fuller bill occurred, it soon became apparent that the demand could not satisfactorily be supplied by merely lifting comic scenes from native plays. What could be more natural, at a time when the importation of foreign singers and dancers was in vogue, than to turn to the wealth of farces and *petite comédies* already established in the French repertory? To make this easier, there was the practice, well fixed in the latter half of the century, of printing even the briefest of French farces. In contrast to the Italians, the French showed no reluctance about making their plays available and were therefore much more exposed to the rifling they underwent at English hands.

It would be pointless to discourse at length on Molière's place in the comic theatre, a subject which has engaged the attention of many writers, but a few observations on the specific problem of the relationship of this greatest of comic dramatists to farce, more particularly to English farce, are necessary.

Molière is one of those rare geniuses in the theatre most remarkable for their multileveled talents. As the theatrical manager in the prologue to *Faust* demands, he could

> plan, that all be fresh and new
> Important matter, yet attractive too.

In possessing this rare and remarkable talent the French writer joins the company of artists ranging in time and medium from Shakespeare, called "many-sided," to Chaplin, whose skilful combination of pathos and farce has won him not only the lasting esteem of the millions but the most extravagant plaudits of the hypercritical few.

Quite understandably, it is easier to isolate the elements in the complex of character and background which are accountable for the farce in Molière than to deal with the more obscure motives which support the strain of high comedy. For one thing, he was an actor given by training and disposition to clowning roles. At the same time he was a manager and therefore acutely sensitive to the demands of a public more intent on being entertained than on being provoked to thought. Add to these his long apprenticeship in the provinces, where the older tradition of French farce survived, and his later intimacy with the Italians and you have more than adequate reason why Molière was devoted to farce—a fact that his enemies were not disposed to forget.

It is perhaps necessary to acknowledge that it was chiefly the lowest levels of Molière's productions that appealed to the English writers and audiences of this whole period. This is evidenced most strikingly in the fact that whereas an out-and-out farce like *Médecin malgré lui* was pillaged repeatedly by English writers, his *Misanthrope* had little appeal—outside of Wycherley's strongly English *Plain Dealer*—to a nation commonly held to be marked by those qualities which mark Alceste. Moreover, in such comedies as *L'Avare* and *L'Etourdi*, where Molière had already included an element of farce but where his primary interest was in the subtler nuances of character, the tendency was to emphasize the farcical elements.

This stressing of the more boisterous passages of Molière was almost inevitable in the Restoration period, when the English theatre had as yet found no place for the afterpiece. With the exception of Otway's adaptation of *Les Fourberies des Scapin*, already noted, the shorter plays were combined in one fashion or another with other materials to make up a full-length play. The first of these borrowings, as we have seen, was the inclusion of *Sganarelle* in Davenant's *The Play-House to be Lett* (1663). This use of a medley of isolated pieces did not result in an established practice.

More commonly the English playwright simply worked scenes from one of Molière's plays into unrelated scenes of his concoction or from other plays, as, for example, in Rawlins' *Tom-Essence* (1676) and in Otway's *Souldiers Fortune* (1680), both of which use scenes from *Sganarelle*. Quite common, too, was the practice of taking parts, usually the most farcical, from one of the French playwright's works and combining them with parts similarly chosen from other plays by the same author. Ravenscroft is especially notorious for this practice, his strongly farcical *Mamamouchi* (1672) being made up from *Le Bourgeois gentilhomme* chiefly but with generous portions of *Pourceaugnac* thrown in. His *Scaramouch* (1677) is also a patchwork of scenes from *Mariage forcé* and *Scapin*, with some scenes added presumably from a *commedia dell'arte* scenario— much in the fashion that Molière himself had used elements from his Italian rivals in *Pourceaugnac* and elsewhere. In his *London Cuckolds* (1681) Ravenscroft managed a somewhat different combination, taking at least one strand of his plot from Molière, another from a novelle of the Decameron type, and possibly some hints from earlier English jigs or drolls.

In other cases the borrowing was confined to one full-length play by Molière, usually with a considerable increase of extraneous clowning. Examples can be found in Dryden's very popular *Sir Martin Mar-all* (1667) from *L'Etourdi*, Betterton's *Amorous Widow* (1670) from *George Dandin*, and Shadwell's *Miser* (1672) from *L'Avare*. Altogether, from *The Play-House to be Lett* in the opening decade of the Restoration to Wright's *Female Vertuoso's* in the closing decade Molière's most farcical pieces underwent wholesale and repeated adaptation.

Though the years from 1660 to 1680 represent possibly the high point of borrowing from Molière, there were two short periods in the first half of the eighteenth century in which his work saw a renewal of popularity. And at both times, it is hardly necessary to add, it was the farcical in him that drew the keenest attention. The reestablishment of competition between rival companies after 1695 and the resulting demand for "entertainments" drove English writers back to Molière, and to his successors also. A long and nondescript piece called *Love without Interest* (1699), turned over to the actor Pinkethman by its unidentified author, represents another—and quite insignificant—attempt to use *Mariage forcé* to provide laughs. With the actual beginning of the century and the custom of tacking on afterpieces, the renewed vogue in farce from Molière really began. Otway's *Cheats of Scapin*, first introduced some twenty-five years earlier, now began to come into its own and was soon a fixture in the repertory of afterpieces. Mrs. Centlivre adopted *Médecin malgré lui* as *Love's Contrivances* (1703); Congreve, Vanbrugh, and Walsh collaborated on an adaptation of *Pourceaugnac* for their *Squire Trelooby* (1704); Swiney used *Amour médecin* for his *Quacks* (1705). Some indication of how high Molière's influence was in this period may be had from John Corey's description of his *Metamorphosis* (1704) as "written originally by the famous Moliere"[16] when in fact there is no Molière in it beyond a brief item from *L'Avare* or its Plautian source, the business about showing of hands. The play was actually based on a pre-Commonwealth English play, Tomkis' *Albumazar*, with the addition of at least one device from Aristophanes' *Clouds*.

[16] Though the current esteem was for Molière the farce writer, and though earlier writers, like Shadwell and Langbaine, had agreed with his enemies at home in Paris to dismiss him as a producer of the merest low stuff, it may be noted that some critics about this time were beginning to accord him the position he deserved. In a letter, from a collection called *Letters of Wit, Politicks and Morality* (1701), quoted by F. E. Budd in his edition of Burnaby, pp. 456-460, we get this enthusiastic appraisal: "Our famous Ben Johnson's *Silent Woman*; *The Fox* and *The Alchymist*, and most of Molière's plays are the surest standards to judge of comedy. . . ."

The last period in which there was a significant amount of borrowing from Molière occurs in the 1730's, when dependence on French sources called forth this typical protest from one native playwright:

> Lately, our audience so capricious grown,
> Will scarce encourage farces of our own;
> For only he your pleasure can advance,
> Who transports humours from the stage of France.[17]

The most notable borrowings from Molière in this period are by Fielding. His adaptation of *L'Avare* in 1733 is among the best of English renderings of the French author, and his farce *The Mock Doctor* (1732) soon established itself in the afterpiece repertory.

Far less popular but scarcely less interesting adaptations were produced by Fielding's contemporary, James Miller, who returned to the practice in vogue seventy years earlier of taking two or three plays and attempting to weld them into one five-act piece. His first attempt resulted in his *Mother-in-Law* (1734), formed from *Malade imaginaire* and the often pilfered *Monsieur Pourceaugnac*. His next play, *The Man of Taste* (1735), combined *Les Précieuses ridicules* and *L'École des maris*. Though some of the blame for Miller's lack of success must be assigned to the persistent antagonism of the law students to his work, some of it must also be placed on his own misjudgment in trying to revive an outmoded practice. In support of the latter suggestion I quote from a current *Prompter*, No. 35: "The two farces in the French tongue, from whence it [*The Man of Taste*] is taken, considered apart, are very pretty for what they are;—but put together, become a very monstrous thing." Apparently Miller took the hint, for his last play, *The Picture: or, the Cuckold in Conceit* (1745), is a one-act afterpiece adapted from the much-used *Sganarelle*.

[17] From the prologue to Robert Drury's *Fancy'd Queen* (1733).

Only a few adaptations of Molière in this period remain unaccounted for. James Ralph's *Cornish Squire* (1734) was an unsuccessful attempt to revive the old "Squire Trelooby" adaptation of *Pourceaugnac*, done thirty years earlier, as a full-length play. Thomas Sheridan's very considerably altered version of the same play by Molière, became, as *The Brave Irishman* (1746 in London, much earlier in Dublin), a highly popular afterpiece, especially in Ireland.[18]

From this brief summary it should be clear that Molière's popularity on the English stage was long-lived and that his influence on farce, especially on the afterpiece, was very great. Reasons for this popularity and influence are obvious. Aside from the fact that his was by far the greatest contribution to a body of comic drama highly regarded all over Europe in its day, Molière would have found English audiences most receptive in any event, since his plays, especially his farces, readily appealed to English taste. It is no accident that such characters as Monsieur Jordain, Monsieur Pourceaugnac, and Sganarelle appear repeatedly in English adaptations; the grossness of character and manner which they represent provided the best of credentials for early naturalization.

Molière did not retain a monopoly over French exports of farce though there were few to dispute his position before 1695. Aside from scattered and insignificant hints, there are only occasional French pieces with considerable farce which Molière could not claim. One of these, appearing in two rival adaptations, was from Thomas Corneille's *Feint astrologue*, itself taken from a Spanish play. In 1668 Dryden brought out his *Evening's Love, or the Mock Astrologer*, which was matched in the same year by an anonymous farce, *The Feign'd Astrologer*. Neither play adds anything to the history of farce, both being largely

[18] For an account of these various adaptations of *Pourceaugnac* in the early eighteenth century, see Hughes and Scouten, *Ten English Farces* (Austin, 1948), pp. 220-221.

comedies of intrigue with some farcical additions. Another French adaptation, also of 1668, comes closer to being a thorough farce. Davenant's title, *The Man's the Master*, gives little more than a hint of the tone of the play, but the name given the original play by Scarron, *Jodelet maître*, indicates something of its author's intention in that the piece is clearly dominated by Jodelet, the great farce actor so long revered by French theatre-goers.

It seems clear, then, that except for Molière no French writer of farce exerted much influence in England before the end of the seventeenth century. However, as we have seen, not long after the secession of Betterton and his colleagues in 1695 the increased competition created a demand for short, farcical plays, and with the demand came a realization of the almost unlimited resources of the French repertory, to which numerous successors of Molière had been contributing. The number of short pieces taken from this rich supply is not as large as might be expected. Still, they constitute an important formative element in the whole picture.

In the early stages, before the establishment of the short, single afterpiece about 1704, there was some experimenting with medleys; and plays borrowed from the French, as well as native materials, were employed as entr'actes or interspersed with musical entertainments. For example, Ravenscroft's *Anatomist* (1696), from Hauteroche's *Crispin médecin*, was given along with a mixture of masque and musical concert called *The Loves of Mars and Venus* by Peter Anthony Motteux. Later that same year Motteux included a French farce, *All Without Money*, as the "comedy" act of his *Novelty*. Vanbrugh's *Country House*, from Dancourt, was produced as early as 1698, doubtless with some such musical or quasi-dramatic addition. It is, incidentally, an early example of a short, non-farcical play, though it was commonly labelled farce and was to take its place in the repertory of afterpieces.

With 1704 and the introduction of what was to become a standard pattern of play plus afterpiece begins a critical period of foreign, especially French, borrowing. As was indicated in Chapter 3, the first afterpiece to find its way into such a double bill was probably a French adaptation, Farquhar's *Stage Coach*, from La Chapelle. At this time, too, appeared the adaptations of *Scapin*, *Mariage forcé*, *Médecin malgré lui*, *Pourceaugnac*, and other plays by Molière. As yet only a few pieces, excerpted from English plays, seemed destined to survive, though several such excerpts had figured prominently in the medleys of a few seasons preceding. In fact, only Cibber's *School-Boy* remained in the repertory for years to come. When we add to these new and revived short French pieces the revivals of certain full-length plays foreign in origin and farcical in content, such as *The Duke and No Duke*, *The Emperor of the Moon*, and *Sir Salomon Single*, we see how important the influence of foreign, especially French, farce was becoming.

With the cessation of steady competition after 1705 and the consequent slackening of interest in afterpieces, this alarming trend toward foreign domination rapidly diminished. The renewal of competition after 1715 began a new trend—or, better, a series of trends—and the influence of French farce waned. It is difficult to account for the failure of Rich's venture into theatrical competition to rearouse an interest in the short French play, especially when we consider the sharp rise in the number of afterpieces played, in both houses, immediately following the opening of the new Lincoln's Inn Fields Theatre, or when we see the long list of foreign bills—many containing afterpieces—performed by visiting troupes in the last years of the second decade. Whatever the cause, both companies got along with surprisingly little direct borrowing. There were a good many revivals of earlier successes and an outburst of creative activity on the part of native farce writers, chiefly among the actors in Rich's new company. Christopher Bullock and Griffin were especially active in turning out novel—a safer word than original—plays to satisfy the increased demand.

In the early 1720's the rise of pantomime revived the interest in foreign pieces but at the same time absorbed most of the importations. Following quickly on this movement came the vogue in ballad opera, which by its very nature stressed native materials both in play and in song.

In the light of these fortuitous circumstances there can be little wonder that the domination of French farce, which seemed so assured in 1705, was terminated, and the native variety, or a mixed breed, took over the stage. The diminishing influence of French farce may be illustrated by a summary of borrowings after 1705. Aside from the plays already specified in the discussion of Molière there are hardly more than half a dozen French adaptations between 1705 and mid-century. Of these a few were highly successful. Regnard's *Retour imprévu* was adapted twice, first in 1715 in an anonymous piece called *The Lucky Prodigal* and again some twenty years later in *The Intriguing Chambermaid*, a popular afterpiece written by Henry Fielding chiefly to exploit the talents of Kitty Clive. Garrick also reworked a play that had already appeared. His *Lying Valet* (1741), a fast-moving farce taken from Hauteroche's *Souper mal apprêté*, became a phenomenal success, whereas Motteux's adaptation of the same play, in *All Without Money*, had been lost in the medley he had placed it in. There remains only Garrick's popular *Miss in Her Teens* (1747), which the actor-author had taken from Dancourt's *Parisienne*, and the list of French adaptations before 1750 is complete.[19]

[19] I am dealing here, to be sure, with farce only. There are several borrowings from short French plays which rise or aspire to the level of comedy, such as Miller's *Coffee House* (1738), based on Rousseau's *Caffé*.

It is no easy matter to assess properly the weight of the various influences, native and foreign, on English farce. I have no doubt that much of the pattern—and something of a pattern is discernible in many of the farces of the period—would have been worked out in time in the absence of any influences from outside, yet it seems equally clear that the establishment of a pattern was considerably hastened by the practice of levying on the French and, to a lesser extent, the Italians.

As an example of this pattern in the composition of farce, we may take Henry Carey's *The Contrivances*, first produced as a one-act farce in 1715, later reworked as a ballad opera in 1729, and long a staple in the afterpiece repertory. *The Contrivances* is, so far as I know, quite original with Carey, and yet it reads like dozens of other plays. The plot involves the attempts, eventually successful, of an impecunious young soldier to win an attractive young girl in spite of the antipathy of her miserly father, who has promised her to a loutish country squire. The fun of this not very novel play depends upon two short but unquestionably lively and laughable tricks employed by the young man to outwit the old. In the first the hero, with the aid of a clever servant, almost succeeds by disguising himself as a bashful country girl. In the second he is finally successful by means of a playful and noisy abduction.

Now *The Contrivances* is intrigue-farce in its least sophisticated form. It seems unlikely that it would have struck an eighteenth-century audience as at all foreign, for it is obviously Plautian and therefore long familiar. Since, however, the Plautian form had long been established on the Continent and had been adapted to the needs of the short farce, it would be equally foolhardy to deny the possibility that the playwright had learned some useful lessons from his foreign rivals.

Whatever the source, this almost stylized intrigue serving as a framework for various farce turns provided the playgoers of that day with just the sort of light dramatic entertainment they wanted, and it still does so. For here are the basic ingredients of the majority of non-serious plays: the successful overcoming of obstacles, the triumph of love, particularly young love, and the discomfiture of persons everyone can safely disapprove of. The most casual survey of the fare provided by the popular theatre today, especially in the movies and on the radio, will reveal the persistent success of such ingredients.

CHAPTER 6

THE ACTORS

✦✦

I am an ass! I! and yet I kept the stage in master Tarleton's time,
I thank my stars. Ho! an that man had lived to have played in
Bartholomew Fair, you should have seen him have come in, and
have been cozen'd in the cloth-quarter, so finely! and Adams, the
rogue, have leaped and capered upon him, and have dealt his
vermin about, as though they had cost him nothing! and then a
substantial watch to have stolen in upon them, and taken them
away, with mistaking words, as the fashion is in the stage-practice.
—BEN JONSON, The Induction to *Bartholomew Fair*

✦✦

As WE RANGE through the texts of farces printed in the
period under survey we are vaguely conscious of missing
something. Where there is so much repetition of the same
device, so little variation from a conventionalized pattern
of intrigue, it is sometimes hard to see how one farce caught
on while a half dozen others, not strikingly different in the
reading, failed. What was the secret ingredient which en-
abled the one to outdistance and outlast the others? Most
often the answer is, I believe, the action or the actor. What
is dead and repetitious on the printed page may well have
been very much alive in the capable hands of a trained
farceur.

Especially in farce, where everything depends upon an
instantaneous and vigorous response from the audience, the
skill of the actor is paramount. Subtle high comedy may
survive a cool first reception and win its way gradually into
high esteem. *The Way of the World*, now acclaimed as
perhaps the finest comedy of manners in English, had just
such a history. But the farce writer cannot afford to be so
patient, cannot depend upon the bright reversion of posterity. He is obliged to take the audience by storm or retire

in defeat. In this sort of desperate campaign the actors are the shock troops. On them depend in large measure all chances for success, as the farce writers of the eighteenth century—many of them, especially after 1715, actors themselves—came to realize and to acknowledge.

The anonymous author of *The City Farce* (1737) provides adequate testimony here when, on publishing his unacted play, he pleads: "I am sensible that every thing of a dramatick kind appears on reading little better than a body without life; and farce, more than any other, suffers by a cool inspection; its business being of such a nature as to borrow more than half its spirit from voice and action."[1]

The same idea is echoed by James Miller in the preface to his *Coffee House* (1738), a play that did see production but was an abysmal failure: "Pieces of this kind are made to depend more particularly on the representation, and must therefore plead for more indulgence in the closet."

John Gay is even more precise in the prologue to his unacted *Mohocks* (1712), in which he provides as a kind of substitute for performance an imaginative picture of how the highly popular buffoons then in the Drury Lane company might have comported themselves:

> This farce, if the kind players had thought fit,
> With action had supply'd the want of wit.
> Oh, readers! had you seen the Mohocks rage,
> And frighted watchmen tremble on the stage;
> Had you but seen our mighty emperor stalk;
> And heard in Cloudy honest Dicky talk,
> Seen Pinkethman in strutting Prig appear,
> And 'midst of danger wisely lead the rear,
> It might have pleas'd; for now-a-days the joke
> Rises or falls as with grimace 'tis spoke.

[1] Nicoll assigns this play to a Mrs. Weddell. It is not actually a farce as the term is used in this study.

Unfortunately we too are obliged to depend largely on our imaginations—unaided by an acquaintance with the actors named—if we attempt to discover anything of the nature of the performances of such famous clowns as Pinkethman and Norris. For earlier performers the task is even harder. We have some few comments to help us imagine Lacy and Nokes in action but they are not only few but lacking in helpful detail also. We do not even have the wealth of anecdotes which crowds the next century and embarrasses the historian of the theatre, who has to winnow so much chaff for a few grains of fact.

There are two quite adequate reasons why the comedian of that day, in contrast to his counterpart today, had no adequate press: For one thing, there simply was not the amount of space available in newspapers and magazines to provide intimate glimpses of the actor at work or play. For another, the low comedian had nothing resembling the following of articulate playgoers enjoyed by present-day actors. To speak warmly in praise of Betterton was not so shameful—actually we know little of this actor's specific qualities. To praise Tony Leigh in anything like the same tone was unthinkable.[2]

Here is a sample of high tribute paid to one of the great clowns of our own age: "Yet to me Chaplin is a poet, even a great poet, a creator of myths, symbols, and ideas, the discoverer of a new and unknown world. I could not even begin to say how much Chaplin has taught me—and always without boring me. Indeed I do not know, for it is too essential to be defined."[3] I shall not argue that so rhapsodic an outburst is misapplied or even that any of the comedians

[2] Cibber is, to be sure, as unrestrained in his praise of low comedians as he is in tributes to more dignified actors, but no earnest person would accept the brazen author of the *Apology* as a model.

[3] Elie Faure, *The Art of Cineplastics* (Boston, 1923), p. 49. While the French commentator probably outdistances others in the extravagance of his praise, he is only one of a throng of Chaplin idolaters.

of the earlier age of which I am speaking in any way matched Chaplin's gifts. I am simply pointing out what seems permissible now by way of comment on a comedian's art as compared to the conventionally acceptable two hundred and fifty years ago when no sane man would have risked such rhetoric—even for a Chaplin.

With the beginnings of modern journalism, heralded in the first decade of the eighteenth century by the first daily paper and the first essay periodical, there are a few scattered instances of more moderate praise, as is indicated by the attention, not always kindly meant, given to the actor Pinkethman. Half a century or more later, at the end of Garrick's career, the praise has turned into strong acclaim. Take, for example, the press reports of Garrick's funeral, in which the note of adulation is of the sort a modern-day movie idol could command. But Garrick was no mere comedian. Ranging as he did through every type of role, he made it possible for many to acclaim him as the great tragedian of the age or of all ages while deploring his fondness for lower roles.

But to return to the period before 1700 when the press as we know it was virtually non-existent. While it will be impossible to do justice to all the players who succeeded in farce roles, I hope to present some facts about a representative group. In speaking of these I shall try to avoid the colorful but unattested anecdote as I say something about their roles, their reputations, and, where the scanty details provide any help, their manner of acting.

Who were the skilled and popular farceurs of the Restoration? For the first decade or so after the reopening of the theatres, until his death around 1673, Edward Angel seems to have been a clown of real promise. For the first two decades, until his death just before the union of the companies, John Lacy of the King's company was even more highly praised. Thomas Jevon shone for some fifteen years, especially in "light-heeled" parts. Cave Underhill played dullard roles for many years from the Restoration on past the turn of the century. Jo Haines flitted in and out of one theatre or the other for over twenty-five years, without making any really great mark as an actor in either. The most accomplished clown of all, perhaps the greatest in the century covered in this study, was James Nokes, who began his career early in the period as a partner and foil to Angel and then joined his talents with those of the almost equally brilliant Tony Leigh to form a team which must have been unbeatable in its day.

It is unfortunate that we do not have more detailed information on John Lacy, the leading farce player and mainstay of Killegrew's company for two decades, for Lacy was evidently a dedicated clown and a successful one. Perhaps he was not quite the paragon suggested by Langbaine's tribute to him,[4] but his playing won the strong favor of Charles II, who had him painted in a famous triptych representing three of his most successful roles. He was as much a favorite of a less influential but no less assiduous playgoer, Samuel Pepys, who saw him a number of times and usually reported favorably. Pepys offers just enough detail to be tantalizing, telling us that Lacy's playing in some piece called *The French Dancing Master* "pleased . . . the best in the world," or that in Robert Howard's *Committee* "Lacy's part, as Irish footman, is beyond imagination." On one of the few occasions when Pepys did not altogether approve of the actor's performance, he does add a few details which indicate what Lacy would do for laughs when left to his own devices. On this particular evening, toward the end of the period covered by the diary, Lacy was responsible for some entr'acte entertainment, "a farce of several dances," as Pepys called it. "But his words are

---

[4] Langbaine thought Lacy "perform'd all parts he undertook to a miracle: insomuch that I am apt to believe, that as this age never had, so the next never will have his equal, at least not his superiour." *An Account of the English Dramatick Poets*, p. 317.

but silly, and invention not extraordinary, as to the dances; only some Dutchmen come out of the mouth and tail of a Hamburgh sow."[5]

Whatever his success with his royal patron or with Pepys, Lacy seems to have followed a practice common among low comedians of aiming to please the humbler playgoers. In this connection it is interesting to see him address his followers in the prologue to his own popular *Old Troop* (1665):

> To you that judges are i'th public street
> Of ballad without sense, or even feet;
> To you that laugh aloud with wide-mouth'd grace,
> To see Jack Pudding's custard thrown in's face—
> To you I do address; for you I write;
> From you I hope protection here to-night.
> Defend me, O my friends of th' upper region,
> From the hard censure of this lower legion.
> I was in hope that I should only see
> My worthy crew of th' upper gallery.
> What made you wits so spitefully to come?
> To tell you true, I'd rather had your room.
> Order there was, and that most strictly gi'n,
> To keep out all that look'd like gentlemen.
> You have e'en bribed the doorkeepers, I doubt,
> Or else I'm sure they would ha' kept you out.
> You must nor censure poet nor his play,
> For that's the work o' the upper house to-day.
> Deal you, Sirs, with your match, your Dryden wit,
> Your poet-laureate both to box and pit.
> It is some conquest for to censure him
> That's filled with wit and judgment to the brim:
> He is for your censure, and I'm for theirs,
> Pray therefore meddle with your own affairs.

[5] *Diary*, 19 January 1669.

Let wits and poets keep their proper stations;
He writes to th' terms, I to th' long vacations.

We may doubt whether Lacy was so alarmed over the reception the critical pit would have given him without denying that his tastes did seem to match those of the upper gallery. In any event it will not be necessary here to repeat any of the action of the play itself to show the kind of performance Lacy gained a reputation for, since I have analyzed the main scenes of buffoonery in Chapter 2.

Lacy's success in such farce roles helped to keep up the fortunes of the King's company for two decades. There seems to be little question that his death in 1681, at a time when the leading actors of serious roles, especially Hart and Mohun, were nearing the end of their usefulness, helped to weaken the company to the point that a union with the Duke's actors seemed the only wise alternative.

We know rather less of Edward Angel than we do of his rival in the opposing company, but there are enough details to suggest that he was a thorough-going clown and that the applause he received encouraged him further in that direction. Like Lacy he was, it will be recalled from an earlier chapter, given to taking liberties with his parts and to cultivating the esteem of what Mrs. Behn called "most o' th' lighter periwigs about the town." Pepys must have seen him a number of times, possibly as the French valet enclosed in a tub in Etherege's *Comical Revenge* (1664), almost certainly as Woodcock in Shadwell's *Sullen Lovers* (1668), one of the parts Downes singles out for praise, but the diarist gives no details until his entry for Angel's performance as Trincalo in Tomkis' pre-Commonwealth *Albumazar*, and even then he is not especially helpful unless we supplement his statement with a few words indicating the nature of the play. *Albumazar* is largely a farcical play, especially in its depiction of Trincalo, who is first tricked into believing he has undergone a magic transformation that has completely altered his appearance and then is beaten, shut up in a beer barrel, tumbled down the cellar steps—in short, submitted to most of the indignities incident to slapstick. It is of Angel's performance in this part that Pepys reports, "The King there, and, indeed, all of us, pretty merry at the mimique tricks of Trinkilo."[6]

Within a few seasons Angel became so closely associated in clownish roles with James Nokes that their names were commonly paired. By 1670 we find Edward Howard casting them together, along with Underhill, in a little quasi-dramatic prologue to his *Woman's Conquest*. It is true that Howard professed to be deeply distressed by the success such fools were gaining. Yet he was not unwilling to take advantage of their popularity by using them in his prologue under their own names while leaving them out of his play. If, as I assume, Howard is presenting the three actors in their own characters it may be of some value to meet them briefly: Angel and Underhill first appear and engage in a quarrel, Underhill being surprised to find that Angel has plans to set aside the new play announced in favor of a farce; in fact, Angel wants a steady diet of farce—"to morrow, and to morrow, and so to the end of our lives." They are about to withdraw to dress when Nokes enters.

ANG. . . . here come Mr. Noakes ready drest. UND. Then I perceive we shall have a Farce to purpose, and 'tis odds, but he personates one beetle-brow'd Fellow or other.

ANG. O, Mr. Noaks, you have habited your self very properly.

NOAK. According to my best apprehensions, Gentlemen. UND. But you should not have entred with your face grim'd, 'twill discover too much of our Farces plot before-hand. NOAK. There's good design in it, I warrant you.

[6] *Ibid.*, 22 February 1668.

UND. But what shall we do for a Prologue? NOAK. Leave that to me, Sirs, I'le give u'm one a new way. ANG. Mark that, Mr. Underhill, and shall we have a novelty in our Prologue, Mr. Noakes? NOAK. I have devised it purposely, because a new way is generally taking in what kind soever. UND. I am much of that opinion, since I have observed that new non-sense is valued in the Pit by looks and grimasks? ANG. A rare and prodigious thought! I have known a device like this, serve well in a Play. UND. And hath been thought a good Scene too. NOAK. And first on you Criticks, I'le leer thus, like a Satyr; for the moderate Wits thus; for ho, ho, ho's, who laugh in such good earnest, when there is no Jest given them, comically thus.

Enter Changling.

UND. No more of your grimasks, good Mr. Noakes. NOAK. And why so, Sir? UND. Because I have consider'd better, and since 'tis resolv'd, we shall have a Prologue to our Farce, here is one shall give it u'm the Farce way exactly.   [*To the Changling.*]

ANG. There's nothing better—the very Pudding of our Farce that must fill the Audience up to the throat with laughter. NOAK. Since you will have it so, you shall find me reasonable; I confess 'tis a pretty toyish way.

UND. And what is most extraordinary, he shall dance out a Prologue.

ANG. A Prologue to be danced, aha, aha, Boys. [*Angel leaps.*]

NOAK. And I make Still-Musick with my mouth the whilst, shall I, Sirs?

UND. 'Tis not amiss; come hither, Changling, and set your feet, and looks in order for the Prologue.

CHANG. Shall it be with my face, feet, and hands, tre-doulding thus?

OMNES. 'Tis very innocent and well.

CHANG. I'le warrant you, I'le tredoudle it so, that it
shall take to purpose.
OMNES. Musick there for the Prologue.
[*The Musick plays, he dances a while, then is heard a
noise with Thunder and Lightning, at which time Ben.
Johnson personated rises from below.*]

With the appearance of this dread apparition representing
true comedy the clowns flee.

In the spring of the same season Howard had another
play produced at the Duke's Theatre, this one called *The
Six Days Adventure*. Again he takes an exalted tone in his
preface and jeers at the rabble for its low taste, but again
he provides two or three roles for extravagant clowning by
the low comedians of the troupe. Angel played Peacock, a
fatuous ass, so in love with himself that he goes about
dressed in a suit of feathers, hugging and kissing himself.
The height of farce—or possibly burlesque since Howard
professes a satirical intent—is reached when a magician
creates a double for Peacock, similarly dressed and similarly
given to self love. Evidently poor Howard, who had only the
most meager dramatic talents, had been forced to bow to
public demand and provide roles for the clowns he professed to scorn.

It is impossible to say what part, if any, Angel played in
Mrs. Behn's *Amorous Prince*, which first appeared about
the same time as Howard's *Six Days Adventure*, but the
prologue to that play has some interest here in that it adds
further evidence that playwrights and playgoers may well
have tended to divide into hostile camps over comedy.
Since this is a prologue in the "huffing" manner we need
not take too seriously the author's professed contempt for
both factions, but her description of them is intriguing:

> First then for you grave Dons, who love no play
> But what is regular, great Johnson's way;
> Who hate the Monsieur with the farce and droll,

But are for things well said with spirit and soul;
'Tis you I mean, whose judgements will admit
No interludes of fooling with your wit;
You're here defeated, and anon will cry,
"Sdeath! wou'd 'twere treason to write comedy.
So! There's a party lost; now for the rest,
Who swear they'd rather hear a smutty jest
Spoken by Nokes or Angel, than a scene
Of the admir'd and well penn'd Cataline;
Who love the comic hat, the jig and dance,
Things that are fitted to their ignorance:
You too are quite undone, for here's no farce
Damn me! you'll cry, this play will be mine A—

Angel, paired as usual with Nokes, acted a clownish role
in Orrery's *Mr. Anthony* (1672), the chief slapstick episode being a comical duel between the two which Downes
was to recall some forty years later. The pair had become
so nearly inseparable by now that we come to expect their
names together in any allusion to farcical acting. Among
the most interesting of these allusions, for example, is one
referred to, from a quite different point of view, earlier. In
The Gentleman Dancing-Master, Monsieur de Paris, char-
acteristically preferring foreign objects to native ones, rates
the famous Italian comedian Fiorilli as vastly superior to
the English clowns. "Angel is a dam English fool to him."
But Hippolita remains loyal.

Hip. Methinks now Angel is a very good fool.
Mons. Nauh, nauh, Nokes is a better fool, but indeed
the Englis' are not fit to be fools; here are ver few good
fools. 'Tis true, you have many a young cavalier who go
over into France to learn to be de buffoon; but for all
dat, dey return but *mauvais* buffoon, *jarni*!
Hip. I'm sure, cousin, you have lost no time there.
Mons. Auh, *le brave* Scaramouche!

HIP. But is it a science in France, cousin? and is there an academy for fooling? sure none go to it but players.

MONS. Dey are comedians dat are de *maitres*; but all the *beau monde* go to learn, as they do here of Angel and Nokes. For if you go abroad into company, you would find the best almost of de nation conning in all places the lessons which dey have learned of the fools dere *maitres*, Nokes and Angel.

The combination of farceurs was not to last much longer, however. Some time towards the end of the following season Angel, who during this last season created at least three new comic roles in Shadwell's *Epsom Wells*, Mrs. Behn's *Dutch Lover*, and Ravenscroft's *Careless Lovers*, died.

Cave Underhill, whom we saw above with Nokes and Angel in the prologue to Howard's *Woman's Conquest* and who appeared in most of the plays mentioned in connection with Angel, was perhaps more of an actor of "heavy" characters than a mere clown, but he managed in a long career to fill a great many farce roles. His chief function in these was to serve as butt for the more sprightly characters. From a very early appearance, along with Nokes, in Cowley's *Cutter of Coleman Street* (1661) to his last performance at Drury Lane as Trincalo in *The Tempest* in the spring of 1710, Underhill acted in numerous low comedies. As Sir Simon Softhead in Ravenscroft's first farce, as Pedagog in *Mr. Anthony*, as Blunt in Mrs. Behn's two *Rover* plays, as Baliardo in her *Emperor of the Moon*, to name but a few of his many, many parts, poor Underhill was beaten and kicked, stripped and ducked unmercifully. Throughout all these indignities he maintained a stolid countenance which in the circumstances was ludicrous in the extreme. In fact, if we may depend upon the memory of Cibber, who knew him for twenty years or more, his stolidity was his chief stock in trade:

Underhill was a correct and natural comedian, his particular excellence was in characters that may be called still-life, I mean the stiff, the heavy, and the stupid; to these he gave the exactest and most expressive colours, and in some of them look'd as if it were not in the power of human passions to alter a feature of him. In the solemn formality of Obadiah in the *Committee,* and in the boobily heaviness of Lolpoop in the *Squire of Alsatia,* he seem'd the immoveable log he stood for! a countenance of wood could not be more fixt than his, when the blockhead of a character required it: His face was full and long; from his crown to the end of his nose was the shorter half of it, so that the disproportion of his lower features, when soberly compos'd, with an unwandering eye hanging over them, threw him into the most lumpish, moping mortal that ever made beholders merry![7]

In contrast with Underhill's fifty years on the stage we have the brief career of Tom Jevon, who built up a considerable reputation, chiefly in low comedy roles, in a scant fifteen years. Jevon's talents, judging from his roles, must have been strikingly different from Underhill's. Where Underhill was heavy and phlegmatic, Jevon was light and mercurial. The latter played Harlequin to the former's Pantalone. Of course the opportunity to play the actual Italian roles was decidedly limited, but even in purely native plays we find the pair similarly contrasted.

Jevon seems to have begun his career as a dancer. Genest's first record of him in a dramatic role is for Osric in a revival of *Hamlet* in 1673, but he very quickly took his place among the great comedians of the Duke's company and for over a dozen years held his own with Nokes, Underhill, and Leigh, the last-named actor having come into the company at about the same time. Though Jevon could play such

---

[7] *Apology,* I, 154-155. Aston thought Underhill overrated by his colleagues in the theatre, but even from his description we get the impression of an extremely ludicrous clown.

straight roles as Young Bellair in Etherege's great comedy of manners, he seems far more at home in more boisterous ones and soon had ample opportunity for slapstick in such farce-comedies as Durfey and Mrs. Behn were rapidly turning out. For a time he was called upon to play character parts running to the stupid or giddy, as Sneak or Harry Jollyman or Sir Frolick Whimsy in some of Durfey's plays, and it may be significant that in the only play he was to write he created a downright English role, the rough cobbler Jobson, for himself. But as we get well into the 1680's we find him giving more attention to the clever and rascally servants of French and Italian comedy. In Otway's coarse *Souldiers Fortune* (1680) he was Fourbin; in Mrs. Behn's *Revenge* (1680), Trickwell; in Tate's adaptation of some other Jacobean pieces, *Cuckolds-Haven* (1685), Quicksilver; and in Mrs. Behn's *Emperor* (1686) and Mountfort's *Faustus* (1688) he played Harlequin.[8] Summers has called Jevon "our first English Harlequin" and thinks the actor "proved the King of all Harlequins, past, present, and to come." I am sorry to say that I know of no evidence to support—or, for that matter, to refute—the latter claim, but the former seems clearly incorrect, for the distinction, such as it is, appears to belong to Jo Haines, who played Harlequin some ten years earlier in Ravenscroft's *Scaramouch* (1677).

The mention of Jevon's rival claimant for the title of "first English Harlequin" introduces a ticklish problem. To many a reader the one name to be recalled as "famous comedian" in this period is Jo Haines. If mere frequency of mention of an actor's name during a period and, more especially, *since* the period were adequate to settle the question, there could be no cause for doubt; Haines would be

---

[8] Jevon by no means deserted English-type roles. To do so would have required him to sever his alliance with Nokes and Leigh. The group may be seen together in such plays as *Mr. Turbulent* (1682), *The Luckey Chance* (1686), and *A Fool's Preferment* (1688).

the acknowledged master comedian of the age, for his name must appear in the various anecdotal histories of the stage at least as often as those of all the others combined. Yet the painful fact seems to be that—setting aside all the numerous stories of him in the role of "humorist" in life and taking into account only those facts which apply to his reputation as an actor—Haines was never much more than a skilful dancer and a mediocre comedian.

It would require far too much space and take us too far afield to set forth all of the evidence on either side of this question. Perhaps two points might be worth mentioning: First of all is the recorded comment during the actor's life or within the span when men who had actually seen him perform were still able to recall his merits. It seems to me quite significant that the most glowing comments all come later. Early in his career he seemed to Pepys "an incomparable dancer." And it was as a dancer that he received the plaudits of Louis and his courtiers at Chambord in the fall of 1670.[9] Later he was noted for his "wit" and his "facetiousness." Even his biographer uses the somewhat equivocal term "famous comedian."[10] After all, comedians, like other men, may gain fame by various means. Colley Cibber, who could be generous with old colleagues and who was almost extravagant in his praises of several of the actors already mentioned, is not even willing to retain the *famous.* His only mention of the actor with whom he spent a decade at Drury Lane labels him as "the noted Jo Haines, the comedian, a fellow of wicked wit."[11] In contrast with these rather faint praises are the glowing accounts of later date.

[9] *The Despatches of William Perwich* (London, 1903), p. 116.
[10] Tobyas Thomas, *The Life of the Late Famous Comedian, Jo. Hayns* (1701). Haines owes much of his fame in later years to his fortune in attracting a lively biographer. Many, if not most, of the anecdotes concerning his witty pranks come from this amusing book, which does not strike the modern scholar as notably careful with facts.
[11] *Apology,* I, 273.

Genest, for instance, recites the tribute of the *Biographia Dramatica*: "The famous Joe Haines . . . , a person of great facetiousness and readiness of wit, which together with his inimitable performances on the stage as a comedian, introduced him not only to the acquaintance, but the familiarity of persons of the first rank."[12]

Yet—and here we come to the second point, the theatrical record—Genest's list of roles indicating Haines' achievement in the theatre is shorter and less impressive than the list he gives for Jevon, though the latter had a scant fifteen years on the stage to over thirty for Haines. True enough, Jo was about as often out of employment at the regular theatres as he was in, for he was by instinct a bird of passage; yet he spent most of the last ten years of his life in fairly steady employment at Drury Lane, acting quite minor roles.[13]

The one commodity which Haines seems to have possessed in abundance was brass. Pound for pound he probably had a greater proportion of the metal in his system than almost any other man in Europe in his day. And it is his brass that earned him such notoriety in his own day and the somewhat spurious fame of later times. It was largely because of his status as a sort of public figure, I

---

[12] II, 236.

[13] In his whole career Haines created three notable but minor roles in major plays: Sparkish in *The Country Wife* (1675), Lord Plausible in *The Plain Dealer* (1676), and Captain Bluff in *The Old Batchelour* (1693). On one or two occasions playwrights seem to have written parts especially for him, but in every case it seems clear that what they intended to exploit was the actor's notoriety rather than his ability. Dryden is said to have had him in mind for Benito in *The Assignation* (1672), but at that point in his career Haines could hardly have had an established reputation in acting; he had, however, recently been on the Continent engaging in some of his characteristic pranks. Dennis's Baldernoe, in *A Plot, and No Plot* (1697), is apparently based upon Haines's character as a trickster; ironically, the role was played by Pinkethman, while Haines had the decidedly minor part of Rumour. In the same year he played himself in Settle's *World in the Moon*.

believe, that he was in such demand for speaking prologues and epilogues, in the rendering of which he began a tradition which later comedians, such as Pinkethman and Spiller, were to carry on. More significant even, in earning him a lasting place in theatrical lore, was his incomparable talent for getting into and out of various scrapes. Most accounts of Haines will be found to consist largely of tales of his "witty pranks," amusing enough in themselves but almost never having anything to do with acting or the theatre. Altogether, Tony Aston's judgment seems to me as nearly sound as any: "Joe Haines is more remarkable for the witty, tho' wicked, pranks he play'd, and for his prologues and epilogues, than for acting."[14] Even Aston could not resist telling half a dozen of his favorite stories of Jo's pranks and closing his *Brief Supplement* with a promise of more to follow in the sequel, which never appeared.

As has doubtless become obvious by now, I find it difficult to treat one of these farce actors without bringing in several others, particularly where they operate over a period of years in pairs or larger groups. In the case of Underhill, for example, I have noted that his forte was to play victim to the sallies and assaults of other clowns in the troupe. It is hardly possible, then, to show him in action without bringing in the others. Similarly, Jevon came to be associated with Tony Leigh, in Harlequin-Scaramouch combinations, for example, so that to talk of one it is almost always necessary to bring in the other.

If it has been difficult to keep the others separate, it is impossible to do so with the greatest low comedians of the Restoration period, Nokes and Leigh. They were not, to be sure, identical in manner. Cibber insists that no one was or could be like Nokes, who was "an actor of quite different genius from any I have ever read, heard of, or seen, since or before his time."[15] Moreover, Cibber continues in his

[14] Lowe reprints Aston's work at the end of his edition of Cibber's *Apology*; the quotation occurs II, 314.
[15] I, 141.

long and superlative-studded tribute, whereas Leigh had his imitators—none quite up to the original, though Pinkethman approached it—Nokes had none.[16]

Yet these two were such excellent foils that they not only paired off in play after play, season after season, but also were joined by name in numerous allusions. To take one set of examples, Mrs. Behn grew fond of alluding to the pair in prologue and epilogue. She closes the epilogue to *The Rover, Pt. I* (1677), with this couplet:

> Oh that our Nokes, or Tony Lee could show
> A fop but half so much to th' life as you.

Two years later her prologue to *The Feign'd Curtizans* has:

> Fops of all sorts he draws more artfully
> Then ever on the stage did Nokes or Leigh.

The epilogue to her *False Count* (1682), possibly written by another, put them into a triplet:

> If to make people laugh the business be,
> You sparks better comedians are than we;
> You everyday out-fool ev'n Nokes and Lee.

Durfey, showing his awareness of the drawing power of the famous team, put them into a curious prologue, not unlike the one referred to above from Howard, to his *Virtuous Wife* (1679). This prologue is too long to give in its entirety here, though one exchange in the mock quarrel that the two actors engage in has a special interest since it has them name some of their best known roles:

[16] Nokes became a sort of byword for foolish appearance or behavior and for primacy in comic roles. The NED cites the *New Dictionary of the Canting Crew*, published about the time of his death, as giving the entry: "*Nokes*, a ninny or fool." Half a century later Dodsley was evidently the inventor of the dictum so often repeated in books on the theatre: "Burbage was the Betterton, and Kempe the Nokes of that age."

NOKES: Ye lye
And you're a Pimp, a Pandarus of Troy
A Gripe, a Fumble.

LEE: Nay, and you 'gin to quarrel,
Gad ye're a Swash, a Toby in a barrel,
Would you were here.

I despair of giving any satisfactory account of either the quantity of roles they played, together or separately, or the quality of their performances. A few representative examples must suffice. In the play by Durfey just mentioned Nokes and Leigh had roles which have little attraction now in the reading—the play is not one of Durfey's best, and Durfey at his best is a mediocre playwright—but they do seem characteristic enough to suggest that they were prepared especially for them. Leigh played Sir Lubberly Widgeon; Nokes had one of his several "nurse" or old woman roles, Lady Beardly.

The reference in Leigh's speech to "a Toby in a barrel" is to a more interesting role in an earlier play by the same author. In *Madame Fickle* (1676) Leigh was Zechiel, former country lout made over, rather botchily, into a town fop; Nokes was his brother Toby, still the incredibly oafish rustic whom Zechiel tries to force into the new pattern. Toby's attempts to learn town manners are highly ludicrous. He cannot get his new name straight; Zechiel in an excess of romantic enthusiasm has renamed himself and his brother Fillo-florido and Rousivell. He has singularly little success in his attempts at courtship; he ruins the carefully laid plans made for his marriage by breaking a vial containing St. Jerome's tears, prize possession of his antiquary father-in-law-to-be. About the only thing he does well is "roar"; that is, when Zechiel urges him to practice his lessons in swashbuckling he pounds Zechiel around the stage in mock rage until the latter is more than content with his progress. The climactic scene between the brothers comes in Act V in a pursuit sequence of the traditional kind. Sought by the watch in a dark street before a tavern, Toby takes cover in a wine-butt; Zechiel climbs to the balcony and thence to the wine bush hanging at the door. Old Tilbury, father of the boys, comes along with a torch and, in anger at Zechiel's pelting him with bits of orange peel, sets the bush on fire. Zechiel's desperate cries bring out the watch, who arrest Tilbury for arson. Toby frightens the watch from his position in the barrel, blows out their lantern, grunts like a pig, and, in general, thoroughly enjoys himself. In short, Durfey's piece, which is two-thirds slapstick anyway, in spite of his usual satirical aim, was obviously designed in large measure for the peculiar talents of the clowns in the Duke's company. Since there are no adequate records of theatrical success in this early period, it is impossible to say just how well they succeeded, but I think it significant that when the rival companies were looking for farcical material in older plays to use in the critical period between 1695 and 1705 they returned to these scenes. At any rate, a later pair of famous clowns, Pinkethman and Bullock, were performing a *Toby and Ezekiel*, which I take to be from Durfey's play, at Bartholomew Fair in 1703.

An examination of the lists given for the pair by Genest will indicate the nature and the number of their roles. It seems obvious from these lists that both actors were indispensable, that the absence of either or both would have had a profound effect upon the fortunes of low comedy in the Restoration period. Of the two Nokes was pretty certainly the more important figure. From Cibber's comments, we may assume that his contribution was unique. We know, moreover, that roles were written specifically for him. For example, Dryden was said to have prepared the leading parts in his two most popular comedies, *Sir Martin Mar-all* (1667) and *The Spanish Fryar* (1680),[17] with Nokes in

[17] Downes, p. 28, is our authority for Dryden's adapting "the part [of Sir Martin] purposely for the mouth of Mr. Nokes." The

mind. There are references also to the damaging effects of the actor's absence from parts designed especially for him.[18] Yet Leigh had his following, too, and, even where we lack positive statements to that effect, it is clear enough that parts were written into several plays with a view to exploiting his talents. Altogether, they were a great comic team, so great that we can hardly suppose that Cibber exaggerates the effects of their retirement: "But alas! when those actors were gone, that comedy [*The Souldiers Fortune*] and many others, for the same reason, were rarely known to stand on their own legs; by seeing no more of Leigh or Nokes in them, the characters were quite sunk or alter'd."[19]

The retirement of a great actor has an effect not altogether different from the retirement of a great champion of the prize ring. So long as the memory of his prowess remains fresh, it is fruitless for new contenders to hope to emulate him. His admirers will endure no comparisons; the day of giants in the earth is over. What makes matters peculiarly difficult, in the case of the aspiring actor, is that while the playgoers wish to see no deviations from the manner of their earlier idol they are unwilling to accept the efforts of the newcomer when he tries to imitate his predecessor. In time, however, successors to Nokes and Leigh did appear. Whether these successors approached—or sur-

---

authority for the second role is somewhat less reliable. The author of *The History of the English Stage* published by Curll in 1741, possibly Oldys, says, p. 32, "Mr. Dryden wrote Gomez in the *Spanish Fryar* in compliment to Mr. Nokes."

[18] In 1685 Tate blamed the poor reception of his *Cuckolds-Haven* on the absence of Nokes from the cast: "The principal part (on which the diversion depended) was, by accident, disappointed of Mr. Nokes's performance, for whom it was design'd, and only proper." Dryden, in some commendatory verses addressed to Southern on the publication, in 1692, of *The Wives Excuse*, apparently consoles his friend after a disappointing reception:

The hearers may for want of Nokes repine,
But rest secure, the readers will be thine.

[19] *Apology*, 1, 148; see also 1, 188.

passed—the earlier pair in ability and acclaim is impossible to decide. The team of Pinkethman and Bullock, or these two plus Dicky Norris, were in time to receive even more press notices, but this may very well have been due to the vast increase in press notices of all kinds. In other words, if the applause they received did not actually exceed that of Nokes and Leigh, it was more faithfully recorded.

Even before the retirement of Nokes and Leigh the united company had recruited an actor of great promise in Thomas Doggett, who had been touring the provinces,[20] and who was to become an impressive figure in the theatre for two decades or more. Maidment and Logan, in their edition of Crowne's works, speak of Doggett as "a comedian of great merit, entirely devoid of buffoonery."[21] The records amply support the claim of great merit, but I cannot see how Doggett can be absolved entirely of the charge of buffoonery. It is true that he is remembered today chiefly as the creator of Ben in *Love for Love*, but he was equally famous in his own day for other, more clownish roles in plays which have not survived in literary anthologies or theatrical repertories. Look, for example, at the low comedy parts Doggett inherited from Nokes: Sir Arthur Addle, Sir Nicholas Cully, Barnaby Brittle, Toby. Or recall his activities at Smithfield during the annual fairs. Summers lists two drolls of 1691 in which Doggett had a share and which seem from the titles to have been somewhat less than dignified. Ned Ward reported seeing him in one of these drolls.[22] For a last bit of evidence take the roles written by and for Doggett. There is some indication that Durfey had him in mind for the

[20] Nicoll, *History*, I, 378, gives a record concerning his coming into the London company, "from being a stroler"; Aston gives some account of Doggett as a stroller; Miss Rosenfeld reproduces some provincial records concerning him.

[21] IV, 226.

[22] In the *London-Spy*, I, 250-252 of the fifth edition of 1718, Ward reports his reactions to a droll which seems pretty clearly to have been the one listed in Summers' *Bibliography*, pp. 137-138.

part of Quickwit in *The Richmond Heiress* (1693) early in his career at Drury Lane: at one point in the play a stage direction marks an exit with the actor's name rather than that of Quickwit.[23] Cibber tells us that, "not wishing to miss the advantage of Mr. Doggett's excellent action," he added a "low character" to his *Woman's Wit* (1696), a part, incidentally, which was to form the nucleus of a popular afterpiece, *The Schoolboy*. Nor is the role of Hob Doggett played in his own *Country Wake* (1696) far removed from buffoonery, though it is not as buffoonish as the roles he played in *She Ventures and He Wins* (1695) or in the short farces adapted from the French around 1704, *The Stage Coach* and *Squire Trelooby*.[24]

Perhaps as unrestrained a piece of buffooning as Doggett ever engaged in occurs not in a play but in one of those zany epilogues Pinkethman became so notorious for. After *Injur'd Love* (1711) Pinkethman appears on the stage to explain, with apologies, that it will be impossible to comply with the usual requirement of having a risqué epilogue delivered by a "pretty maid," maidens being notoriously scarce. He hopes, however, that the audience may not object to the substitution of his own sister, and then proceeds to haul on Doggett in woman's clothes—the costume he had worn in the play. After some conventional clowning, with Doggett repeating both prompts and comments, he obliges with a burlesque version of the suggestive epilogue.

To picture Doggett as wholly a buffoon of a class with Pinkethman would of course be wrong. He was a careful and judicious actor as well. Wilkes tells in some detail how carefully Doggett dressed for his playing of Moneytrap, exaggerating certain traits to be sure, but keeping a close eye on the demands of character.[25] The anonymous *Essay on*

---

[23] I realize the possibility that the error may have occurred in printing the play shortly *after* its first performance.

[24] See Downes, p. 49: ". . . Mr. Dogget acting Trelooby so well, the whole was highly applauded."

[25] *General View*, p. 147.

Acting (1744) goes even further in reproducing what the author admits is only hearsay to the effect that "The late celebrated Mr. Dogget, before he perform'd the character of Ben, in *Love for Love,* took lodgings in Wapping, and gather'd thence a nosegay for the whole town."

We may suspect that Doggett knew his own limitations from the fact that he gave up the part of Lory in *The Relapse* to his sprightlier colleague Pinkethman. Aston, who had toured the provinces with Doggett, tells a story of his venturing out of his depth, in a serious role, and of his being laughed back into his senses by the audience, which saw too much of Hob in the part.[26] Yet Aston's general opinion of Doggett is very high. He calls him "this nonpareil" and "the best face-player and gesticulator, and a thorough master of the several dialects, except the Scots (for he never was in Scotland) but was, for all that, a most excellent Sawney." The remark about dialects confirms the tributes to Doggett's care in studying parts.

Perhaps the finest tribute to Doggett's care and subtlety comes from Steele, who thus describes his performance as Hob:

There is something so miraculously pleasant in Doggett's acting the awkward triumph and comic sorrow of Hob in different circumstances, that I shall not be able to stay away whenever it is acted. All that vexes me is, that the gallantry of taking the cudgels for Gloucestershire, with the pride of heart in tucking himself up, and taking aim at his adversary, as well as the other's protestation in the humanity of low romance, that he could not promise the squire to break Hob's head, but he would, if he could, do it in love, then flourish and begin: I say, what vexes me is, that such excellent touches as these, as well as the squire's being out of all patience at Hob's success, and venturing himself into the crowd, are circumstances hard-

[26] See Cibber's *Apology,* II, 309.

ly taken notice of, and the height of the jest is only in the very point that heads are broken.[27]

Another successor to the roles of Nokes and Leigh was William Bullock, of whose buffoonishness there seems to be no doubt. In fact, "old" Bullock, as he is often called to distinguish him from his actor sons, paired with Will Pinkethman to become one of the most popular comedians during the reigns of the last Stuarts.[28] Bullock did not make his appearance on the stage until the secession of Betterton and his companions in 1695, so that Pinkethman had some three years' start, but he outlasted his partner a dozen years or more.

Among his first roles, if not the very first, Bullock played the old landlady in Scott's *Mock Marriage* (1695). In this part, we may assume, he made something of a name, for we find him playing a bawd, Frowzy, in Dennis's *Plot and No Plot* (1697), and another bawd, Mrs. Mandrake, in Farquhar's *Twin Rivals* (1703), and, some years later, his manner of acting such parts is offered as a model of coarse manners among old women.[29]

In 1714 Bullock deserted Drury Lane and Pinkethman to spend the latter half of his long career in Rich's company, playing with Griffin and Spiller and his own sons in numerous farce roles, chiefly heavy fathers and stupid cuckolds. For the first twenty years of his career, however, he was an almost constant stage companion of Pinkethman, and we find as frequent mention of the pair in prologue and epilogue as we do of Nokes and Leigh.[30]

[27] *Spectator*, No. 502.

[28] Critick, in A *Comparison between the Two Stages*, p. 106, calls him "the best comedian that has trod the stage since Nokes and Lee. . . ."

[29] See above, p. 38.

[30] Bullock and Pinkethman appear, often in company with Norris, by their name in several plays, both in references within the play and in prologue or epilogue. See, for example, Cibber's *Love Makes a Man* (1700) and *Rival Fools* (1709); Thomas Baker's *Humour*

From almost the very first of his *Tatlers* Steele paid re-peated tributes to Bullock and Pinkethman, though it must be admitted that his praise is always qualified by a strong dash of irony. As we saw earlier, Steele did not approve of their frequent practice of ad-libbing, and we may assume that his attitude towards their furious clowning was at best a mixed one. Yet whether he approves or disapproves he acknowledges their popularity with London theatre-goers. In *Tatler* No. 7, for example, he describes their performance in *Epsom Wells*, Shadwell's comedy, in which Nokes and Angel had played Bisket and Fribble thirty-five years earlier:

This evening, the comedy, called "Epsom Wells," was acted for the benefit of Mr. Bullock, who, though he is a person of much wit and ingenuity, has a peculiar talent of looking like a fool, and therefore excellently well quali-fied for the part of Biskett in this play. I cannot indeed sufficiently admire his way of bearing a beating, as he does in this drama, and that with such a natural air and propriety of folly, that one cannot help wishing the whip in one's own hand; so richly does he seem to deserve his chastisement. Skilful actors think it a very peculiar hap-piness to play in a scene with such as top their parts. Therefore I cannot but say, when the judgement of any good author directs him to write a beating for Mr. Bul-lock from Mr. William Pinkethman, or for Mr. William Pinkethman from Mr. Bullock, these excellent players seem to be in their most shining circumstances, and please me more, but with a different sort of delight, than that which I receive from those grave scenes of Brutus and Cassius, or Antony and Ventidius. The whole comedy is very just, and the low part of human life represented with much humour and wit.

Much later, in No. 188, Steele returned to the pair, again

of the Age (1701) and *Fine Lady's Airs* (1708); Motteux's *Farewel Folly* (1705).

in the same ironic tones. In No. 182 he had undertaken to compare the talents of Wilks and Cibber, both excellent actors. Now he reproduces a request from the two low comedians asking for the same sort of attention and obliges with a brief sketch of their talents:

> Mr. William Bullock and Mr. William Penkethman are of the same age, profession, and sex. They both distinguish themselves in a very particular manner under the discipline of the crabtree, with this only difference, that Mr. Bullock has the more agreeable sqawl, and Mr. Penkethman the more graceful shrug. Penkethman devours a cold chicken with great applause; Bullock's talent lies chiefly in asparagus. Penkethman is very dexterous at conveying himself under a table; Bullock is no less active at jumping over a stick. Mr. Penkethman has a great deal of money, but Mr. Bullock is the taller man.

In time, however, Steele drops his bantering tone, not so much to disapprove of the farceurs as to admonish the audiences which encourage them to overdo their slapstick. In the passage from the *Spectator* quoted above, in which the fine acting of Doggett as Hob is praised, it will be recalled that Steele lamented that the actor's nuances of characterization were wasted on the average audience. In this same essay he goes on to show the kind of acting the audience did appreciate and in doing so expresses his own feelings toward the actors involved:

> I am confident, were there a scene written wherein Penkethman should break his leg by wrestling with Bullock, and Dicky come in to set it, without one word said but what should be according to the exact rules of surgery in making this extension, and binding up the leg, the whole house should be in a roar of applause at the dissembled anguish of the patient, the help given by him who threw him down, and the handy address and arch looks of the surgeon.

The surgeon of Steele's imaginary scene is of course the actor Norris, who was nearly as popular as Bullock and Pinkethman, with whom he shared many scenes at Drury Lane and elsewhere. His career might serve as an example of how an apparent disadvantage could be turned into an advantage. Being a tiny man with odd face and voice,[31] he managed so well his curious talents that in his very first role in London he secured a reputation and, quite literally, a name. In Farquhar's second play, *The Constant Couple or a Trip to the Jubilee* (1699), he was cast as Dicky, a part which will strike the present-day reader as inconsequential. Yet Norris became "Jubilee Dicky" overnight and from then on was known as Dicky Norris rather than by his given name of Henry. Without overlooking Wilks' sensational triumph as Sir Harry Wildair, we may assume that Norris helped to make Farquhar's play the success it became. A disappointed rival, John Corey, brought out a comedy at Lincoln's Inn Fields probably during the triumphant run of *The Constant Couple* and, failing to match Farquhar's success, complained in the dedication of his play that his own failure had been due to the poor taste of the day: "I am afraid that true comedy will be rare, the encouragement for such labours being very small. We must believe this, when we find an audience crowding to a *Jubilee-Farce*, and sweating to see Dicky play his tricks. . . ."

Farquhar amply repaid Norris by providing him another opportunity to play Dicky in the sequel to *The Constant Couple, Sir Harry Wildair* (1701), by creating for him the highly original role of Costar Pearmain in *The Recruiting Officer* (1706), and, finally, by giving him one of the most famous oafish servant roles in English drama, Scrub in *The Beaux Stratagem* (1707).

[31] See the story Genest reproduces, II, 590-591. Norris's size is clearly aimed at in the names of characters written for him. In addition to the most famous of these, Scrub, there are Petit in *The Inconstant* (1702) and Shrimp in Baker's *Fine Lady's Airs*.

Norris was not relegated by his size to playing only diminutive servants. He acted a great many pantaloon roles as well and on a few occasions played old women, as, when Doggett was out of the company around 1708, he acted First Witch in *Macbeth*.[32] In addition to numerous roles he created himself, he inherited some well known low comedy parts from famous predecessors, Dashwell from Leigh, Barnaby Brittle, Sir Arthur Addel, and two or three others from Nokes, First Gravedigger from Underhill, Solon and Nicompoop from Doggett. Altogether Norris proved a resourceful and highly popular low comedian, belonging, if not in the very first rank, at least high in the second.[33]

Few would be disposed to question the claims of William Pinkethman to the highest rank among farceurs in the first quarter of the eighteenth century. Pinkethman's talents were of a sort that any age would have applauded publicly. Cibber considered him almost the equal of Leigh as a stage clown. The *almost* itself does not, upon examination, reduce Pinkethman to a secondary level as a player of farce, for the very qualities with which Cibber finds Pinkethman oversupplied are the stock in trade of the farceur.

Pinkethman made his debut in the united company at the very time when Nokes and Leigh left it, but it was several seasons before he was given anything but bit parts. Like Cibber, who had come into the theatre only a season or two earlier, he was obliged to wait until the secession of 1695 for his first real opportunity. Once having found a scope

[32] He also created the part of Duenna in Dennis's *Gibraltar* (1705) and played Old Woman in a revival of *Rule a Wife* in 1710-11.

[33] Other low comedians of a similar class at this time were Benjamin Johnson, who seems to have been something of a copy of Underhill though hardly the older actor's inferior, and Escourt, whom Steele greatly admired. The latter's estimate (see especially *Spectator* No. 468) is clearly too high. Less intimate and less biased acquaintances, like Cibber, dismissed him as chiefly a mimic.

for his extravagant brand of clowning he made rapid progress. Parts were soon being added to plays to show off his
talents, as when in 1696 Vanbrugh added Sir Polidorus
Hogstye to his adaptation of Boursault's *Esope*. By the end
of the century he had begun to emulate and even outdo Jo
Haines in speaking comic prologues and epilogues and was
prominent enough to be mentioned by name in several
plays. In Burnaby's *Reform'd Wife* (1700), for example,
Sir Soloman Empty recommends the acting profession
to Freeman, just back from France: "They'll try your
talent, Tom, not but thou mayst get as much honour from
acting a cobler, as acting a lord, as an old moralist said of
the world, and I had rather see a Scaramouch than an emperor! for there's that dog! that sly rogue, that arch son of
a whore, that Pinkethman, there's always more in that fel-
lows face than in his words, and to see that rascal act does
me more good than railing against the court party."

At this time Pinkethman also began to profit from an increase in the number of spectators whose tastes ran to slapstick, when Christopher Rich, determined to have some sort
of an audience even in hard times, opened the upper gallery gratis to footmen, who had previously been barred from
the theatre until late in the evening. Here was a group disposed from the start to encourage Pinkethman's robust
form of comic acting, and a close rapport was soon established between the actor and the "parti-colored gentry
aloft." From the many anecdotes and allusions to this relationship we may take one example. In the prologue to
his *Love Makes a Man* (1700) Cibber professes to be following the custom at public feasts of providing a varied bill
of fare for the hungry diners. For the critics, he begins, we
have "faults without number," since critics delight in faults.
For the sophisticated man-about-town there are fops and
wits and rakes. For the ladies the usual love scenes are provided. And finally,

To please all tastes, we'll do the best we can;
For the galleries, we've Dicky and Will. Penkethman.

Years later Cibber was forced to admit that the low comedians had the best of the bargain in choosing to play to the galleries, for their occupants were not shy about showing their gratitude for the new privilege: "This additional privilege (the greatest plague that ever playhouse had to complain of) he [Rich] conceived would not only incline them to give us a good word in the respective families they belong'd to, but would naturally incite them to come all hands aloft in the crack of our applauses: And indeed it so far succeeded, that it often thunder'd from the full gallery above, while our thin pit and boxes below were in the utmost serenity."[34]

About this time also Pinkethman, possibly following Doggett's lead, began to exploit another opportunity to gain followers by acting in the annual London fairs and was soon as much at home in Smithfield or Southwark as at Drury Lane. The speakers in *A Comparison between the Two Stages* (1702) refer to his activities:

Sull. But Penkethman the flower of—
Crit. Bartholomew-Fair, and the idol of the rabble. A fellow that overdoes everything, and spoils many a part with his own stuff.

Six years later Downes testifies to the actor's success in his booth at the fair when he describes Pinkethman as "the darling of Fortunatus, [who] has gain'd more in theatres and fairs in twelve years, than those that have tugg'd at the oar of acting these 50."

Evidently Pinkethman had no compunctions about deserting the regular company when a more profitable opportunity at the fairs beckoned. At one time, in fact, he seems to have first drawn his pay and then absconded without

[34] I, 233-234.

fulfilling his commitments. Miss Rosenfeld reprints this passage which appeared originally in *Heraclitus Ridens*, 24-28 August 1703:

> Deserted from her Majesty's company of stage players at Bath with all his cloaths and accoutrements after having receiv'd advanc'd money: a man that writes himself a *famous comedian*: Suppos'd to have enter'd himself among the socks and buskins in Bartholomew Fair, and taken his journey through the allurement of a thirty pound bag. If he will return to his quarters at the Bath in 14 days, he shall be kindly receiv'd; otherwise his twelve-penny admirers will proceed against him with the utmost severity, and have no more claps at his service, when the money shall be spent, and he come upon the stage again.[35]

Miss Rosenfeld is content to accept the conjecture of R. J. Smith that this passage applies to Tony Aston. It seems to me to be clearly aimed at Pinkethman. "Her Majesty's company of stage players" would hardly fit Tony's "medley" troupe, whereas it does fit the Drury Lane company, which, Cibber tells us and Genest confirms, was acting at Bath while Queen Anne was vacationing there. And "famous comedian" would appear to have come from a bill that had appeared in the *Daily Courant* at this very time, 24 August:

> At Pinkeman's, Bullock's, and Simpson's Booth, over against the Hospital-Gate in Smithfield (during the Time of Bartholomew-Fair) will be presented an extraordinary Entertainment after the best Manner, call'd, Jephtha's Rash Vow, or, The Virgin's Sacrifice. With the Comical Humours of Nurse and her Two Sons, Toby and Ezekiel. Together with the Pleasant manner of Didimer Toby's Man. Also several Diverting Performances of Singing and Danceing. The Comedy being all new Writ. And the

[35] *Strolling Players*, p. 169.

Parts of Toby and Ezekiel perform'd by the Two Famous Comedians, Mr. Pinkeman and Mr. Bullock.

Of the numerous references to Pinkethman in Steele's papers I have already called attention to several, both in connection with his notorious practice of tampering with the scripts of plays he acted in and with his work with other actors. I wish now to return briefly to one of these references which shows the actor in a bit of gagging that evidently became famous. In *Tatler* No. 188 Steele had undertaken to satisfy the alleged request of Bullock and Pinkethman for some tribute to their skills. Among these Steele singles out the latter's proficiency in eating: "Penkethman devours a cold chicken with great applause." This is apparently a reference to some business introduced in Cibber's *Love Makes a Man* (1700), in which Bullock and Pinkethman played foolish old men. That Pinkethman's performance in the scene added further to his reputation may be judged from the fact that Steele came back to it ten years later when in No. 21 of his *Theatre* (1720) he refers to the actor's eating "two chickens in three seconds." But it remained for Alexander Pope to immortalize the episode in his ironic *Epistle to Augustus*:

> And idle Cibber, how he breaks the laws,
> To make poor Pinky eat with vast applause!

By the time Pope had recorded this bit of slapstick for posterity in 1737, however, the contriver had been dead a dozen years. During the last years of his career the actor devoted more and more time to his theatre and his followers in suburban Richmond. His early successes at the fairs seem to have given him a taste for playing the role of theatrical impresario as well as stage clown and, when in 1709 the authorities put a stop to the very formidable enterprise he seems to have built up at May Fair, Pinkethman turned to the districts lying just outside reach of the city fathers. For a time he had a successful theatre at Greenwich but he turned finally to Richmond where after several years of almost continuous applause he brought his career to a close.

With the opening of John Rich's first theatre in 1714 the renewed competition also revived the evidently moribund farce afterpiece and called forth a new group of farce players to compete with Pinkethman and his colleagues at Drury Lane. Rich was able to recruit a part of his company from his rivals, though the only low comedian with an established reputation to desert Drury Lane was "old" Bullock. Along with Bullock came his son Christopher and James, popularly "Jemmy," Spiller. The most notable new farce actor not from Drury Lane was Benjamin Griffin. These four, with some assistance from the rest of the troupe, played a number of old and new farces, more in fact than any other company had ever offered. It must be admitted that they did not play to crowded houses, for Rich found the going exceedingly difficult the first ten years. They did manage, however, to build something of a reputation for themselves and on several occasions forestalled their more popular competitors at Drury Lane.

There is nothing very remarkable recorded of the younger Bullock's career as an actor.[36] He did play a number of farce roles, but we have little knowledge of the nature or the success of his performance. Clearly he was not the actor his father was. In any event his career at the new theatre was cut short by death in less than a decade. His most notable contribution to the stage was in writing and adapting pieces, chiefly short farces, for the company.

Griffin, too, wrote plays. He started with tragedy, adapting Massinger's *Virgin Martyr* under the title of *Injured Virtue* and appearing in it in 1714. After being taken into Rich's new company, he abandoned the buskin for a long

---

[36] I refer here to the best known of Bullock's sons, of whom there were three engaged at the theatres. Genest identifies all three, III, 593.

career as a successful buffoon and a writer, not quite so successful, of farces. His forte seems to have been foolish old men, and he paired off with old Bullock, just as Bullock and Norris had played together for some years at Drury Lane.

In the first farce Griffin produced for Lincoln's Inn Fields, *Love in a Sack* (1715), he provided himself with the ridiculous role of Sir Arthur Addlepate, "an old humourous citizen," who is, like Wycherley's Alderman Gripe,[37] enticed into putting aside his cloak of sanctimoniousness to engage in a night's intrigue. The choice of disguise is significant, however, of the farcical objectives of the piece. Sir Arthur dons the garb of stammering old Smut the chimneysweep to begin a series of slapstick adventures winding up with his taking refuge in his own "swoot-sack" and employing such farce properties as a nightshirt and a blunderbuss.

Among numerous other farce roles played by Griffin at Rich's theatre, as interesting as any was the part he played in Christopher Bullock's *Woman's Revenge* (1715), adapted from the common theme of Mrs. Behn's *Revenge* and Marston's *Dutch Courtezan*. Bullock both shortened and coarsened the melodramatic plot in the older plays and increased the buffoonery. Then, having designed the leading comic roles of Vizard and Mixum for himself, he added some new roles and expanded others to take care of other clowns in the troupe. Spiller doubled in the "padder" and the servant Tim. But the most striking change made by Bullock was to build up the part of the nameless bawd into Mother Griffin. This extremely coarse and farcical creature must be taken as some indication of Griffin's own traits in acting on the one hand and as a link with such earlier roles

[37] Though Genest gives an earlier play, Chapman's *May Day*, as the source of this character, the resemblance of the name of Addlepate to Addleplot, another character in *Love in a Wood*, suggests the possibility that Griffin may have been going back no further than the Restoration playwright.

as those played by "Nurse" Nokes on the other. Griffin seems not to have specialized in these roles, however, though we do find him playing Dorcas Guzzle in Christopher Bullock's *Cobler of Preston* (1716) and, according to Genest, an "Old Woman" in *Rule a Wife* at Drury Lane fifteen years later.

In 1721 Griffin deserted Rich's company for Drury Lane, where he also abandoned authorship and to a large extent the farcical kind of role he had specialized in at Lincoln's Inn Fields. Whether—as the author of *Tyranny Triumphant* (1743) charges—the triumvirate at Drury Lane enticed Griffin away just to weaken Rich and then proceeded to deprive the actor of significant roles for some years, there seems no way of knowing. At any rate he did wind up a long career in somewhat more elevated parts than those he played at Rich's theatre in the lean years after that house first opened.[38]

Of John Rich's first company the most exuberant personality was certainly Spiller, who, like Haines and Pinkethman before him, courted notoriety on and off the stage. Unlike Pinkethman, he had no talent for profiting from his notoriety and died before he reached forty, broken in health and fortune. Spiller made his first appearance five years before his big chance came under Rich. When Collier was successful during the fall of 1709 in wresting control of Drury Lane from the elder Rich, who had been silenced, he was obliged to recruit a number of new players in order to compete with Swiney's far more seasoned troupe at the Haymarket. Among these was young Spiller, who at once assumed such roles as Harlequin in *The Emperor of the Moon* and Corporal Cuttum in Aaron Hill's new play, *The Walking Statue* (1710). He then played in Pinkethman's summer theatre at Greenwich and might have been well launched on his career, had not Collier caused a union of

[38] For an account of his later career see Genest, III, 615-616.

the two companies and obliged Spiller, after a season or so of apparent unemployment, to take bit parts at Drury Lane. With such actors as Doggett, Pinkethman, Bullock, Norris, Estcourt, and Johnson in the company, there was no hope for bigger things until John Rich restored competition.

Rich's new venture provided Spiller with an opportunity to shine, and shine he did, though often to empty seats. He acted a great variety of roles, chiefly the giddy or the ultra-stupid. His specialty seems to have been servant parts, either of the dull English variety, as in Bullock's *Slip* (1715), where he played Roger, or of the clever French valet sort, as in Merlin in *Wit at a Pinch* (1715) or Crispin in *The Anatomist*. There are grounds for supposing that Spiller, like Norris, could make much of even small parts. One testimonial to this ability occurs in the second edition of Christopher Bullock's *Woman's Revenge*, which is dedicated to "my merry friend and brother comedian Mr. James Spiller: I shall content myself with acknowledging the many obligations I have to you, particularly for your good performance in this farce, especially in your last part; I mean that of Padwell." Spiller had played both Tim and Padwell, the latter a very small part. Unfortunately, we have no details concerning Spiller's acting in the most famous role he ever created, also a mere bit, that of Matt o' the Mint in *The Beggar's Opera*, which Bullock alleged to have been stolen from his play.

Not all of Spiller's roles, however, were small ones. Not infrequently he was called upon to assume the lead, especially in farces. Among older parts, in addition to the Harlequin already mentioned, he played Jobson in *The Devil of a Wife* and Hob in *The Country Wake*. On one rather famous occasion he took the lead in Bullock's *Cobler of Preston* in rivalry to the redoubtable Pinkethman, who played the corresponding part in Charles Johnson's play of the same name. Again we have no way of knowing how he came off in the competition.[39]

By the time Spiller had spent a decade in and out of debt he had become so notorious a figure of the sort called "humourist" in his own day that we find him capitalizing on his misfortunes both physical and financial—he seems from the first to have had only one eye and to have been in debt continuously. Genest reproduces an entry for 31 March 1720 and attaches to it an advertisement which had appeared two days earlier in the *Anti-Theatre*. Both reveal something of the one-eyed actor's brazen, or insouciant, manner. The bill reads: "For the entertainment of Robinson Crusoe [Defoe's famous novel was then just a year old] —for the bt. of Spiller. A collection of farces after the English manner—viz. Walking Statue—Hob or Country Wake and Cobler of Preston. . . ." The advertisement from the *Anti-Theatre*, a mock-challenge addressed to the lesser known young Bullock, Hildebrand, reads,

I have a great desire to engage you to be my friend, and recommend me to the town; and therefore I take the liberty to inform you, that on next Thursday will be acted, for the benefit of myself and creditors, a collection of Farces, after the English manner; and as I am a curious observer of nature, and can see as much with one eye as others do with both; I think, I have found out what will please the multitude. . . . I have tolerable good luck, and tickets rise apace, which makes mankind very civil to me; for I get up every morning to a levee of at least a dozen people, who pay their compliments, and ask the same question, "When they shall be paid?" all I can say, is, that wicked good company have brought me into this imitation of grandeur. I loved my friend and my jest too well to grow rich: in short, wit is my blind side; and so I remain," &c.

[39] See Hughes and Scouten, *Ten English Farces*, p. 147, for the story told by Spiller's biographer, George Akerby.

From an assortment of testimonials we may assume that Spiller could count on a certain section of the public to assist him in appeasing his creditors. We have already seen, in an earlier chapter, that at least one playwright was willing to depend upon his comic ingenuity as an actor.[40] His biographer testifies that from his apprenticeship in the provinces he was highly successful in certain ridiculous roles: ". . . When he came upon the stage for Hob in the *Country Wake*, the Widow Lackit's foolish son, Daniel in *Oroonoko*, Costar Pairmain in *The Recruiting Officer*, and many others of the like sort: his looks, his most significant shrugs and gestures, would oftentimes set the whole audience a laughing before he had spoke one word."[41] Spiller might well have become the leading farceur in London after the death of his old rival Pinkethman in 1725 if his irregular habits had permitted.

The last two decades before mid-century are marked by a scarcity of great clowns. There were competent, even excellent, low comedians in this period, but almost none of them built their reputations on farce roles exclusively, and few attracted the sort of following enjoyed by the earlier clowns. Though I am unable to suggest one "sufficient cause"—mere chance is possibly as important as anything else but to resort to it is merely to avoid the issue—I would like to suggest two or three possible contributory causes.

For one thing there is the popularity of pantomime. After the great triumphs of 1723-24 both Rich and his rivals were able to satisfy the demand for spectacle and sheer fun by this silent kind of drama. And though it is true that the clowns of the regular companies found a place in pantomime, it is hardly possible that they could profit from such an opportunity as much as they had been able to in spoken drama. The records show, in fact, that the stars of panto-

[40] See above, p. 59.
[41] Akerby, *The Life of Mr. James Spiller* (1729 [obviously old style]), p. 7.

mime were a quite different set of actors. Several foreign dancers came to be leading attractions, and John Rich himself, as Lun, became perhaps the most famous pantomimist.

Another possible cause was the tendency to limit the number of farces in the repertory by repeating the same ones over and over. As a study of the stage calendar will reveal, such old standbys as *Hob, The Devil to Pay, The Stage Coach*, and *The Intriguing Chambermaid* were given season after season. The result of this practice, so far as actors were concerned, was to diminish the chances for a low comedian to build up a reputation by *creating* roles. We know from ample testimony that it was traditional in the repertory theatre for an actor to copy the manner of successful predecessors in established roles, that to depart from the known pattern was to court public disapproval. Hence the tendency to identify a role with its original performer or the performer with the role. Hob, for example, suggested Doggett, even though there were many successful Hobs after him or even a few during his day. Pinkethman was referred to years after the first performance of *The Constant Couple* as Beau Clincher, and Norris took his stage name of Jubliee Dicky from the same play. While I have no proof, I would assume that Norris left his stamp upon Scrub, though in time the role was returned to the public domain by so original an actor as Garrick. Harper's name remained attached to the part of Jobson and Mrs. Clive's to Nell in *The Devil to Pay*, though again in the course of a very long life on the stage these roles, too, were occupied by new favorites, Munden and Mrs. Jordan taking them over years later.

Some influence may also be assigned to the change in farce styles, especially after 1728. The practice, following the tremendous success of ballad opera, of introducing new songs into the texts of old farces is bound to have reduced the emphasis on mere slapstick and to have created a demand for actors who could sing as well as clown through their roles. Another tendency, much less marked, to follow the lead of the French in fast-moving intrigue farces of the kind represented by *The Intriguing Chambermaid* or *The Lying Valet* must have limited even further the scope of the vigorous native clown best represented by Nokes.

Some of the actors in the remaining decades deserve at least mention here. Chapman was a steady if not sensational low comedian in Rich's company for some twenty years, though Genest's list of his roles indicates an amazing versatility, which may well have come, as Davies tells us, not from any native ability in more serious roles but from the actor's insistence upon being allowed to act in parts in which he had no real competence. If the charge is justified, it serves as some testimony to his talents in low comedy, which he seems to have used for bargaining purposes.

Harper of the rival Drury Lane company was without question a versatile performer. He was especially acclaimed in native rustic characters and made capital of a good voice in ballad operas. His most famous part was that of Jobson in *The Devil to Pay* (1731), but he ranged from the royal role of Henry VIII—in which Davies recalls seeing a little too much of Jobson—through Falstaff on down to old women's parts in such coarse characters as Betty Kimbrow in *The Strolers* (1723), Ursula the Pig Woman in *Bartholomew Fair*, and Lady Termagant in *The Boarding School* (1733), the last a role created by Leigh in the play by Durfey from which the farce was taken. Harper seems to have been one of the stage pioneers in a comic "specialty" of the soil best known in modern vaudeville, for he gained some fame in his performance as a "Drunken Man."

An even more famous "Drunken Man"[42] was John Hippisley of Lincoln's Inn Fields and Covent Garden, companion to Chapman and, though perhaps not so versatile

[42] See Wheatley, *Hogarth's London* (London, 1909), p. 280. *The Theatrical Museum* (1776) gives a sketch of what purports to be Hippisley's "Drunken Man."

as Harper, a superior clown in the older tradition. Like Spiller, with whom he acted for the first five or six years of his career, Hippisley was disfigured, his face having been scarred by a severe burn.[43] Also, as Spiller had done, he turned his disfigurement into a trade-mark. He played a great variety of low comedy roles: Scaramouch, Scapin, Barnaby Brittle, Gregory in Italian-French adaptations; Hob, Dogberry, Shallow, Ananias in more English roles. Like Harper, and their more famous predecessor, Nokes, Hippisley also played old women's parts. His most famous creation was probably that of Peachum in *The Beggar's Opera*, but in his own day he was more closely identified with Welsh or West Country parts, such as Fluellen, the Welsh Collier in *The Recruiting Officer*, and David Shenkin in his own farce, *A Journey to Bristol: or, The Honest Welchman*, first performed in Hippisley's theatre in his native Bristol and later, in 1731, at Lincoln's Inn Fields. There is some evidence that it was Hippisley whose superb performance of Old Gerald in *The Anatomist* impressed the Italian actor Luigi Riccoboni so favorably on his visit to England in 1727.[44]

---

[43] See Genest, IV, 253.

[44] Victor misled scholars on this point for years by his positive assertion that Riccoboni was describing the performance of Spiller. Genest quoted Victor without question, and W. J. Lawrence, in his "Player-Friend of Hogarth," was even more misled. It remained for E. T. Norris, in "The Original of Ravenscroft's *Anatomist*, and an Anecdote of Jemmy Spiller," *Modern Language Notes*, XLVI (1931), 522-526, to point out that the acknowledged fact that Spiller played Crispin was completely irrelevant since Riccoboni was describing the performance of Old Gerald and not that of the valet. Professor Norris does not venture to identify the Old Gerald. It does not seem possible to identify him positively, but in this limited space I should like to call attention to three items pointing to Hippisley: (1) We know from the stage calendar that he commonly acted old men's roles from the start of his career in London in 1722. (2) The advertisement of his benefit in *The Craftsman* for 20 March 1736 suggests that he may well have been known to London theatre-goers in the role of Old Gerald, and the 1743 notices in the

Other farce players were serving their apprenticeship or had already done so before Hippisley had played his last role. Among these one of the best was Woodward, called Lun Junior because of his success in pantomimes. His career lies for the most part, however, on the other side of the mid-century mark and therefore does not so much concern us here. Much the same may be said of Shuter, a very capable actor. Others gained fame in somewhat circumscribed patterns. Blakes, for example, was a superb mock-Frenchman as is indicated by the number of roles of that sort he performed and, more strikingly, by the fact that older roles were adapted to suit his talent, as when Ravenscroft's *Anatomist* was revised with Blakes in mind. Taswell was similarly restricted to a few parts. Montague Summers has spoken of him as "a great farceur,"[45] but I have found little evidence to support the phrase. Genest says, without giving his source, that Taswell was "a confined actor" but, among other things, a superb Dogberry.

More names might be mentioned, but these are perhaps enough to indicate the continuance of a tradition in English low comedy. We may suppose that the Abbé Le Blanc's somewhat biased observations, from around 1741, were made with some of the above comedians in mind:

> You find at this time more pitiful buffoons on the stage at London, than tolerable actors; which seems to me the effects of the national taste. The English, if you'll permit me to use a term of painting, which can alone express my

---

Daily Advertiser announcing a Bartholomew-Fair droll at Hippisley and Chapman's booth entitled *The French Doctor Outwitted, or the Old One in Danger of being Dissected* add some weight to the conjecture. (3) Miss Kathleen Barker of Bristol informs me that Mr. L. G. Turner, the best authority on Hippisley, has discovered the date of the actor's birth to be 14 January 1696; that would make him thirty-one, not unreasonably far from Riccoboni's "jeune homme de vingt-six ans tout à plus."

[45] *Restoration Comedies* (Boston, 1922), p. xxxiii.

idea; love caricaturas: they are more struck with a large face and great nose, designed by Callot, than with a noble and graceful countenance, trac'd by Corregio's pencil. For this reason, their comic characters are always more over-strain'd than ours; and the actor in following his own taste, imagines he only follows the genius of the author. The more he finds in the caricatura in his part, the more he thinks there ought to be of it, in his action; and thus, he endeavours to express the humour of it, more by the grimaces of his face, than the proper modulation of his voice: and he succeeds the better in it, as 'tis the less difficult to do. When farces supply'd the place of comedies, grimace supply'd the place of action.[46]

The discussion to this point has been confined to *actors*; nothing has been said—except for comments on the coarse impersonations of buffoons like Nokes and Bullock in old women's roles—of the players of feminine roles. There is little to be said on this subject, simply because English farce, like most of the continental variety, provided no great scope for the actress in low comedy. At the most she was called upon to be pert and clever; the more boisterous scenes were handed over, as a natural right, to her male companions. As in Italian and French farce, she commonly provided an excuse for clever tricks as the object of amorous pursuit. Occasionally she was given a chance for broader comedy in assisting, in servant roles, in the pursuit, but her place was always clearly secondary.

It would be an injustice, however, to pass over without comment the work of at least one English actress of farce roles, Kitty Clive. Not that Mrs. Clive was merely a feminine Pinkethman confined to low comedy roles; she was, in fact, a highly versatile actress and a very fine singer as well. But she did bring into the numerous parts she played

[46] *Letters on the English and French Nations* (London, 1747), II, 40-44.

in farces a sprightliness and gusto which not only made her famous as Lucy or Nell but also helped in a small way to change the tone of farce after 1730.

Kitty Clive is too well known to the students of the English stage to require any elaborate introduction here, but I do wish to comment on a few of her triumphs in the lighter vein. Her charming voice seems to have won her first chance at Drury Lane, where she soon rose from small roles to leading parts in which she was widely acclaimed. The author of the list in Whincop tells us how her acting of Nell in *The Devil to Pay* (1731) brought her into prominence and earned her an increase in salary. Unquestionably the role became one of her favorites. Her superb voice—quite early in her career we find a writer calling it the best outside Italian opera[47]—also won her a reputation as one of the finest Pollys in Gay's immortal ballad opera.

One of the first to recognize and to make use of her talents in light comedy was Henry Fielding, always her warmest admirer. His first public expression of gratitude to the actress appears in the preface to his *Mock Doctor* (1732), in which she played opposite young Cibber. Some months later, Fielding expanded a female servant role in his adaptation of another play by Molière, *The Miser*, in order to exploit further the young actress's skill. The most striking demonstration of both her talent and the author's appreciation of it followed a year later when Fielding, in adapting still another French play, Regnard's *Retour imprévu*, made a radical change in the farce. He transformed the clever valet, Merlin, really the leading actor in the play, into Lettice, "the intriguing chambermaid."

Fortunately we have an account given by an eyewitness of this performance, one of Mrs. Clive's favorite roles. John Hill, in his treatise called *The Actor* (1750), describes in

[47] *The Comedian, or Philosophical Enquirer*, No. 7. (October 1732).

some detail her brilliant acting in one of the key scenes in the play:

> There are [scenes] in which the performer has three instead of two parts to play at the same time; where there are two people to be deceived by two different stories at the same instant, and the performer is all the while to express also to the audience a sense of the difficulty of what is doing, and a continual dread of being discovered by one or other of the persons deceived. We have an eminent instance of this kind in one of our farces, where an intriguing maid-servant finds it necessary for the good of her young master to delude his father, and the aunt of the lady he courts, into an opinion of one another, as persons out of their senses. While the actress is here construing every look and gesture of Mr. Goodall into madness to Mrs. Highmore, and every glance and accent of that lady into frenzy to him; she is expressing to the audience all the while the utmost terror in the world, lest one or the other of them shou'd discover her: Nay, she even adds to the necessary perplexity of the part she has to act, by blending with her very terror the pert self-sufficiency, that marks out the rest of her character; and gives us one of the strongest modern examples it is possible to quote, of the application of the rule deliver'd in the last chapter, that the same passions are to be express'd very differently, as acting upon different characters. The person who understands this merit in Mrs. Clive's playing this short character, will not wonder if it appear very insipid when perform'd by any body else.[48]

When we add to the tributes paid her by Fielding and Hill the weighty voice of Dr. Samuel Johnson,[49] we may

[48] p. 163.
[49] Boswell quotes Johnson to the effect that "Mrs. Clive was the best player he ever saw." *Journal of a Tour to the Hebrides* (Pottle-Bennett edition), p. 93.

well believe that Mrs. Clive was an outstanding comedienne. The editor of the works of another Hill, the critic and playwright Aaron, is perhaps voicing a common judgment when, in reminiscing about bygone days in the theatre, he singles out her brilliant performance of Nell in *The Devil to Pay*: "She has had many followers, some imitators; and, 'tis but justice to add, no equal. She then promis'd to be, what she has since prov'd, one of the first performers of the stage: and, when judiciously examined in the general various cast of parts she acts, 'tis imagined she will be allow'd not to be inferior to any performer of her time."[50]

I turn, finally, to a word on Garrick and his influence on farce and farce acting. His history falls largely outside the confines of this study, but even in his first decade he made a mark upon farce. Before the beginning of his long and brilliant career—there have been longer ones but none more brilliant—farce had won its place in the theatrical bill. Still the marks of his influence upon the genre are obvious at a glance. For one thing, Garrick's triumphant first season at Goodman's Fields caused some sweeping changes at the two patent houses, where Rich and Fleetwood had been engaged since the passing of the Licensing Act in outmonstering each other in pantomimes and freakish displays, to the detriment of the more legitimate forms of drama. Within a short time after Garrick's descent upon the town, a change for the better occurred, and we hear gratifying comments upon the great improvement his presence had brought about. It would be a grave error to picture Garrick as altogether the high-souled devotee of Melpomene and Thalia. He could himself resort to pantomime and show without too much justification, as audiences were later to protest.[51]

[50] *The Dramatic Works of Aaron Hill* (1760), II, 332.

[51] What may be described as Garrick's official position is neatly stated in his prologue at the opening of Drury Lane on 8 September 1750:
> Sacred to Shakespeare was this spot design'd,
> To pierce the heart, and humanize the mind.

But his own talents naturally led him to support legitimate drama when doing so did not entail too great a sacrifice.

The chief influence of Garrick on farce came about, however, through his writing farces and acting in them and thus giving the genre a kind of support it had often lacked in the past. From the very start of his career he gave nearly as much attention to low comedy or farce as he did to the more elevated kinds of drama, for his greatest talent was his versatility, a talent which he—a notoriously vain man— was always quite proud to display. Davies speaks of the abandon with which he threw himself into his new career: "To a very long and fatiguing character in the play, he would frequently add another in a farce. The distresses which he raised in the audience by his Lear and Richard, he relieved with the roguish tricks of the Lying Valet, or the Diverting humours of the School-boy."[52]

Garrick seems to have been undecided at the start of his career whether his abilities were greater in comedy or in tragedy. His enthusiastic public gave him no help, for they applauded him in everything. During his first weeks of triumph he wrote to his brother Peter: "The valet [Garrick's farce *The Lying Valet* (1741)] takes prodigiously & is approved of by men of genius and thought [the] most diverting farce that ever was perform'd; I believe you'll find it read pretty well, & in performance tis a general roar from beginning to end; & I have got as much reputation in the

---

But if an empty House, the Actor's curse,
Shows us our Lears and Hamlets lose their force;
Unwilling we must change the nobler scene,
And in our turn present you Harlequin;
Quit Poets, and set Carpenters to work,
Shew gaudy scenes, or mount the vaulting Turk:
For though we Actors, one and all, agree
Boldly to struggle for our—vanity,
If want comes on, importance must retreat;
Our first great ruling passion is—to eat.

[52] *Memoirs of the Life of David Garrick, Esq.* (1780), I, 39.

character of Sharp & is [*sic*] in any other character I have perform'd tho far different from the other."[53]

Some of the men of genius and thought were presumably not so ready to applaud an actor of farces, and Garrick found it necessary to defend his practice. In the above letter he is even obliged to deny a rumor that he had been playing Harlequin. But Garrick's persistence in producing and acting farces seems eventually to have won over all but the most intransigent opposition, to the great advantage of farce itself. A revealing letter from an old Lichfield friend, the Reverend Thomas Newton, indicates how significant Garrick's influence must have been in winning converts. Mr. Newton says he is none too happy over his friend's stooping to such low parts as Fondlewife, "nor should be of 'The Lying Valet,' if it were not of your own writing."[54]

Comments describing Garrick's performance in comedy and farce are so plentiful and so laudatory that it seems hardly necessary to quote any details here. It is safe to assume that in spite of the sprightliness of his acting in Sharp and Fribble and other farcical roles he was always more restrained and subtle than the great mass of his predecessors[55]

---

[53] D. M. Little, *Pineapples of Finest Flavour* (Cambridge, Mass., 1930), pp. 28-29.

[54] Joseph Knight, *David Garrick* (London, 1894), pp. 44-45.

[55] Samuel Foote, in *The Roman and English Comedy Consider'd and Compar'd* (1747), pp. 38-39, gives us a detailed contrast between Garrick's performance in a low comedy role and that of Theophilus Cibber and, by implication, of Hippisley and others: "But, for the sake of Brevity, suffer me to confine the latter to two, the Comic, and the Comical. And, in order to give you a clear Idea of what I mean by the Distinction, cast your Eye on the Abel Drugger of G. and the Abel Drugger of C. I call the simple, composed, grave Deportment of the former Comic, and the squint-ey'd grinning Grimace of the latter Comical. The first obtains your Applause, by persuading you that he is the real Man. The latter indeed opens your Eyes, and gives you to understand, that he is but personating the Tobacco-Boy: But then to atone for the Loss of the Deception, you are ready to split with Laughter, at the ridiculous Variations of his Muscles. It may indeed be objected, that this Conduct destroys all Distinction of Characters,

and that the effect of his acting was to raise farce to the level of *petite comédie*. In any event, his contribution to the cause of farce was of the highest significance.

---

and may as well become Sir John Daw, or Sir Amorous La Fool, as honest Nab. Well, and what then? Don't Folks come to a Play to laugh? And if that End be obtained, what matters it how? Has not he the most Merit, who pleases the most? Suppose G. has the Approbation of Twenty or Thirty Judges in the Pit, shall I give up my Fun, which makes the Inhabitants of both the Gallerys my Friends, for his Humour? No, hold a little, that will never do. And to convince the Public, that Mr. C. is not single in his Judgment, Mr. H——Y, W— d—d, Mr. Y——s, both approve and pursue his Plan."

CHAPTER 7

FAIRS AND STROLLERS

++

For once be courteous to a country muse
Untaught such tricks the wits of London use;
And in short time, he may find out the way
To write fine poppet plays as well as they.
—*The Muse of New-Market* (1680)

++

IN Christopher Bullock's *Slip* (1715) we get a fleeting picture of country theatricals. Trickwell and his fellow conspirators act out a little play, supposedly for the benefit of his uncle Sir Anthony Bounteous, actually to cover up their plans to rob their host. Sir Anthony is delighted with this rare treat but eager also to have his tastes catered to: "Let the play be short and very comical," he cries out before the curtain rises, "for I love to laugh heartily." Whether or not we may take Sir Anthony's attitude as widely representative of rural tastes in the eighteenth century, we may assume that his demands were not at all singular. In short, we may safely say, on the basis of a great deal of accumulated evidence, that farce flourished as vigorously in the provinces as it did in London.

There is no need here to present the story of the provincial theatre in detail. That task has been done—and done well—by Miss Rosenfeld. But something should perhaps be said about repertories, on which she and others[1] have pre-

[1] In addition to Sybil Rosenfeld's *Strolling Players & Drama in the Provinces* (Cambridge, 1939) there are several informative articles, often stressing the period after 1750 but nonetheless significant for strollers in general: Alwin Thaler, "Strolling Players and Provincial Drama after Shakespere," *PMLA*, xxxvii, No. 2 (June 1922), 243-280; Elbridge Colby, "A Supplement on Strollers," *PMLA*, xxxix, No. 3 (September 1924), 642-654; Herschel Baker,

sented a wealth of evidence, and something about audiences and their reception of farce specifically—two points on which the evidence is much slighter but quite adequate for some speculation.

The most striking observation, which may be made at once, is that a close parallel exists between the repertory of the provinces and that of London. In many cases it amounts to virtual identity, at least for those more ambitious troupes whose activities are recorded. Of course the influence of the capital should not surprise us. For one thing, the actors were often recruited from the London theatres or, if they had not as yet risen to such eminence, they aspired to Drury Lane and Covent Garden. In either case they would tend to ape the leading theatres even though, as we frequently see, their properties and costumes were pitifully inadequate to the demands of such a repertory. The audience too, wherever it can be seen clearly enough to discern its composition, would seem to have called for a fashionable production. Strolling companies were often sponsored by noblemen,[2] until the Licensing Act rendered the practice illegal, and they frequently acted in the houses of the country gentry. Thus they were not entirely dependent for an audience upon farmers and laborers and could count on at least a minority whose tastes had been formed in the metropolis.[3]

The lists of plays which have come down to this day are sufficient indication of the attempts of provincial companies to keep the pace set by London. Shakespeare and his contemporaries were, if not so popular as in the capital,

---

"Strolling Actors in Eighteenth Century England," University of Texas *Studies in English*, 1941, pp. 100-120. The files of *Notes and Queries* are also useful on this subject; those of the more recent *Theatre Notebook* are indispensable.

[2] See the various references in Nicoll and Miss Rosenfeld to companies traveling under the aegis of the Dukes of Monmouth, Norfolk, Ormond, and so on.

[3] The evidence here can be contradictory. See Miss Rosenfeld, pp. 27-28.

at least popular enough to maintain a reasonably firm hold on provincial audiences.[4] And the standard plays of more recent times, from Dryden to Fielding, were given numerous performances, comedy possibly getting more attention than tragedy, but the proportion not differing too greatly from what it was at Drury Lane.

The farce afterpiece was distinctly popular in the provincial theatre. Miss Rosenfeld tells us that "afterpieces were sometimes included in the programme as early as 1711, but were not advertised as a regular feature until 1730, when the success of *The Beggar's Opera* had established a vogue for ballad operas such as *Damon and Phillida*, or *Flora*, which could be called 'after the manner of *The Beggar's Opera*.' "[5] The clear implication here that the triumph of ballad opera had a direct effect of creating the vogue of the double bill is, as I have shown in Chapter 3, more than a little misleading, but the fact that by the early 1730's the afterpiece was a fixture in the provincial bill is not likely to be disputed.

The list of plays already cited in Chapter 3 as having been given in Kent is perhaps not altogether typical since it represents the offering of a summer company recruited from London. Yet it does not differ greatly from lists we may reconstruct from the researchers of Miss Rosenfeld and other students of the provincial theatre. To recapitulate, the Kentish strollers professed to be ready to perform anything from a list of twenty-seven tragedies, thirty-nine comedies, and twenty afterpieces, the bulk of the last-named being farcical.

[4] The case of French provincial drama is interesting if not strictly parallel. In addition to the evidence provided by such students as Liebrecht and Fransen we have the summing up of Lancaster, *History*, III, 35. The latter says, in effect, that there were some few strictly provincial dramatists and that in the more remote provinces especially the repertory might be a trifle old-fashioned; yet on the whole it follows the Parisian theatre fairly closely.

[5] p. 72.

Let us take a similar list from Professor Colby's brief study of strollers. This seems to be the record of a genuinely provincial troupe for they are playing small towns in Wales and Western England and the only actor's name reproduced by Colby is that of a Morrison, not a London actor. The parts listed for Morrison probably constitute the bulk of the repertory of these West-Country strollers in 1741; there are fifteen tragedies, seventeen comedies, and nineteen "entertainments." But these last ought perhaps to be specified, to show both how familiar they would have been to a Londoner and how nearly they approach the usual proportion of farce, burlesque, and sentiment: *"Devil to Pay, Mock Doctor, Virgin Unmask'd, [Honest] Yorkshire Man, Lover his own Rival, Damon & Philida, Chrononhotonthologus, Strolers, Tom Thumb, King & the Miller [The Lucky Discovery: or,] Tanner of York, Flora or Hob in the Well, Cobler of Preston, Wife Well Manag'd, The Lovers Opera, The Vintner in the Suds, [The Walking Statue, or] The Devil in the Wine Cellar, Stage Coach, Toy Shop.* We also learn from the record of this troupe that they made good use of their repertory. Of the twenty-one productions listed by Colby for May-July 1741 only three are without afterpieces. Yet, in spite of the varied list available, they offer *The Honest Yorkshireman* five times and a piece not listed above, *The Parting Lovers*—which I take to be another of Carey's plays, the two-year old *Nancy, or the Parting Lovers*—seven times.[6]

It may be noted that neither this troupe nor the strollers in Kent two summers earlier offered any pantomimes. The

[6] In the Harvard Theatre Collection there is an interesting little MS record of a strolling troupe in the 1760's, traveling under the leadership of Roger Kemble, father of two very famous theatrical personages. The repertory of this company parallels those already given quite closely. A prominent feature, for our purposes, is the repetition of the "standard" farce afterpiece: *The Devil to Pay, Hob, The Sham Doctor* [doubtless *The Anatomist* rather than Fielding's equally popular *Mock Doctor*].

reason is obvious: since the successful production of pantomimes required costumes and, more especially, "machines"
too elaborate and cumbersome for a company constantly
on the move, this more elaborate form of fashionable entertainment could scarcely be staged in the provinces.[7] Here
at least farce had a distinct advantage over its rival. Yet
there was some pantomime in the provincial theatre. The
list of productions in Miss Rosenfeld's index contains a
number, most of them differing, in titles at least, from those
current in London.

The parallel between the non-pantomimic theatrical repertories of London and the provinces, though close, is by
no means perfect. There is evidence for a distinctly provincial repertory and, what is of especial importance here,
a distinct repertory that emphasizes the farcical. Again
referring to Miss Rosenfeld's list of productions, we observe
a scattering of titles which do not coincide with the list
for the metropolitan theatres. Unfortunately most of these
pieces were never published and it is therefore impossible to
make any positive statements about them as a group. From
what little can be gleaned from titles it seems that the
majority represent the provincial pantomimes mentioned
above or, where actual plays are indicated, are merely alternate titles of known plays. Most of these titles have a
distinctly comic or farcical tone; it seems unlikely that we
should discover some rural *Hamlet* or *Lear* among them if
these pieces were somehow miraculously restored to view.

There still remain some few items which have been published and which do indicate a distinctly provincial label.
The Commonwealth collection of drolls called *The Wits*,
frequently referred to above, does not of course represent

[7] Everyone is familiar with Hogarth's "Strolling Actresses Dressing in a Barn." These strollers, we are assured by Miss Bowen, are
preparing to give an elaborate production with grand mythological
figures. Marjorie Bowen, *William Hogarth* (London, 1936), pp.
194-195.

the provincial theatre, since these drolls were originally designed for what might be termed the "underground" theatre
in London. There are some vague hints, however, that these
drolls continued to thrive, especially in the provinces or the
non-patent theatres in London.[8] In any event they suggest
certain features of the country theatre in their departure
from the established pattern. They are not full-length plays.
In fact, the typical droll is as much a medley of miscellaneous scenes as a unified five-act play. And, most significant here, they incline toward buffoonery, though bombast
or sentiment is by no means an uncommon ingredient.

One of the first examples of a clearly provincial drama
is to be found in the collection called *The Muse of New-
Market* (1680). The three three-act plays which make up
this collection are not at all original but are derived from
pre-Commonwealth plays, the hands of Nabbes, Massinger,
and Davenport being clearly traceable.[9] Without going into
any detail, I may say that all three are marked by coarseness of language and action. And while the third, *The
Politick Whore*, is possibly the worst offender on this score,
the first two, *The Merry Milkmaid* and *Love Lost in the
Dark*, contain more farcical action though neither is a true
farce. Perhaps the most striking feature, especially of *The
Merry Milkmaid*, is the use of traditional farce devices. Both
a tub and a buck basket are used for extended scenes of
rough and tumble in this play; somewhat less boisterous
use is made of a chest in the second piece.

An even more interesting collection of provincial plays
appeared sixty years later, and, while it is said to be aimed
at audiences in the London fairs, it pretty certainly represents a common form of drama still popular in the provinces. The whole title page is interesting enough to be
quoted in full.

[8] See especially J. J. Elson's introduction to *The Wits*, pp. 23-26.
[9] See J. G. McManaway, "Philip Massinger and the Restoration
Drama," *ELH*, 1 (1934), 276-304.

The Strolers Pacquet Open'd. Containing Seven Jovial Drolls or Farces, Calculated for the Meridian of Bartholomew and Southwark Fairs. Representing the Comical Humours of Designing Usurers, Sly Pettifoggers, Cunning Sharpers, Cowardly Bullies, Wild Rakes, Finical Fops, Shrewd Clowns, Testy Masters, Arch Footmen, Forward Widows, Stale Maids, and Melting Lasses.

The seven pieces in this collection are in either one or two acts. Like the Newmarket collection they are coarse and filled with pratfalls. Also like the earlier plays they are drawn largely from other plays though here the range is greater, extending from Fletcher in Elizabethan days through Congreve in the Restoration period on up to Mrs. Centlivre and Christopher Bullock in more recent times, though these last two have themselves done more borrowing than original work in the materials they have provided.

Not all of the drama of the provinces was borrowed, however. Here and there a local playwright, usually a member of some provincial acting company, supplemented the fare of plays drawn from the London repertory by providing a droll, or sometimes even a more ambitious full-length play of his own. These, as might be supposed, often run to farce.

One example of this type is a play by Essex Walker called A *Trip to Portsmouth* and evidently produced in the Portsmouth region about 1710, for the edition in the Huntington Library has the imprint "Gosport: Printed and sold by James Philpott, in Middle-Street, 1710." The list of actors includes, in addition to the author, the names of Dyer, Harper, Thomas, and the Mesdames Maris and Baxter, most of whom do not appear in the London bills. As this play has escaped the vigilance of both Professor Nicoll and Miss Rosenfeld, I may be excused for giving it somewhat more attention than its real merits warrant. For one thing, it is possibly one of the first one-act pieces on record for the English theatre—if we may exclude the somewhat baffling case of *The Stage Coach*.[10] At least it is as early as the only other rival I know of for this not very important distinction, Aaron Hill's *Walking Statue* (1710). A *Trip to Portsmouth* starts out on a clear note of topical satire, the prologue and the opening scenes being devoted to a partisan attack on the Whigs by means of a burlesque of a local contest for parliament. The satire and the slight originality soon run out, however, and the play winds up in a slapstick bedroom farce not unlike Ravenscroft's popular *London Cuckolds*.

Of all the provincial companies in this period that have been traced by Miss Rosenfeld one, the York company, is especially interesting as a producer of more or less indigenous drama. "York," she tells us, "is unique in producing its own dramatists."[11] None of these playwrights proved to be a genius, but they managed to stay quite faithful to the droll tradition. Their plays would have pleased Sir Anthony Bounteous, for they are invariably short and boisterous. Two York playwrights, Yarrow and Ward, chose independently to publish versions of the old "vintner tricked" farce much like the one in *The Strolers Pacquet*. Even when there are attempts at originality, we get boisterous intrigue farce, as, for example, in the work of Joseph Peterson or of John Arthur, whose *Lucky Discovery: or, The Tanner of York* we saw in the repertory of the West-Country strollers above.

In brief, then, it seems clear that farce and especially the short farce afterpiece did a thriving business in the provinces. After the pattern of double-billing, so important in nurturing the short farcical play, had been firmly established in London after 1715, the practice soon spread to theatres even far removed from the capital and farce was at home everywhere in the English theatre.[12]

[10] The first edition of this farce, the early history of which is still obscure, appeared in Dublin in one act; the first English edition, which appeared the following year, 1705, is in three acts.

[11] p. 106.

[12] I omit any mention of the suburban theatres, which are

What has been said of the fortunes of farce in the provinces applies pretty generally, with some interesting exceptions and additions, to the various outlaw theatres in
London: the booths at the annual fairs, the temporary es-
tablishments in several inns and alehouses, the "wells"
which begin to appear in increasing numbers from about
the date of the Licensing Act. These outlaw activities, while
in many ways paralleling those of the provinces, are different enough to warrant separate treatment, especially
since they have not drawn as much attention from modern
scholars as the provincial theatres have.

Just how early the performances by live actors at the
London fairs began is hard to say. We know that there is
nothing to match the venerability of the *théâtres de la foire*
in Paris, where plays had been given at least since the time
of Henri IV,[13] just as the performers in the London fair-
booths in the eighteenth century fail to match the significance of the *forains* in contemporary Paris. We know from
Pepys and others that the usual offering at Bartholomew or
Southwark Fairs shortly after the Restoration was likely to
consist of rope-walking or puppeteering. Take, for example,
the account by the indefatigable diarist of his visit to Southwark 21 September 1668 and his interview with the noted
funambulist Jacob Hall. From other accounts we gather
that the puppets attracted their share of spectators.

Still, there are fairly early signs of the presence of real
actors at the fairs. It may be that Pepys is referring to a
real play in his entry for 29 August 1668. The early date
would seem to point to a puppet-show, but Pepys dis-

---

treated at some length by Miss Rosenfeld, with some additions by
Avery and others. From our comparatively limited knowledge of
the theatre in Ireland, Scotland, and even the American colonies,
we see clearly that the practice of double-billing set by London
was very quickly adopted in these theatres, both near and remote.

[13] Maurice Albert, *Les Théâtres de la foire* (1660-1789) (Paris,
1900), p. 3.

tinctly says "stage-play": "To Bartholomew Fair, and there did see a ridiculous, obscene little stage-play, called 'Marry Andrey'; a foolish thing but seen by every body."

By 1680 there are clear indications of acting at the fairs.[14] Take, for example, this notice from *The Loyal Protestant and True Domestick Intelligence* for 26 August 1682: "At Mrs. Saffry's a Dutch-womans booth, over against the Grey-hound Inne in West-Smithfield, during the time of the Fair, will be acted an incomparable entertainment, call'd the Irish Evidence; the Humours of Tiege; or, the Mercenary Whore; with variety of dances. By the first New-Market Company." It will be noted that though this is almost certainly the company which produced the plays collected in *The Muse of Newmarket,* published two years before, they do not perform one of the plays from that collection but a sort of play which, to judge from the title, is quite distinctive, a droll of the fair-booths.

To be sure there were plays from the standard theatrical repertory in productions of later years, plays which may not have differed greatly from those at the patent-theatres. Tom Brown suggests a movement in this direction for the period around 1700:

> As I have observed to you, this noble fair is quite another thing than what it was in the last age. It not only deals in the humble stories of Crispin and Crispianus, Whittington's cat, Bateman's ghost, with the merry conceits of the little pickle-herring; but it produces operas of its own growth, and is become a formidable rival to both the theatres. It beholds gods descending from machines, who express themselves in a language suitable to their dignity; it traffics in heroes; it raises ghosts and apparitions; it has represented the Trojan-horse, the workmanship of the di-

[14] George Daniel, nineteenth-century antiquarian and bibliophile, had in his library a *"Life of Mat. Coppinger,* once a player in Bartholomew Fair, and since turned Bully, executed at Tyburn, 27 Feb. 1695. London: 1695."

vine Epeus; it has seen St. George encounter the dragon, and overcome him. In short, for thunder and lightning, for songs and dances, for sublime fustian and magnificent nonsense, it comes not short of Drury Lane or Lincoln's Inn Fields.[15]

Brown's statement must be taken critically, however. What he describes is, in spite of the parallel he insists upon, not really the fare of the regular theatres. In fact, his satiric intent is obvious; he is not so much describing performances at the fairs as calling the patent theatres to account.

In later decades we find much clearer evidence of borrowing from the theatres. For example, *The Beggar's Opera* was being offered to audiences in Smithfield in the first summer following its sensational premiere at Lincoln's Inn Fields. There are records of performances of *The Devil to Pay*, of *Hob*, of *The London Merchant*. Then there are numerous borderline cases, plays with titles suggesting pieces from the standard repertory but about which it is difficult to be sure. In 1733, for instance, there is *A Cure for Covetousness, or the Cheats of Scapin*, which would seem to be Molière's play. Or in the same season we find an advertisement in the *Grub-Street Journal* for *The Forc'd Physician*, which is most likely an adaptation of Fielding's adaptation of Molière's farce. The pieces in *The Strolers Pacquet* were "calculated for the meridian of Bartholomew and Southwark Fairs" and, while they are not precisely plays from the standard repertory, they are *from* pieces long familiar at Drury Lane and Covent Garden.

In spite of these parallels and borrowings, however, there is a distinctive form of drama offered year after year in the booths at the annual fairs, and it is a form of considerable interest in a study of farce. Not that the fairs ran at all exclusively to farce. Ned Ward, in *The Dancing School* (1700), in a note of expostulation with some real or imag-

[15] *The Compleat Works of Mr. Thomas Brown*, p. 241.

inary correspondent, alludes to the love of buffoonery at the fairs: "But till I find you affect weeping rather than laughing, and are sooner to be frightened into pity, than jested into gratitude; I shall proceed to gain your good opinion, as Bartholomew-Fair players do to please their audience, more by farce and jocularity, than tragedy and fine speeches." Yet an inspection of the numerous titles of drolls given at the fairs—dozens of them are still preserved in eighteenth-century newspapers and periodicals—or, even better, an examination of some of the pieces which found their way into print will show that the audiences in the fairbooths loved bombast if not fine tragic speeches. In fact, the typical droll is a combination of melodramatic rant, melting love story—often the "nut-brown maid" sort— hearts-of-oak British patriotism, and rough-and-tumble farce. In keeping the mixture pretty much the same as it had always been, the droll writer was not following the trend noted in Chapter 3 toward separating the genres. Rather this folk-drama was arch-conservative in form. To find plays at all similar in the theatrical repertory we must go back to such early seventeenth-century plays as the highly popular *Mucedorus*. Like the groundlings of an earlier day the spectator at the fair wanted to run the gamut of feelings —all at once or in close alternation.

Almost any of the titles of the drolls advertised at fair time will serve to indicate the mixed nature of these pieces. The one quoted above for the Newmarket company in 1682 indicates that political satire was not unknown at the fairs. Sometimes only one element comes out in the title. Examples may be found in the list of plays and drolls by Elkanah Settle. *St. George for England,* in which poor Settle performed the part of dragon in a suit of green leather, according to Pope's account, represents the interest in patriotic or pious legend. His masterpiece, *The Siege of Troy,* reveals the universal fondness for combat and spectacle. More commonly, however, the title reads like a theatrical bill of fare. Doggett's performing in a droll was mentioned in the last chapter. The title of this piece is fairly typical: *Fryar Bacon; or, The Country Justice. With the Humours of Tolfree, the Miller, and His Son Ralph.* Or, to take an even more varied offering, we find Pinkethman and Norris offering this droll in 1725: *The True and Famous History of Semiramis, Queen of Babylon, or, The Woman Wears the Breeches. Containing the Distressful Loves of Prince Alexis and the Princess Ulamia; the pleasant Adventures of Sir Solomon Gundy and his Man Spider and the Comical Humours of Alderman Doddle, his Wife and Daughter Hoyden.* With true history, distressful loves, pleasant adventures, and comical humours all being offered for a single admission, the entrepreneurs must have felt confident of pleasing everyone's taste.

In spite of intermittent warfare between the city fathers and the proprietors of the acting booths,[16] this particular form of folk-drama seems to have done a thriving business throughout much of our period. Possibly with the Restoration or shortly thereafter the official period for the fair of three days was extended to a fortnight, thus making more ambitious productions worthwhile.[17] The extension itself, however, constituted a *casus belli,* for it was chiefly over this point that the battle raged. As in most contests, fortune shifted from one side to the other until, sometime shortly after mid-century, the forces of morality and prosperity won a clear victory. Meanwhile there were two fairly distinct periods when the actors in the fair booths had their innings, the first one during the opening decade of the eighteenth

---

[16] I use the term *intermittent* advisedly, with the French parallel in mind. In Paris the chief enemies of the *forains,* after 1680, were the actors in the regular theatre, and, as Campardon and others indicate, they were almost constantly alert to protect their monopoly.

[17] The dates are uncertain, but there was much talk of the extension in the litigation around 1708. Henry Morley, *Memoirs of Bartholomew Fair* (London, 1880), pp. 293-299.

century, the second during the late twenties and early thirties.

In the earlier period not only Bartholomew and Southwark Fairs but even such less famous ones as May Fair were so successful that during some of the theatrical seasons the regular theatres abandoned all attempts to compete and closed their doors. We may take 1703 as a high point of the triumph of the English *forains*. On 29 April *The Daily Courant* announced a performance at Drury Lane for the following day, the bill beginning with the warning "Being the last time of acting until after May-Fair." And during the fairs in August and September the patent companies suspended activities. This particular summer the Drury Lane company had moved to Bath, to return in October. As I have pointed out in connection with the activities of Will Pinkethman, this "darling of the fairs" joined forces with his fellow clown Bullock and an obscure actor named Simpson in a booth at the fairs, while Doggett had teamed with a certain Parker in a rival booth.[18]

The only text of a droll from the fairs of this season I have been able to examine is Settle's *Siege of Troy*, a steady favorite with audiences in the booths, just as a similar piece at about the same time, Fuzelier's *Ravissement d'Hélène, le siège et l'embrasement de Troye*, was being offered for the delight of spectators at the Foire Saint-Germain.[19] We gather from Tom Brown's remarks quoted above that Settle's droll was already being offered around 1700. I have examined two editions of the play at the Huntington Library. One is dated 1703 and is said to have "been often acted with great applause." It is accompanied by a long (146 pages) chapbook account of the legendary events. The

---

[18] Morley gives, p. 302, an account of a certain John Edwards, who was a quack horse-doctor during the rest of the year but "Penkethman's Merry-Andrew" during fair-time.

[19] Lancaster, *Sunset*, pp. 312-314.

other, of the play alone, is dated 1707 and is quite definitely tied to the fairs of that year:

The Siege of Troy, a dramatick performance Presented in Mrs. Mynn's Booth, over against the Hospital-gate in the Rounds in Smithfield, during the time of the present Bartholomew-Fair. Containing a description of all the scenes, machines, and movements, with the whole decoration of the play, and particulars of the entertainment. London, Printed and sold by Benj. Bragge at the Black Raven in Pater-noster-Row. And also at the booth all the time of the fair, 1707.

Settle's address to the reader is interesting, both in what it suggests of his pronounced persecution complex on the one hand and in what it reveals of his persistent ambition on the other. He is unwilling to label his piece as a droll since he has spent "near ten months" in preparing it, with the result that he is willing to match it against "any one opera yet seen in either of the royal theatres." All these elaborate preparations, a conspicuous item being a wooden horse seventeen feet high, were admittedly designed to attract something better than the mere rabble, especially since "their happier brethren undertakers in the fair, more cheaply obtain even the engrost smiles of the gentry and quality at so much an easier price."

The comic scenes of The Siege of Troy, which are our only concern,[20] are typically foreign to the main action and obviously thrust in to provide more laughs than it would have been possible to get out of the Trojan story itself. An extremely coarse and thoroughly English cobbler engages in a running battle with his wife. He straps her, she cuckolds him, he leads the mob as Captain Bristle, and so on. Some of these scenes of domestic strife have obviously been suggested by Jevon's Devil of a Wife.

[20] Morley gives a detailed summary of the entire droll, pp. 284-291.

The opponents of these spectacles at the fair were aroused to renewed activity by the successes in the early years of the century. In 1708 the Court of Common Council moved to limit Bartholomew Fair to its original three days, "viz. on the Eve of S. Bartholomew, that day and the morrow after, being the 23rd, 24th and 25th days of August." An even more vigorous attack on May Fair followed shortly, with the grand juries of Westminster and Middlesex moving to forbid all acting whatsoever at this fair. The showmen were not completely routed, however, and in less than two decades were again in full swing, at least at the two major fairs in August and September. Again they set up as formidable rivals to the patent theatres and to the several new companies which had been formed at Goodman's Fields and the Little Haymarket, for the period from about 1728 to 1737 was a bustling time in the London theatres. Again their successes aroused strong opposition, and in 1735 the city moved against them, with greater, though still far from complete, success.

Since it is not my purpose to rewrite the history of the London fairs but to examine some of the plays in the booths at these fairs, particularly the farcical materials in these plays, I wish to pause here, finally, for it is here that the largest number of extant drolls have been preserved. Of these plays it is possible—and necessary—to distinguish between the real drolls prepared specifically for the fairs and the few plays designed primarily for the theatre but offered at the fairs as well.

I have already mentioned that *The Beggar's Opera* was produced at both Bartholomew and Southwark Fairs in 1728 with, according to the newspapers, "all the songs and dances set to music, as performed at the Theatre in Lincoln's Inn Fields." This must have been a fairly regular production of Gay's ballad opera rather than a mere droll. At the rival booth of Lee and Harper—*The Beggar's Opera* was offered by "the company of comedians from the Haymarket" at Fielding and Reynold's booth—the visitors to Southwark Fair were able to see a similar spectacle in Thomas Walker's *Quaker's Opera*. Though this performance represents the premiere of *The Quaker's Opera* the piece is in no sense a droll; it is an out-and-out copy of its more famous and artistically superior rival. Walker simply turned back to an anonymous piece called *The Prison-Breaker* (1725), which had evidently been submitted to Rich at the time interest in Jack Sheppard's escapades was running high but which Rich, noting the failure of the Drury Lane pantomime on the same theme, had ultimately refused to produce. Walker simply transformed it into an even more topical *Beggar's Opera*. The characters, most of them taken directly from the unproduced play, are mainly from life: Jack Sheppard, Jonathan Wile, and Kate Hackabout mingle with fictitious persons like Nym, File, and Hempseed. The fate of Walker's ballad opera indicates that Rich's judgment had been sound when he refused *The Prison-Breaker* three years earlier, for it had no real success. It is of some interest to us, however, in that it was performed both at the fairs and, a little over a month later, at the Little Haymarket.

In the summer of the following year, Charles Coffey, soon to gain some measure of fame as author of *The Devil to Pay*, wrote a play called *Southwark Fair: or, The Sheep Shearing* which stands somewhat nearer the borderline between regular drama and droll. Still, though Coffey's play seems not to have been received at the regular theatres, it is less a droll than a ballad opera of the more conventional sort, with the standard wares of a match of wits between a heavy father and a clever pair of lovers. The setting does, of course, provide for certain items suggestive of the fair: a merry-andrew—more fashionably named Harlequin—a showcloth, and some trading in and shearing of sheep.

There is no problem over classifying three pieces published in the summer of 1730, a season which may mark an all-time high in activities at the fair. All three are out-and-out drolls though one, *The Generous Free-Mason: or, the Constant Lady, with the Humours of Squire Noodle, and his Man Doodle, a Tragi-Comi-Farcical Ballad Opera,* appeared later in the year at the Little Haymarket. A second, called *Robin Hood,* also poses in the latest fashion as "an opera . . . with the musick prefix'd to each song." No amount of disguise could hide the fact that this is a traditional folk-play of the fairs. Not only the romantic scenes—showing the English folk-hero rebelling against tyranny and fleeing to the free life of the forest, to which his loyal Matilda follows—but also the farce episodes stem from the people. We must go all the way back to the Commonwealth droll for a parallel. See, for example, the episode in which the wild boy Darnel (Little John) is forced into extravagant farce as he attempts to cuckold the gullible Pindar of Wakefield. Darnel hides under a table during a meal and is obliged to bark like a dog, eat scraps, bite the Pindar's finger. Later he is put into the cradle and rocked, while the Pindar wonders about this strange infant's bristly face. Here is the kind of primary farce turn discussed in Chapter 2.

Wat Tyler and Jack Straw, the offering at the rival booth, is cut from the same material but lacks any sign of farce. From a comment on this piece in the *Grub-Street Journal* for 27 August 1730 we gather that the droll was boisterous enough to please the rabble. In a news item for that date the five different offerings of five different booths at the current fair are listed, with a few gratuitous comments by the scornful editors. The first of the five reads, "At Mr. Penkethman [son of the famous actor] and Mr. W. Giffard's great theatrical booth, is acted a new droll, called Watt Tyler and Jack Straw, in which are presented my Lord Mayor, four mobbs, and a great deal of hollowing, singing and dancing."

As indicated above, one of the pieces acted at the fairs

this season, and duly noted by the *Grub-Street Journal*, was *The Generous Free-Mason*, which is no less a droll than the other two, even though it was later performed at the regular theatres. The serious part of the play is sheer clap-trap in strained heroic couplets. The faithful lovers Sebastian and Maria fly a cruel father in England, are captured in a sea-fight by the infidel Mirza, taken to Tunis, threatened with martyrdom for their faith, and in general match the adventures of such popular plays of Elizabethan days as *Fair Maid of the West*. Accompanying all this are the most extraneous farce episodes which rise to the wildest *lazzi*, and which for sheer coarseness of language and action would be hard to match in the whole period. Noodle and Doodle are subjected to every conceivable indignity known to the farce actor. They have snuff and urine thrown over them, have their pockets picked, are lathered (actually blackened) for shaving, are thrust into sacks—in short run through fully half of the ageless routine of English farce.

The three drolls just discussed make up a large, and typical, part of the offerings at the fairs in this crowded season. Other items which I have not been able to examine in detail but which are listed faithfully by the *Grub-Street Journal* are, with one exception, well within the droll tradition. There is a *Scipio's Triumph: or, The Siege of Carthage. With the Comical Humours of Noodle, Stitch, Puzzle, &c*; a *Siege of Bethulia; containing the antient History of Judith and Holofernes; together with the comical Humours of Rustigo and his Man Terrible*, all of which evidently preceded the *Robin Hood* I have described; and a *Whole History of Herod and Marianne*. The sole exception to this offering of drolls accompanies the last item, which was to be followed by "that celebrated opera call'd *Flora or Hob in the Well*." In short, the dramatic activities at the fairs did not remain entirely unaffected by those of the regular theatres; there was traffic between them, in plays as well as

in actors, though most of the traffic was in one direction.[21]
Only a few more years of untroubled activity remained
for the showmen at the fairs. With 1735 begins a period of
the most intense struggle which ran more and more in
favor of their enemies. In the summer of that year Sir John
Barnard, who had recently moved with considerable force
against the non-patent theatres and had stopped short of
victory only because of his reluctance to join forces with
the officials of the national government,[22] led the aldermen
in an attack upon the fairs. *The London Magazine* for 25
June informs us that "The Court of Aldermen came to a
final resolution touching Bartholomew-Fair, that the same
shall not exceed Bartholomew-Eve, Bartholomew-Day, and
the Day after; and . . . no acting be permitted." When, at
the time of the fair itself, their courage or their powers
failed them, fate played into their hands. According to
Fog's Weekly Journal for 30 August there had been a serious mishap at Bartholomew Fair on the preceding Tues-
day, the 26th. In the crush of the mob a five-year-old child
had been killed. With this unlooked-for stimulus to their
flagging resolution, the aldermen moved swiftly. "No more
such accidents will probably happen this year in that place,"
continues *Fog's*, "for that evening the city marshalls put an
end to fair with the accustomed ceremonies, to the great
sorrow of all the strolers, rogues, whores, and pickpockets,
who resort thither during the time of the fair." When the
time of the fair across the Thames came, the aldermen did
not wait for any providential assistance. *Grub-Street Jour-*

[21] I hesitate to subscribe completely to Professor Noyes's theory:
"Although the fair was giving the legitimate stage some competition,
there was one virtue not discerned by Brown [i.e., Tom Brown].
The farces and drolls were developing a school of comic actors, like
Johnson, Pinkethman, and Jo Haines, where the managers of the
theatres found many of their best players." *Ben Jonson on the
English Stage* (Cambridge, Mass., 1935), p. 235.
[22] Watson Nicholson, *The Struggle for a Free Stage in London*
(Boston, 1906), p. 59.

nal No. 298 quotes an item from the *Daily Post-Boy* for 10 September: "Last night the city marshalls went to the Borough of Southwark, and put an end to the fair with great exactness."

These effective maneuvers of Barnard and his colleagues unquestionably did great damage to theatrical activities at the fair, even though they did not bring activities to a full stop. For the next few years the advertisements call attention more sharply than ever to "the short time" of the fairs.

A counter-maneuver to set up fairs in addition to the two regular ones may have resulted from these early victories of the aldermen. In any event we find notices in great number about this time for May Fair, Tottenham-Court Fair, Welsh Fair, and others. These are not all new fairs called into being by the opposition of 1735, for we find activities noted in the *Daily Courant* for Tottenham-Court Fair as early as 1717. But the greater frequency with which notices of all these fairs began to appear shortly after 1735 does suggest a causal link. An interesting feature of these fairs is that the showmen there, with even greater frequency than the actors at the better-known festivals, began to produce more ambitious shows on the pattern of the "entertainments" at the regular theatres and, to judge from the titles, even an occasional play, though this last may well have been altered to fit the needs and the limitations of the booths. *Jane Shore*, for example, seems to have been a favorite, as, considering its origins, it might well have been.[23] To give a sample of other productions, we find, mixed in

[23] Consider the opening lines of Rowe's prologue:
> Tonight, if you have brought your good old taste,
> We'll treat you with a downright English feast—
> A tale which, told long since in homely wise,
> Hath never failed of melting gentle eyes.
> Let no nice sir despise our hapless dame
> Because recording ballads chaunt her name;
> Those venerable ancient song-enditers
> Soared many a pitch above our modern writers.

with the more conventional drolls, such pieces as *The Honest Yorkshireman, The Author's Farce*, even *Henry V.* Equally interesting is the generous sprinkling of pantomimes—if we may safely assume that such titles as *Harlequin Restored, Harlequin Sorceror*, and *Jupiter and Juno* announce a silent rather than a spoken form of drama.

Whatever trend there may have been away from the traditional droll, this and all other activities at the fairs came under the zealous scrutiny of the authorities. *The Daily Advertiser* for 28 April 1748 offers a presentment of the county court indicating that some move was about to be made against the "several fairs or pretended fairs . . . not warranted by law, to wit, Tottenham Court Fair, Hampstead Fair, in Holborn Division, the Shepherd's Bush Fair in Kensington Division, the Welsh Fair in Finsbury Division, Mile-End Fair and Bow Fair, commonly called Green-Goose Fair, in the Tower Division, and May Fair in Westminster Division. . . ." Just what specific move the authorities contemplated or eventually carried out I am unable to say, but there seems to be little doubt that the glorious days of acting at the fairs were about over. Morley's interesting account of the principal one in Smithfield begins to run out about mid-century. According to him no actor of note after Shuter had any connection with Bartholomew Fair, and his own account turns farther and farther away from the drama toward the exhibition of freaks.

The story of the smaller outlaw theatres in London, those in addition to the half dozen well known theatres I have been dealing with, is not yet as fully known as we might wish. Enough facts are available, however, to make possible some tentative observations about their place in the history of farce. With even less knowledge than we do have, we would be reasonably safe, I feel, in assuming that whatever influence these smaller houses had would be greatest where such popular forms of entertainment as farce were concerned. Except for an occasional attempt at the more exalted kind of drama, often by "ladies and gentlemen for their own entertainment"—genuinely amateur theatricals, that is, and therefore outside the range of our interest here—most of these outlaw activities went on at the various "wells" which sprang up, chiefly in the suburbs, in the last two decades of our period.

In the earlier years of the eighteenth century,[24] such activities as have come to my attention were largely in the hands of one entrepreneur, Anthony Aston. This interesting character had a long and adventurous career in the provinces, too, evidently even straying as far abroad as the American colonies.[25] We have already commented on his early relations with the much greater actor Doggett. Miss Rosenfeld and others have chronicled a number of his adventures in the theatre outside London.

But Tony was not content with always being exiled from the capital and repeatedly tried his fortunes there. Genest gives us but one season's records of his performing in a patent theatre, when he was with Rich's company in the 1721-22 season. He also quotes Chetwood to the effect that Aston played in "all the theatres in London," and, while this may possibly be somewhat extravagant, it finds partial support in the actor's own cryptic statement of 1743 that

[24] Allusions to actors performing outside the regular theatres, the royal entertainment halls, and the fairs before 1700 are bafflingly few and obscure. Perhaps the clearest suggestion of such activities is a quite familiar one. In Etherege's *She Wou'd If She Cou'd* (1668) Courtall teases Sir Oliver, who is dressed in his penitential suit, "Bless me, Sir Oliver, what, are you going to act a droll? How the people would throng about you, if you were but mounted on a few deal-boards in Covent-Garden now!"

[25] See Watson Nicholson, *Anthony Aston Stroller and Adventurer* (South Haven, Michigan, 1920). Aston's name appears in several studies of the early American theatre, such as those of Miss Willis and Professor Odell. Aston also acted at the London fairs. A notice in the *Daily Advertiser* for 18 August 1733 says that "the famous Tony Aston, so remarkable for his performances thro' great Britain and Ireland," is to team up with Paget, of Drury Lane, at Bartholomew Fair.

he had recently been "denied at both theatres . . . though initiated and often there."

If his better placed rivals could keep Tony out of the regular houses, they could not prevent him from setting up on his own in London. At three or four different periods in the first half of the eighteenth century the London newspapers carried advertisements of his attempts to draw people to his unconventional productions. His forte throughout his long career was the "medley," a series of wholly disconnected scenes—largely farcical if we may judge from the ads—from standard plays, the sort of production that had a brief season of popularity in the regular theatres at the time Aston was beginning his career at the turn of the century. Notices in *The Daily Courant* for January-March 1717, for example, tell us that "Tony Aston's Medley from Bath" is to present a variety consisting of "Drunken Man" scenes and bits from such plays as *The Spanish Fryar*, *Aesop*, *Venice Preserved* (no doubt the "Nicky Nacky" scenes), *The Plain Dealer*, and *Love for Love* at a tavern in Fleet Street. Perhaps as remarkable as his repertory is his method of evading the law against non-approved performances. Anticipating by more than twenty years the ruses which the Licensing Act was to foster, he announced: "Mr. Aston performs to divert his friends gratis, and hath toothpickers to sell at 1s. each."

In the fall of 1723 he was back in London, according to *The Daily Post*. On this occasion he was still producing his "Medley," with scenes from some of the same plays but with interesting additions more in line with recent developments in the farce afterpiece such as *Love's Contrivances* and "The Humours of Hob in *The Country Wake*." He also moved about town rather more this time, working his way from the Dog Tavern near Billingsgate to the Globe and the Bull-Head in Fleet Street to the Three-Tun Tavern in the Borough. Aston was evidently not greatly encumbered by props or personnel and therefore highly mobile. In the advertisements six years earlier he had listed his troupe as consisting of himself, his wife, and his ten-year-old boy.

After the passing of the Licensing Act he was still further reduced in the size of his company and, it appears, in fortune. In advertisements for March and April 1740, this time in *The Daily Advertiser*, he is "by himself" and doing a sort of music-hall routine:

> At the desire of several gentlemen, Tony Aston, by himself, at Ashley's Punch-House on Ludgate-Hill, this present Friday exhibits his learned, humorous, and various oratory, on the head and face; with several English, Irish, and Scots songs, and Pasquin,[26] all his own making; beginning at seven o'clock. Price one shilling. [The Latin motto which comes at this point I am unable to decipher—regrettably, for Tony's Latin is often rewarding.] N. B. If his few creditors please to take part or all his debts in tickets, he'll give 'em a bowl of punch, and extra merry songs.

By 1743 fortune must have been smiling again, probably not very warmly. From Boxing Day until 29 March, when he had advertised "this last, last night"—he had started on his "last night" routine two months earlier—he offered some parts of his old medley, along with "Negro songs" and his "Pasquin." On this occasion he was assisted by a Mrs. Motteaux, who became "the Widow Motteaux" for her benefit in March.

[26] Whether or not this is a reference to Fielding's play, the author of *Pasquin* took the occasion of Tony's appearance to jibe at the government censors in *The Champion* for 5 April 1740: "The noted Tony Aston, having lately taken upon him to exhibit certain sarcastic faces, which are said to be copied from the life, at the most frequented levees in town; 'tis expected that he will be call'd upon to rehearse his said faces at the Dramatical Excise office, that such as are judged obnoxious, may be superseded, and a regular permit be taken out for the rest: It not being consistent with the intention of a late act, that the very looks or gestures of the great should be made the jest or laugh of the vulgar."

It is hardly necessary to claim any great influence on the development of farce for Aston. As the previous chapters have shown, farce did a sufficiently thriving business within the patent theatres themselves. Yet his activities represent one more phase of the competition, especially in the early years of the century, which was to assure the short farce a permanent place in the repertory. Aside from this, Aston's career can be taken as one more manifestation of the sort of activity represented by the Commonwealth droll: the irrepressibility of the determined actor and the permanence of at least some kind of audience to applaud his attempts.

Aside from the activities at the fairs and from Aston's repeated attempts to restore the centuries-old practice of using inns as the center of theatrical activities, the bulk of outlaw performances were given at the various "wells" about London, chiefly after the Licensing Act. There were some activities, however, before 1737. Particularly during the mid-thirties, when as many as five or six companies were in operation, there were attempts to start still more.

Perhaps the most active of these little-known houses was one—if there was but one—commonly labelled as the "Tennis Court in James Street, near Haymarket." From scattered advertisements in *The Daily Advertiser*, ranging from at least as early as 1732 on to 1749 and beyond, there was a succession of theatrical companies with such familiar names of minor actors and actresses as Hallam, Norris, and Charke. The real owner or impresario throughout much of this time, to judge from evidence of ticket-sales, was Pinchbeck, probably the son of the famous watchmaker and inventor of the metal which has succeeded in keeping his name alive. The bills at this theatre ran chiefly to the same type as those at such better known houses as the Little Haymarket. Commonly there were double bills of play and farce. Invariably the farce afterpiece was a prominent feature.

Much the same history is indicated for the theatre commonly labelled "York Buildings" or "The Great Room in

Villers St., York Buildings." This theatre seems not, however, to have survived the Licensing Act, the last performance I have seen listed in *The Daily Advertiser* being for 2 May 1737.

The history of the various wells theatres is even more complex. Perhaps the earliest is the one which was in time to become the most famous, Sadler's Wells. Nicoll says that "There was a music room here from 1683, but the theatre was not set up until 1740."[27] There are signs of some kind of theatrical activity before 1740, however. Bills in *The Daily Advertiser* as early as March 1733 call for performances of *The Harlot's Progress*. Even more interesting evidence comes from a rare little book in the Huntington Library dated 1730. The title reads: *"The Prisoner's Opera. To which is added, several other entertainments, interchangeably perform'd at Sadler's Wells, during the summer season. Where also the best of wines, excellent ale, brew'd of the Well-water, and all other liquors may be had in perfection. London printed: and published at the Wells 1730. Price six-pence."* *The Prisoner's Opera*, obviously one of the earlier attempts to profit from the acclaim of Gay's hit, is hardly more than quasi-operatic. It consists of a number of songs with some continuity and linked by an occasional direction calling for gesture or dance, but there is no true dialogue or recitative carrying out a detailed plot. In fact *The Prisoner's Opera* more nearly resembles the Elizabethan jig than it does the newer form of ballad opera. The few advertisements of Sadler's I have seen in later newspapers indicate a trend even farther away from legitimate drama. There may have been other attempts at this house to provide a more conventional sort of theatrical fare. Miss Rosenfeld informs us that in 1741 the people of Ipswich, who had recently seen the debut of Garrick, acting under

[27] *History*, II, 430. References in Fielding's *Pasquin* to Sadler's Wells indicate that at that time (1736) the usual offerings were rope-dancing and tumbling.

the name Lyddall, were offered a succession of farces and pantomimes by "Yeates's Company from the New Sadler's Wells."[28] But from the widely scattered bills I have seen for the Wells itself it does not appear that any date can be selected as marking a definite shift in the type of production. In September 1740, a year before the visit to the provinces noted by Miss Rosenfeld, the company was doing a variety bill which suggests dancing and pantomime. According to *The Daily Advertiser* for 9 September, for instance, the offering was in three parts: a *Birth of Venus*, a *Tambourine of Tambourines*, and a piece called *Bonus*, labelled in the bill by a term which carries us back to the early years of the century, "a night scene." On the preceding evening there had been a pantomimic dance called *The Cobler* in which Newton played Jobson and which was said to include a new interlude called *The Parting Lovers*. This kind of theatrical melange differs very little from the sort being offered three or four years later. In April 1744 there was a succession of performances of *The Birth of Venus* plus *Zypherus and Flora*; in May began a long run of *The Happy Despair* followed by *Le Bergère in the Temple of Flora*.

What has been indicated for Sadler's Wells may stand pretty generally for the other "wells" about London. Of these, two stand out. One was in Goodman's Fields and was usually labelled in the newspaper bills "New Wells, bottom of Lemon St., Goodman's Fields." This should not be confused with the Goodman's Fields Theatre, which assured itself a lasting fame, just before passing out of existence as a theatre, by introducing Garrick to the London public. The Goodman's Fields Wells dates from at least as early as June 1739 and ran in opposition to the theatre much of the time till May 1742, when Garrick's moving to Drury Lane extinguished the lights in that house for good. The

[28] p. 101.

other of the more important wells was in Clerkenwell and was called "the New Wells, London Spaw, Clerkenwell."[29]

Both these wells presented, usually, programs of the sort listed for Sadler's Wells. Unfortunately we have little beyond titles to go on, but these seem clearly to indicate dancing and pantomime, possibly with some rough-and-tumble farce. There are a great many "harlequin" titles: *Harlequin Hermit, Harlequin Statue, The Escapes of Harlequin,* and the like. There are also titles suggesting masque and pageantry: *The Temple of Diana at Ephesus, Bacchus and Circe, Hymen's Temple, Baucis and Philemon.* Only occasionally are there plays from the standard repertory, performed, as best we can tell, by scratch companies hoping to draw upon the plentiful supply of playgoers. There are plays advertised in the newspapers for Clerkenwell in October and December 1740 and again in November 1748, evidently isolated performances parading hopefully as actors' benefits. For three seasons, from November 1744 to April 1747, a company, or succession of companies, ran fairly regularly during the winter seasons at the Lemon Street Wells, offering a conventional repertory of plays and afterpieces, but after that this theatre went back to the fare more commonly associated with the "wells" theatre.

It would be foolhardy to claim any great influence upon farce for these outlaw houses. They are to be looked upon as symptomatic rather than influential. In the theatre, at least, the traditional insistence on a repertory of regular five-act plays had long since lost much of its weight.

[29] For details of another wells see Sybil Rosenfeld, "Shepherd's Market Theatre and May Fair Wells," *Theatre Notebook,* v, No. 4 (July-September 1951), 89-92.

CHAPTER 8

SOME REPRESENTATIVE FARCES

++

> They who are born to taste with pleasure throng
> To Shakespeare's sense, or Farinello's song:
> The tasteless vulgar, as experience tells,
> Warmly espouse their Harlequins and Nells.
> —Epilogue to *The Mournful Nuptials* (1739)

++

HAVING elaborated the complex background against which farce developed from the Restoration to mid-eighteenth century, I turn now to an examination of some of the specific farces presented during this span. To talk about every one of the dozens and dozens of plays containing farce would be pointless if not downright confusing. Many of them—candor suggests that *most* would not be too severe—are quite uninspired attempts to get laughs by repeating endlessly hard-used but durable formulas. Most of them failed to survive more than a few short seasons. Here and there, however, we find one which merits closer attention, either because of what it reveals of the development of the theatre in general and farce in particular, or because of some slight touch of originality or cleverness the writer managed to introduce. After all, some of these plays did survive through generations of performances. Such exceptional pieces as *The Devil to Pay* match the enviable records of some of the outstandingly popular plays of the century, even such hits as *The Beggar's Opera* or *The Beaux Stratagem.*

The development of farce types, already outlined in preceding chapters, may be described, in what I hope are not too highly oversimplified terms, as follows: From a beginning in the traditions of the English stage of an earlier day, when farce served as filler or comic relief in full-length plays and where it was often mixed with pageantry or stage-magic, farce followed divergent paths—showing some tendency to go in the direction of the *commedia dell'arte* but being displaced there by the pantomime, showing an even greater tendency to carry to extremes the tradition of over-drawn "humours" characters, but eventually settling upon a formula of intrigue involving three or four brief *lazzi*. In many cases, where a given play is not taken directly from an earlier piece, the native stress on ridiculous character and the Continental tradition of intrigue are both in evidence. In a comparatively few instances the introduction of more subtle comedy raises the play above the level of farce to that of *petite comédie*.

In this chapter it is my plan to survey some of the higher —and where possible, brighter—points in the period by examining specific plays. To avoid the awkwardness of cross-reference I shall be obliged to repeat here and there some ideas already touched upon earlier, though I shall attempt to keep actual duplication to a minimum.

It is difficult, and possibly unnecessary, to single out a representative from the many revivals of five-act plays with farce early in our period. During the first decade after the theatres reopened, several plays answering to this description were produced, some of them being revised by the addition of more slapstick. Among these were such plays as Cowley's *Guardian*, reproduced in 1661 with considerable farcical alteration as *The Cutter of Coleman-Street*, and Shakespeare's *Taming of the Shrew*, which received similar treatment at the hands of the star comedian John Lacy and was renamed *Sauny the Scott* (1667). Other plays seem to have contained satisfactory amounts of slapstick and therefore called for little revision. Tomkis' *Albumazar*, a mixture of satire on astrologers and rousing farce, was revived in 1668. If we may depend upon Pepys' reaction, already quoted, as being representative of the current attitude, we can see clearly enough which of these elements were most pleasing to a Restoration audience: Pepys was delighted to report that even King Charles agreed with him in singling out for special applause "the mimique tricks of Trinkilo." Marlowe's *Dr. Faustus* enjoyed a renewal of popularity in these early years, though what proved most pleasing in it may well have been the scenes of the marvelous and the magic, the sort of attraction which in the eighteenth century accounts for the craze over pantomimes. A commentator in 1681 singles out this element in the play in an allusion to the heated politics of the day: "Since the Salamanca Drs. rrmoval [*sic*] into the City, the Whigs are so generous in their supplies, that pigs, geese, and capons fly in at his windows in as great plenty as ever they did to Dr. Faustus."[1] A little later *Faustus* was revised by the actor Mountfort, principally by having some Italian harlequinery added.

In addition to revived full-length plays with farce from the earlier English repertory, there were some original plays of similar structure in these early years. Lacy's *Old Troop* is an example of such a mixture. Into a surprisingly realistic and cynical picture of the recent civil wars the actor-playwright managed to work a series of basic farce turns already described in the chapter on structure. Rather similar in the use of hilarious slapstick are Boyle's comedies, *Guzman* and *Mr. Anthony,* both of which were apparently designed largely to exploit the talents in clowning of Nokes and Angel.

The demands for farce in the early days of the Restoration were usually satisfied, however, without any great expenditure of effort in original composition. The common practice, rather, was simply to lift plays or combinations of plays from contemporary French comedy. In the discussion of sources I pointed out the dependence of Davenant and

[1] *The Loyal Protestant and True Domestick Intelligence,* 20 September 1681.

Dryden and Mrs. Behn and a host of others upon Scarron and Thomas Corneille and, most of all, Molière. Of all the riflers of Molière the chief one, it will be recalled, was Edward Ravenscroft. Almost any of his several early farces, *Mamamouchi* or *Scaramouch*, for example, might serve as a model of the adaptation of farce from Molière. His *London Cuckolds* (1681), though perhaps less typical a borrowing, might serve better to illustrate the work of this leading farce writer in the Restoration period. It was not only his most popular full-length play—only the shorter *Anatomist* competes with it as a popular favorite—it is perhaps as ingenious a compilation of miscellaneous farce tricks as the English theatre has ever seen.

The basic plot of *The London Cuckolds* has to do with the cuckolding and eventual disillusioning of three pompous London aldermen, Doodle, Wiseacres, and Dashwell (played by Nokes, Underhill, and Leigh). Each is confident that he has discovered the certain way to keep a wife faithful: by depending on her youth and naïvete, or on her wit and sophistication, or on her strict moral upbringing. Of course each is completely taken in by his own arrogant folly. Now this basic theme may well have been suggested by Molière's "school" comedies, but the individual scenes in which the disillusionment is brought about depend upon a great variety of suggested sources. True, as Langbaine originally pointed out and as Montague Summers has insisted, much of this can be found in the seventeenth-century French collection of novelle, d'Ouvilles' *Contes aux heures perdues*. Still the lines ramify out in a dozen directions into folk literature of various sorts, and the whole play, episodic as it is, somehow manages to crystallize into a racy piece which was to retain a place in the esteem of the less staid theatre-goers for a whole century, or until its salaciousness proved too strong for the refining tastes of the eighteenth century.

Two or three scenes of this long and very full yet fast-moving farce-comedy will serve to show what it is like. In the first scene of Act II we have an age-old deception which, though Ravenscroft may have gone no farther than d'Ouville for it, is to be found in a number of folk-tales. In our own day it is perhaps best known, in bowdlerized form, as Andersen's "Great Claus and Little Claus."[2] In the play, Loveday, "meanly habited, in black," comes to Dashwell's house to claim hospitality since he has a letter of introduction from Dashwell's brother. But Dashwell being away from home and his supposedly pious wife Eugenia being on the impatient lookout for her lover Ramble, Loveday gets a cool reception and is hastily packed off to the poor accommodations of the attic. From this position he sees Eugenia receive Ramble and place a handsome dinner before him. Dashwell's unexpected return sends the food and the lover into hiding and brings Loveday down from the attic for a more adequate welcome by his host. They sit down to eat the plain food set before them. But now Loveday is in charge of affairs. Taking advantage of Eugenia's compromising situation and Dashwell's gullibility, he "conjures" a fine meal out of its hiding place and even lets his host get a fleeting glimpse of the devil (Ramble) who is then allowed to escape.

This scene and one or two others, particularly the "Lady No" scene[3] in Act IV, have perhaps a sophistication not quite in tune with most of the play, which runs very much to boisterous physical action. Perhaps the wildest scene of farce occurs in III, i, at Doodle's home. Arabella, the wit, has sent a note to Townly to inform him of her husband's

[2] The story also appears in the collection of fairy stories by the Grimm brothers, under the title of "The Little Farmer," in Hans Sachs' "Farendt Schuler mit dem Teuffelbannen," and in a number of other versions.

[3] I judge from Professor Lancaster, *History*, IV, 935, that this "no" motif had some currency at the Parisian fairs. He describes *Le Marchand ridicule*, which I have not read but in which the theme is used.

absence, but her maid Engine delivers it by mistake to Ramble, who comes at once. There follows a dialogue studded with the most salacious *double-entendres* as Ramble talks Arabella, pretending coyness, into granting his wishes. No sooner have they withdrawn to her bedroom, however, than Doodle returns unexpectedly. After rescuing the lover through much ingenuity on the part of maid and mistress, they find that he is locked in the house for the night and, wishing to lose no opportunities, they suggest that he go to bed with Engine until Doodle is asleep. But before any exchange can be made satisfactorily, Roger, Ramble's man, in a desperate attempt to save his master yells "Fire!" just outside the house and quiet again gives place to pandemonium. In the excitement Ramble shows himself but is able to give a satisfactory account of his presence. But now that he is locked out rather than in, he tries to enter the cellar window, gets stuck halfway, has his hat and wig stolen, is hit on the head by a linkboy, has a chamberpot emptied over him, and is only after a long ordeal rescued by the watch. Or, better, he is apprehended on suspicion of burglary. Again the house is aroused, Doodle rushes out in his night shirt, thrusts his blunderbuss into the window after any possible accomplices, fires, and is kicked head over heels. In short, as this somewhat detailed summary of one bit of action is designed to show, *The London Cuckolds* is full of noisy action which is scarcely edifying but undoubtedly laughable.

Though no other five-act play in the century covered here can quite match *The London Cuckolds* in its abandoned pursuit of the risqué and the risible—here indeed rather than in the comedy of manners is the Cloud Cuckoo Land which Lamb was seeking—or in its ingenious use of a host of motifs, there are plays in which similar devices are employed. Mrs. Behn and Tom Durfey come to mind as nearest rivals and followers of Ravenscroft. Mrs. Behn's *Rover* plays, especially Pt. II (1680), follow the same pattern of noisy and racy intrigue.[4] If "fair Astrea" did not quite succeed in putting everyone to bed, she tried hard to pop everyone behind or under the bed, into closets, down trapdoors. Durfey pursued much the same course while pretending to be intent upon satire. Not to linger over the long list of his plays, most of which have at least some admixture of farce, I might point out that one of the most farcical, A Fool's Preferment, or, The Three Dukes of Dunstable (c. 1688), follows a pattern quite typical of Durfey's pieces yet very much like that of Ravenscroft's play in that it is obviously intended to exploit the talents of Nokes, Leigh, and Jevon in a sequence of boisterous scenes.

But to return to Mrs. Behn, it might be well to select of her numerous plays the one which proved to be most popular through the years and which will illustrate at the same time a particular kind of play, the full-length borrowing from the Italian comedians. Not that The Emperor of the Moon (1687) was the first English play to be taken directly from the commedia dell'arte. Even before 1660 Sir Aston Cokain had written a play called Trapolin creduto principe, or Trapolin suppos'd a prince, which he professed to have copied from a performance he saw in Italy. Cokain's play may have been performed in London between 1660 and 1675, but it was obliged to wait until 1685 for Nahum Tate to take it in hand and turn it into A Duke and No Duke before it became at all popular. In any event, Mrs. Behn's play became much more popular and shows in several ways a more revealing use of the exotic materials of the commedia dell'arte. It held the stage for a number of years and was eventually dropped only because of the rise of the pantomime, which it clearly anticipates.[5]

---

[4] The burlesqued farce in Shadwell's True Widow (1678) seems to have been aimed at just the sort of noisy slapstick Durfey and Mrs. Behn were turning out, not that in this case the accuser was quite beyond reproach himself.

[5] For the stage history of this play, see Hughes and Scouten, Ten

The framework of *The Emperor of the Moon* is typical of the Italian pattern. The romantic young men, Cinthio and Charmant, are unsuccessful in their attempts to marry Elaria and Bellemonte until, with the aid of Harlequin and Scaramouch, they convince the father and uncle of the girls, the crack-brained old astrologer Dr. Baliardo, that they are emissaries of the emperor of the moon. This fantastic plot is obviously designed only to provide a number of scenes of pageantry and scenic display on the one hand and a series of extraneous *lazzi* on the other. These latter are of greatest interest to us. Scaramouch and Harlequin (played by Leigh and Jevon) not only assist the young lovers but carry on a sort of counterplot or antimasque in which they outbid each other for the hand of Mopsophil.

The several *lazzi* in which the two Italianate clowns engage are all quite interesting as clever novelties, such as the night scene in which they grope about in the dark, getting fingers in each other's mouths and so on, or the extravagant scene of Harlequin's desperate attempt to commit suicide by tickling himself to death. We may single out one for somewhat more extended notice as an example of the Italianate type of farce. At the beginning of Act III there is a wholly extraneous bit of clowning in which Harlequin almost drives a customs officer or tax collector out of his wits. The scene is set at the town gate where the official has his post. Harlequin appears, well-dressed, and riding in a calash, and is immediately called upon to pay the tax the city of Naples requires of all gentlemen. But, Harlequin protests, he is no gentleman but a mere baker riding in his cart. While the officer goes off to bring a clerk to assist him in proving his contention that Harlequin is really a man of quality and substance, the *zanni* whips on a baker's gown and drops the rear of the calash to form a cart. Of course

---

English Farces. Several of the representative plays described in this chapter are reproduced and discussed in that collection.

the clerk loses his temper over what he supposes to be the officer's folly and departs in a huff. While the officer's back is turned Harlequin doffs his gown, turns the cart back into a calash, and is once more ready for the whole sequence. As might be surmised, the whole thing is repeated more than once. The Italians had long since arrived at a stylized kind of farce in which all the familiar motifs figured.

Several other plays with a considerable farcical content appeared in the period between 1682 and 1695 when a single company was providing all the theatrical fare for London playgoers. Most of these were original plays or derived from native sources. Comparatively few plays with a notable farce content were borrowed from abroad; of these only Dryden's *Amphitryon* (1690), Wright's *Female Vertuosos* (1693)—both from Molière—and the trilogy by Durfey from *Don Quixote* are worth noting. Perhaps the most significant plays with farce taken from sources right at home were Mrs. Behn's *Revenge* (produced just before the union, in 1680) and Tate's *Cuckolds-Haven* (1685). Even more interesting from our point of view are two evidently original plays: Jevon's *Devil of a Wife* (1686) and Doggett's *Country Wake* (just beyond the period, in 1696). Since all of these latter plays except Tate's will appear again reduced to short farces, I shall not take them up in detail here.

With the splitting up of the one theatrical company into two in 1695 a new era began and a demand for short farces was soon created. Though in time much of this demand was to be satisfied by native talent, there was a tendency in the early years to draw upon the full repertory of short French plays available in great quantity. As early as its second full season the company under Betterton was making use of such borrowings, not for afterpieces to be sure—the afterpiece is still some five seasons away—but as parts of hastily contrived medleys. Motteux turned Hauteroche's *Souper mal apprêté* into a second act, called *All without Money*, of his *Novelty* at the end of the 1696-97 season. Here again, however, is an interesting little piece which may well wait until we meet it again in Garrick's far more popular version. We may pass, then, on to another, equally notable, borrowing from Hauteroche which had already appeared the preceding November at Lincoln's Inn Fields.

The Anatomist, or the Sham Doctor, taken, with important alterations, from Hauteroche's *Crispin médecin*, was Edward Ravenscroft's last venture in farce. His handling of this play differs significantly from his handling of earlier French materials. This time, instead of gathering together a number of scenes from various plays or stories to make up a full evening's bill, Ravenscroft anticipates the sort of production which was soon to come into vogue by combining his own efforts on a single play with those of Motteux, who produced a series of musical interludes under the title of *The Loves of Venus and Mars*. In later years it was a simple matter to drop the musical scenes and play *The Anatomist* as an afterpiece.

Crispin médecin is a lively farce making clever use of traditional materials. The play is centered around a stereotyped intrigue: young Gerald is obliged to make use of his clever servant's talents to win the hand of Angelica, daughter of the Doctor. Since the Doctor's wife runs the affairs of the family, and since she readily approves of her daughter's choice, it seems perfectly clear that this bit of intrigue is only technically central and that Hauteroche was actually concentrating on the fun to be had from Crispin's trickery. Ravenscroft went even further in this direction, and in his most significant alteration, multiplied the *lazzi* until in the last act everything turns into the most abandoned horseplay.

In the original the big farce scene comes in the middle of the play, after a first act devoted chiefly to exposition. Crispin finds himself trapped in the Doctor's office and to avoid detection follows Beatrice's suggestion that he pose as the cadaver the Doctor has been eagerly awaiting. When she is conveniently unable to find the instruments for dissection, Crispin is saved from any serious consequences but not before he has undergone a harrowing period during which the surgeon discourses learnedly on poor Crispin's anatomy and points out the various cuts and slashes he proposes to make. A second farce scene taken from the French play has Crispin himself posing as physician and prescribing, chiefly cathartics, for various ridiculous ailments. Then Ravenscroft abandons his French original and, quite possibly using his knowledge of Italian *lazzi*, repeats the earlier dissection scene in even more laughable form. This time old Gerald poses as the cadaver while Crispin plays surgeon. Brandishing an assortment of axes and cleavers, the sham doctor matches the real doctor's discourse on anatomy, with several hilarious mistakes in nomenclature and with appropriately bloodthirsty gestures, until Old Gerald is almost reduced to a real corpse from fright. Eventually Crispin gets down to business but, with the first incision, ripping Old Gerald's waistcoat from top to bottom, the poor cadaver takes to his heels, knocking down the real doctor and his wife, who are just entering for the final scene of reconciliation.

This play met with great success from its very first appearance. A contemporary witness offers quite adequate testimony: "There has been for four or five days together at the play house in Lincolns Inn Fields acted a new farce translated out of the French by Mr. Monteux called the Shame Doctor or the Anatomist, with a great concert of music, representing the loves of Venus and Mars, well enough done and pleases the town extremely. The other house has no company at all, and unless a new play comes out on Saturday revives their reputation, they must break."[6]

The Anatomist went through successive stages of altera-

<hr />

[6] Leslie Hotson, *The Commonwealth and Restoration Stage* (Cambridge, Mass., 1928), p. 307.

tion after about 1704 when the era of afterpieces arrived. First it was divested of its musical context and later cut down from three acts to one. The last recorded change seems to have been made with Blakes, a minor comedian of Garrick's time, in mind when the Doctor was changed into a stage-Frenchman. Ravenscroft's farce continued for generations as a most popular afterpiece.

In the period of 1702-05, when the custom of adding an afterpiece was first adopted on the English stage, we have a whole series of more or less novel pieces in two or three acts. While it is perhaps unnecessary to describe more than an example or two at length, it might be of some interest to indicate the several patterns. The practice, followed in the first season or two after the turn of the century, of linking several scenes taken from full-length plays to make up a medley led easily to a similar means of providing afterpieces. One of these very first afterpieces is Cibber's *School-Boy* (1702), a two-act play adapted from his own *Womans Wit* (1696).

The *School-Boy* has little intrinsic interest; it consists of nothing more than the comic scenes of a weak play, itself derived from earlier works, notably Wycherley's *Plain Dealer* and Mountfort's *Greenwich Park*. Its real interest to us lies chiefly in the circumstances of its production. Though Doggett had created the original Mass Johnny or "school-boy" role, Cibber took over the part when the play became an afterpiece.[7] The *School-Boy* was a success from the beginning, even though it was, as Cibber says in his preface, "a kind of adjective, and seldom stood by it self,

[7] In the preface to *Womans Wit* Cibber tells how he had originally written the play without a "Mass Johnny" and then added the part for Doggett on the latter's returning to Drury Lane. But he himself took over the role when he took out the comic scenes for an afterpiece, as we see from the bill in *The Daily Courant* for 21 October 1702. He is also down for the part in a cast for about 1716-17 reproduced in the 1761 edition of the play. As late as 1743 a speaker in *Tyranny Triumphant* recalled Cibber as Master Johnny.

yet with what other play it was ever acted; it generally diverted the audience. . . ."[8]

A simpler means of filling the demand for farces was, as I have indicated, to borrow directly from the French, who had a wealth of plays of the requisite length. There was a revival of interest in Molière's farces, as shown by the appearance of two or three adaptations of his *médecin* plays as well as a reappearance of Otway's twenty-five year old *Cheats of Scapin*. One of the first afterpieces to appear has a special interest in that it represents an early use of *petite comédie* to complete an evening's bill. As early as January 1698 Vanbrugh had translated Dancourt's *Maison de campagne*, a one-act piece which Professor Lancaster quite accurately labels "comedy of manners," as *The Country House*.[9] This little play quickly earned a permanent niche in the repertory of afterpieces, to which several other non-farcical pieces were to be added in time.

Among the most popular French borrowings in the period before 1705 was a genuine farce already alluded to a number of times, Farquhar's *Stage-Coach*, taken from LaChapelle's *Carrosses d'Orléans*. In this play the stock intrigue of a young man's winning a girl whose father has promised her to a booby country squire is given some touch

---

[8] This remark indicates clearly enough that as late as 1707, when *The School-Boy* first appeared in print, the afterpiece was still something exotic on the English stage. Cibber goes on to explain why he bothers to publish this "adjective" play, the reason being one which I have anticipated in Chapter 3. After its early popularity, from about 1702 to 1705, *The School-Boy* had been dropped from the repertory, along with other afterpieces: ". . . by the separation of the players [not into two strong rival companies but, in Rich's long and involved machinations, into noncompetitive groups, one stressing plays the other music and dancing], it lay idle and could not any sooner divert the town again, than by putting it under the character it now stands in [in non-Cibberian English, by having it printed]."

[9] Hotson reproduces a record, p. 377, indicating a performance on 18 January 1698. Since it is listed alone, we may assume that the bill was filled up with music and dancing.

of novelty by having the principals thrown together in a provincial inn at which they have arrived by stage coach. By one of those helpful coincidences on which farce thrives even the parson who marries the couple at the end has just happened to arrive in the same coach as the young captain-suitor. The fun of the piece depends chiefly upon two characters, the booby squire, who belongs to the Latin tradition of the braggart, and the rough coachman, and upon one big night scene in which there is much scrambling about, pursuit and escape, and general head-knocking. At one point, reminiscent of the Italianate scenes of *The Emperor of the Moon*, a servant groping about in the dark mistakes the coachman's mouth for a keyhole and almost loses a finger.

Why such crude and elementary clowning should have been so well received may seem puzzling at this distance but it apparently was. In fact, *The Stage-Coach* long remained one of the most popular of afterpieces, though it did not, as Professor Lawrence thought, bring about of itself "the firm establishment of the principle of the afterpiece."[10]

Moving on into the interim decade betwen 1705 and 1715, when the initial momentum behind the farce afterpiece showed signs of becoming spent, we find only a mere handful of new farces. Of these, however, one or two are worth some attention. Aaron Hill's *Walking Statue, or, The Devil in the Wine Cellar* (1710) has considerable interest, both because it was to stay in the repertory of afterpieces and because it represents perhaps the last borrowing directly from the *commedia dell'arte* before the Italian influence was channeled in the direction of the pantomime. Of the three main episodes in the play one seems quite domestic, another seems pretty certainly to have come from the Italians, the third may or may not have been im-

[10] See above, p. 81, for Lawrence's conjecture.

ported. The whole piece adds up to a loud and lively farce, a wholly stylized play in which the supposedly central intrigue of a contest between a pair of lovers and a testy father is shoved into the background and attention is focused upon a series of *burle*.

In the first episode, the one which can safely be claimed as English, the young hero's servant, Toby, disguises as an "Exchange girl" and attempts to circumvent old Sir Timothy Tangle in order to deliver his master's letter to Leonora. Toby falls considerably short of being a clever valet, however, and, taking fright when Sir Timothy thrusts a blunderbuss in his face, neglects to disguise his voice. The attempt is easily foiled and the whole scene winds up in a series of beatings as the irate father lays about him with vigor. Obviously the whole point of the scene rests in the ridiculous disguise, the fright, the beatings.

The second episode is the foreign one and must, from its central position and from its providing the main title of the play, have been designed as the big attraction. Again Toby disguises, this time as a Jew, and delivers a statue which—by one of those convenient accidents we do not question in farce—Sir Timothy has recently ordered. The statue is of course false too. Corporal Cuttum poses as the man of stone. What follows is a traditional Italianate *lazzo* of "the clock-work statue," later to provide one of the marvels in the first sensation in pantomime, *Harlequin Doctor Faustus*.[11] Poor Toby once more proves insuffi-

---

[11] The scenario printed in Thurmond's *Three Entertainments* in 1727 gives some details on the operation of the statue, which seems to have been somewhat more of a showpiece than a mere farcical device. Years later, however, we find the two definitely tied together. In the MS transcript made by J. P. Kemble from Dublin papers and now preserved in the Harvard Theatre Collection we get this interesting item for 18 March 1751: "Benefit of Mr. Cibber The Provoked Wife. . . . To which will be added a dramatic petite piece of two short acts (taken from La Comedie Italienne) called the Statue or the Devil in the Wine Cellar—with alterations. The part of Corporal Cuttum by Mr. Cibber—in which character will be repre-

ciently clever to fool suspicious Sir Timothy and the latter, not having his blunderbuss handy, attempts to snatch a leg off the statue with which to brain him. The statue kicks Sir Timothy sprawling but neglects to resume the exact posture he had been in so that the old man's suspicions are aroused. While he is searching for his spectacles, Cuttum resumes the correct position, to Sir Timothy's utter bewilderment. Eventually the scene must end with the statue in flight.

The source of the third episode is uncertain. It could be from a foreign play but is almost as likely to derive from a droll background. Again Toby is near the center of things but this time he does the frightening. Seeking refuge after his last defeat, he hides in a sort of well or wine cellar, from which he thrusts out his face, now disguised in a devil mask. This time even Sir Timothy, who has come to chide and support his timid servants, takes fright and flees. During all this noisy business the young lovers manage to slip off and marry—as if they might not have done so previously.

The episode of the well may have been suggested by an Italian farce; the one involving the statue almost certainly was. Though I have been unable to discover such a play antedating Hill's, I assume that one produced by the Italian comedians who visited London in 1726 and published in an English version at that time had been in the commedia dell'arte repertory previously. The English title of the play is *The Most Knowing, Least Understanding: or, Harlequin's Metamorphosis.* A full length piece in five acts, it suggests some of the episodes in the seventeenth-century *Empéreur de la lune*[12] but is much closer to Hill's play.

---

sented the Clockwork Statue, in the manner it was originally perform'd by him, upwards of fourscore nights, in the first run of the pantomime called Doctor Faustus in Drury-Lane."

[12] In the scenario, which I have consulted at the Huntington Library, there is a Pantalone mad over astrology and some other items

The statue, nothing more than Harlequin passing as a "Blackamoor," appears twice. In Act II it is brought in and laid on the floor, in which position it manages to eat a "bisket" and drink some wine. In Act IV it is placed on a pedestal and there plays several of the tricks Cuttum does, at one point kicking Pantalone head over heels. There is little more than a suggestion of the wine cellar in Act V. Harlequin, attempting to send a message up to the young ladies locked in a tower, is fired upon by Pantalone's watchman and drops into a well. From his place of concealment he calls out to the young lovers and "tells them of a hole that corresponds with Pantalone's cellar, advises them to come to him." If, as I suspect he did, Hill had seen this or a similar piece he may well have developed it into the sequence we have in his farce.

An episode involving a well appears in a better known afterpiece which made its appearance at Drury Lane two seasons later. Beyond the slight parallel, however, *Hob: or, The Country Wake* is at opposite poles from *The Walking Statue,* for it is thoroughly English and much less farcical. Thomas Doggett made but one venture into writing plays when, back in 1696, he composed a mixture of rough, realistic comedy and farce called *The Country Wake. Hob* is, with some minor alterations, merely a one-act version of scenes from the earlier play; and, though it has long been ascribed to Colley Cibber, there seems to be no good reason for taking it away from Doggett, who played Hob with brilliant success in both versions.

Though there is farce here, *Hob* is far from being mere farce. Severe cutting has reduced the weight of the central plot, which is a traditional but not altogether stereotyped love story, but it has not spoiled the portrait of the doughty English servant, whose reliance on the law and, when that

suggesting *The Emperor of the Moon,* such as the actors' posing as signs in the zodiac.

threatens to fail him, on his cudgel, gives him an air quite different from that of the clever or stupid servant of the usual run of farces. There are two or three scenes which deal largely in boisterous physical comedy if not in downright slapstick. In the first, Hob attempts to deliver a letter at night, is caught, beaten, and thrown into the well. His mother and father search for him until the former, not aware that Hob is in the well, attempts to draw water, takes fright on drawing up her own son, and gives the lad another ducking. In the final scene Hob, whose father has rescued him from the well, engages in cudgel-play with Sir Thomas Testy and by lustily beating his opponent gains a measure of revenge as well as providing the young lovers an opportunity to escape. When at the very end Sir Thomas too retains his British stubbornness and, departing from the conventional ending, refuses to be reconciled, Friendly's man Dick[13] remarks, "Won't you? Why then, Mr. Pack give out the play, and Mr. Newman let down the curtain."

In the period 1715-24, the period, that is, between the revival of theatrical competition and the rise of pantomime with its devastating effect upon farce, farces become too numerous to be represented adequately by a few models. Two or three trends can be indicated. For one thing, there is a striking falling off in foreign borrowing. One full-length play with some farce, Molloy's *Perplex'd Couple* (1715), taken from Molière, and one short farce afterpiece, *The Lucky Prodigal* (1715), from Regnard's *Retour imprévu*, represent the chief importations of the period. Gay and his collaborators were accused of having lifted the ill-fated *Three Hours after Marriage* (1717) from Gherardi's *Théâtre Italien*, though there is little to support the charge. The majority of the numerous farces in the period are either more or less original pieces thrown together hurriedly by

[13] One of the more interesting items in the one-act revision is the addition of this part for "Dicky" Norris, who had not appeared on the scene in London when the original *Country-Wake* was written.

some of Rich's actor-playwrights or plays drawn from the older English repertory.

Before taking up a few plays representing the latter types it might be well to dispose of the plays of foreign extraction mentioned above. The first two we may safely ignore for the present. Molloy adds nothing to the story of domesticating Molière. And the discussion of *Le Retour imprévu* may well be put off till we need to take it up in connection with Fielding's much more skilful and successful adaptation in 1734. *Three Hours after Marriage*, for which Gay seems to have been chiefly responsible but in which Pope and Arbuthnot shared, is hardly to be listed as a representative farce. As it was not an afterpiece, it did not, apparently, fill a need; at any rate, it did not find a home in the English theatre. In fact its chief interest, in addition to the fame of its authors, lies rather in its being so different from the usual farce-comedy fare, for here we have an attempt to do on the London stage what the Italians had more and more come to in Paris: namely, to join extravagant farce with bold satire. As I have suggested, they were accused of having pilfered the *Théâtre Italien* for the material for their play though one accuser gets himself involved in some contradictions and indicates fairly clearly that he has no real basis for his charge.[14] Yet the charge is not so far wide of the mark. It seems that Gay and his confederates, doubtless familiar with the materials in the Gherardi collection, borrowed something more basic: the plan of hiding some sharp personal satire behind a screen of apparent buffoonery. Thus their imitation of the Italians led them, not to the empty entertainment which the

[14] Nicoll, *History*, p. 144, n. 1, suggests that "the basis of this play itself seems borrowed from a farce contained in the collection called *Le Théâtre Italien*." If this is a reference to Regnard and Durfresny's *Momies d'Egypte*, as I take it to be, it is misleading. Beyond the one incident of a man's posing as a mummy there is virtually no resemblance.

pantomime too often represented, but to something very much like burlesque.

To a modern reader *Three Hours* seems to consist of the wildest clowning. Dr. Fossile has just married a young sophisticate, Mrs. Townly, only to discover that heroic efforts will be necessary to prevent his being cuckolded by two resourceful rivals, Plotwell and Underplot. This pair assumes various disguises, first as foreign doctor and patient, later and more fantastically as mummy and crocodile. Plotwell almost gets past the vigilant doctor by being brought in in a chest but Underplot betrays him. Fossile himself resorts to various disguises in his counterplotting. Meanwhile other doctors, Possum and Nautilus, appear as well as an apothecary, Ptisan. These carry on a consultation à la Molière and engage in learned disputes over the curios mentioned above. A female poet, Phoebe Clinket, manages to have a tragedy rehearsed, providing occasion for some jeering at poetasters and poor actors.

Beneath all this, as Gay's contemporaries could be counted on to recognize, was a good bit of rough satire, personal and general. From the keys published in connection with the play and from the remarks of contemporaries we can gather something of the nature of the satire and identify some of the targets. Fossile is Dr. Woodward. Mrs. Townly is not, however, Mrs. Woodward; according to a later key, "Another prominent physician's wife sat for that picture." Phoebe Clinket, the female poetaster, is the Countess of Wincheslea.[15] The hypochondriac Countess of Hippokekoana is the Duchess of Monmouth. In short, Gay and his friends were producing half farce, half burlesque with the obvious intent of ridiculing some public

[15] Though these identifications have stood for generations, one or two of them have been vigorously questioned in recent years. See the article on this play by George Sherburn, "The Fortunes and Misfortunes of *Three Hours after Marriage*," *Modern Philology*, XXIV (1926-27), 91-109.

figures, while giving Johnson, Pinkethman, Norris, and Cibber a chance to evoke some hilarious laughter. The same purpose seems to have motivated Louis XIV's Italian troupe, with the possible difference that their satire was likely to be more general. It was, however, an attack or the suspicion of an attack on Madame de Maintenon that caused their eviction from Paris in 1697.

The majority of farces in this decade were not new borrowings from abroad. Those that were not actually original were based upon earlier English plays. Of these, two items—really three but two of them are close enough to be treated together—will serve to represent the type: Christopher Bullock's *Woman's Revenge* (1715) and the two *Cobler of Preston* afterpieces of 1716, one by Bullock, the other by Charles Johnson.

Woman's Revenge is a transition piece. Derived from Mrs. Behn's *Revenge*, which was based upon Marston's *Dutch Courtezan*, it represents a somewhat anachronistic combination of melodrama and farce. On the other hand it has reduced the Marston plots to three acts and in doing so stressed the farce turns. The next stage, represented by three or four brief pieces in quick succession, shows the farce materials on their own.[16]

Ignoring the serious plot—once the main item of interest but rapidly losing its importance in the long series of adaptations—we may examine briefly the highly durable farce episodes. Of these there are three principal ones, the first two and the beginning of the third all crowding into the middle act of Marston's play. The first is the ageless "shaving" trick, a device well known to droll-performers. Vizard, the clever rogue of the play, borrows shaving equipment

---

[16] For details on the long and involved history of these farce materials see Hughes and Scouten, "Some Theatrical Adaptations of a Picaresque Tale," University of Texas *Studies in English*, 1945-46, pp. 98-114; Hughes, "Trick upon Trick; or, Methodism Display'd," *ibid.*, 1950, pp. 151-161.

from a naïve barber's boy and goes to shave his enemy Mixum, vintner and cheat. What he actually does is to lather the unsuspecting vintner so vigorously that he is blinded and, keeping him beguiled with a series of tall tales, slips out with Mixum's purse. A second episode, equally suggestive of such folk-types as the droll or the *fabliau*, is a bit more involved. Again the vintner is the victim but this time his wife is the innocent accessory. Vizard talks her out of a silver punchbowl in trade for a salmon and then returns to cap the trick by talking the poor woman out of the salmon. The final episode is even more complex, involving a change of scene. Vizard robs a fiddler of his cloak, only to be caught by his pursuing enemy, who just manages to snatch off the newly acquired garment when the watch arrives with the fiddler-plaintiff and arrests him. This sequence ends in jail, where Vizard comes as a parson to console the condemned vintner and to pick his pocket, thus recovering the deed to his own estate of which Mixum had originally cheated him. This being merely a farce, everyone winds up reconciled. A few years later these farcical episodes, freed from the matrix of the serious love and revenge plot, became highly popular both in the provinces and, as a droll, at the fairs.

In his version of *The Cobler of Preston* Bullock went back once more to the Elizabethans, this time to a greater dramatist than Marston, for the latter play is based upon the induction to Shakespeare's *Taming of the Shrew*. Before treating Bullock's play we must link with it a rival *Cobler of Preston*, written for the Drury Lane company by Charles Johnson. It would require too great a digression to outline the entire story of this minor skirmish in the continuous warfare between the two patent companies. In brief what happened was that word got out of Johnson's preparing an afterpiece based on the induction to Shakespeare's farce-comedy and of Johnson's plan to name his play *The Cobler of Preston*, thus linking his cobbler-hero—transformed from Shakespeare's tinker—with the recent Jacobite rebellion. Bullock hastily got up a similar play, stole Johnson's title, and introduced his piece at Lincoln's Inn Fields before his rivals knew what was happening. As a result we have not one but two cobbler plays to deal with.

Of the two plays Bullock's is somewhat the superior. Staying fairly close to Shakespeare—many lines echo the original—he plunges into the first episode of carting home a drunkard and then treating him in rough fashion. Then follows the reawakening, which may be original but is more likely a copy of Sancho's sitting in judgment in *Don Quixote*. "The one-eyed Cobler of Preston"—Bullock obviously wrote the part for his friend and fellow-actor Spiller—has two squabbling women brought before him: the alewife, Dame Hacket, and his own consort, Dorcas Guzzle—again Bullock is aiming at a colleague; Griffin, who had acted the bawd Mother Griffin in *Woman's Revenge*, played Dorcas. Toby soon grows impatient with the litigants when they profess to recognize him as a mere drunken cobbler and prescribes a sound whipping and ducking. After one or two more cases of rough but shrewd justice, Toby again succumbs to liquor and is carried home, only to be pounced upon by the bedraggled women. The farce ends in the usual brawl and reconciliation.

Johnson, too, starts with Shakespeare but allows himself to wander from his source. For one thing, he attempts the standard farce device of doubling by having the lord's drunken butler sent home to the cobbler's house, possibly borrowing from Jevon's *Devil of a Wife*. Having got so far, he seems to have forgotten the butler and nothing comes of the episode. His greatest error comes from another attempt at repetition, this one prompted by his political bias. In order to satirize the Jacobites he has Kit carried home and then returned to the manor house in order to have him taught a lesson in politics. As Genest long ago pointed out, this last episode is both anticlimactic and implausible, since a sober cobbler would scarcely be so easily deluded as a drunken one.

Whatever the respective merits of the rival pieces it is interesting to note that the eighteenth century was still turning back to the older drama for successful farce materials. Yet, in spite of the evidence of the last three plays, it must be admitted that by no means all of the farces in this period are traceable to specific forerunners. Many of them can best be described as farce-players' farces, plays made up by stringing a number of tested *lazzi* on a thin and worn thread of plot. Among a few examples, we may consider the play linked with the Bullock *Cobler of Preston*. This farce, also by the busy actor and writer Christopher Bullock, is entitled *The Adventures of Half an Hour*, candid admission that it is nothing more than some scenes designed to fill up the requisite half-hour devoted to afterpieces. *The Adventures* is no more than a series of disguises, pursuits, and beatings in which a jealous and cowardly military officer is abused by his wife and her gallant. Or, for two other examples of pieces formed by linking farce episodes together, we may take *Love in a Wood* (1714), which is the merest—and the noisiest—slapstick, or *Love in a Sack* (1715), the title of which is adequately descriptive.

Perhaps the best representative of this type of farce is one which by its long career shows clearly the kind of reception such pieces were sometimes accorded. Henry Carey is perhaps best remembered, when he is remembered at all, for "Sally in Our Alley," but in his own day he was thought of primarily as the composer of burlesques—*The Tragedy of Chrononhotonthologos* and *The Dragon of Wantley* were the two best received—and of farces. His first play was a farce, *The Contrivances* (1715). In spite of its long success *The Contrivances* is hardly more of a play than the less successful pieces just mentioned above. As the title suggests, it is a mere intrigue farce. A highly conventional plot involving the usual penniless but gallant young man and his attempts—inevitably successful—to win a willing young lady from the hands of a less than willing father, this brief farce must have depended upon lively turns to keep afloat so long. Since I have already described the play in an earlier chapter, I need not devote much time to analysis here. There are two "contrivances," the first ineffectual and the second successful. The earlier episode involves a disguise scene, the gallant posing as a green country girl and his servant acting the loutish brother. The second is of the noisier sort, old Argus, the testy father, being assaulted and tied up by his enemy's allies and rescued by a watch very much in the tradition of Dogberry and Verges. This quite English and not strikingly original concoction was, in 1729, to undergo the kind of revision which most plays of the sort saw after the success of *The Beggar's Opera*: it was revised by having a dozen songs to familiar tunes added. In this state it kept the stage for years.

With the mention of the ballad farce[17] we are carried

[17] Gagey says, *Ballad Opera* (New York, 1937), p. 101, "The eighteenth century made a broad and rather careless distinction between pieces of three acts, which were called ballad operas, and pieces of one or two acts, which were labelled ballad farces." An examination of a run of ballad-opera title pages reveals no such distinction. About all that can be safely maintained is that when, on occasion, a piece is called ballad farce, it is likely to be shorter than three acts. There was a tendency on the part of a few commentators to look upon all ballad operas as farces. In *The Players, a Satyr* (1733), sometimes attributed to Edward Phillips, we get this kind of comment:

Who wonders now, that Harlequin's advance,
And drama falls, transfixt with song, and dance?
Rank ignorance usurps the place of wit:
Shakespear, and Ben to abject farce submit;
Farce void of sense, imperfect in its sound,
Felonious phrase, in jingling fetters bound.

In the same year, in *The Stage Mutineers*, appears the phrase, in an inventory of plays, "six old comedies farcify'd with songs," the only instance I recall in the period, by the way, of the use of *farce* in its original and literal sense.

forward some fifteen years, bridging the decade of the 1720's when pantomime triumphed and things looked very dark for the farce afterpiece, to the period when theatrical enterprise flourished and farce made its remarkable recovery. In this period the difficulty of choosing a few representative pieces from the many offered becomes greater than ever. If, however, we impose as a criterion the requirement of success in the theatre the task is appreciably lightened. That is, if we eliminate those plays which did not gain a secure position in the repertory, we narrow down the list to where it is manageable. For, as I have previously indicated, one of the remarkable features of the eighteenth-century repertory is the tendency to present a few afterpieces over and over even where a great variety of main plays is offered.

If, then, we take the criterion of success as paramount, our choice of plays to represent the booming thirties is made easy. We might, in fact, narrow down to one play, since no other farce could possibly match the success of *The Devil to Pay* (1731). Like *Hob, The School-Boy,* and a number of other afterpieces, *The Devil to Pay* was taken from an earlier and longer piece, the actor Jevon's *Devil of a Wife.* The earlier version had been highly successful on the stage and had gone through at least three editions in the fifteen years between its first appearance and the close of the century. The adaptation proved even more successful, after a rather slow start. As a three-act ballad opera it had only modest success in the summer of 1731, but on being reduced still further to one act and offered as an afterpiece it began a truly remarkable career. It was still being performed a century later; meanwhile it had gone through more than forty editions and had been adapted into French and German. As the quotation at the head of the chapter referring to the cobbler's wife in this play suggests, the play came to stand almost as a symbol of the farce afterpiece.[18]

[18] Horace Walpole confirms this suggestion that *The Devil to Pay* came to be looked upon as representative when, in a letter to

It is not easy to assess the particular qualities which made *The Devil to Pay* so successful. Certainly it is not abandoned slapstick, though it has its share of noisy beatings. Then, too, the basic idea of the transformation, which the spectator is asked to accept as real, goes "beyond nature" too far for mere comedy, if I may conveniently adopt the eighteenth-century point of view. Fundamentally, one may suppose, the piece depends upon its rapid movement, upon the amusing contrast in situation and character the sudden transformation affords, and upon that age-old requirement, the happy ending.

The story of *The Devil to Pay* is about the termagant wife of a kind-hearted gentleman, Sir John Loverule, and her equally meek and lovable foil, the "innocent country girl" wife of a forthright cobbler, Zekel Jobson, who has one cure for all domestic difficulties, a stout leather strap. A magician passing through is provoked by Nell's kindness and Jobson's surliness into exchanging the positions and the persons—though not the personalities—of Lady Loverule and Nell, with amusing results. Nell first baffles and then overwhelms with her instinctive kindness her new servants, who have been used to quite different treatment. Lady Loverule storms about in a rage over her new surroundings but is no match for Jobson's strap. A few encounters with this mighty equalizer and she is ready to return to the hall, a much chastened woman. At the end Nell too is eager for her old home, for she has found her new surroundings a trifle heady. Even Jobson is sufficiently impressed by the realization of his fortune in having so sweet-tempered a wife that he hangs up his strap for good.

West dated from Paris 21 April 1739 he writes, "Tomorrow we go to the *Cid*. They have no farces, but *petites pièces* like our *Devil to Pay*." His distinction of genres is equally interesting though not altogether conventional. The French translator who included it, as *Le Diable a quatre*, in *Choix de petites pièces du théâtre anglois* in 1756 refers to the play as *"une de ces pièces burlesques que les anglois appelent farces."*

Whether or not this play can be forced into the limits set here for farce, it is unquestionably a fresh and clever production. It was, moreover, fortunate in the cast it drew on its first performance at Drury Lane as an afterpiece. Harper as Jobson made a name for himself for the rest of his acting career. Years later Tom Davies, on seeing Harper in *Henry VIII* found it impossible to get Jobson out of his head.[19] Kitty Raftor—she had not then become Mrs. Clive— can be said to have launched Nell on her career; and with equal justice Nell can be said to have launched Kitty. John Mottley, who was involved in the revision of the play and therefore in a position to observe, said, "Mrs. Clive owes great obligations to this farce, for it was her playing the part of Nell in *The Devil to Pay*, that made her first taken notice of to any purpose, and for that, if I am not mistaken, the little salary she then had was doubled."[20]

The reputation Mrs. Clive attained by her performance of Nell was further enhanced in parts written with her specifically in mind by one of her leading admirers, Henry Fielding. As I have shown in the discussion of actors in Chapter 6, Fielding was not at all hesitant about publicly acknowledging his esteem for this actress and his obligations to her, especially in connection with his *Mock Doctor* and *Intriguing Chambermaid*.

Before examining these plays, I need to pause for a moment to appraise Fielding's position in this genre. The term "Fielding's farces" appears so frequently that an ill-informed reader may get the impression that the author of *Tom Jones* made no weightier contribution to the theatre than a few plays of the type Christopher Bullock is credited with. Actually the phrase is as often misleading as not, since what is commonly meant is his work in burlesque form: *Tom Thumb*, *Pasquin*, and the rest. On the other hand, Fielding did contribute farces to the repertory, some

---

[19] *Dramatic Miscellanies* (London, 1785), I, 357.
[20] Whincop, p. 200.

of the best and the most popular. In addition to the two I have mentioned there are the "Lucy" plays, *An Old Man Taught Wisdom* (1735) and its sequel *Miss Lucy in Town* (1742), in which Fielding had a share only; *The Letter-Writers* (1731), the first of his actual farces; and *The Lottery* (1732), which is on the border between farce and *petite comédie*.

Mention of *petite comédie* brings up a problem which would take us too far afield here but which has some real significance in this last span of our whole period, for several writers, notably Fielding and Garrick, at one time or another expressed a wish to raise the level of farce. In the prologue to *The Lottery* Fielding indicates this desire when he says:

> As tragedy prescribes to passion rules,
> So comedy delights to punish fools;
> And while at nobler game she boldly flies,
> Farce challenges the vulgar as her prize.

The attempt to raise the level of farce to that of comedy, which in our judgment would be the effect here, is always perilous to the genre. The hazard, to be sure, is only a technical one, for what is lost by the one form is gained by an admittedly higher one. Yet a real danger, in the theatre, remains. Since the span of attention of a given audience is limited, the farce which proves to be more subtle and thought-provoking than farce is supposed to be runs a grave risk of not being accepted at all.

The two most successful of Fielding's farces, to which I now return, ran little risk of failure at the start, for the formula he applied in preparing both of them was a well tried one. The case of *The Mock Doctor* is especially revealing. Fielding's burlesque *Covent Garden Tragedy* had been written as an afterpiece to his *Old Debauchees* in June 1732. The latter play was just scandalous enough to assure success, especially since the scandal involved a French Jesuit, but *The Covent Garden Tragedy* proved too strong for the tastes of the time, and Fielding quickly replaced it with a succession of tested afterpieces, chiefly *The Devil to Pay*, and went about preparing a new farce. From some remarks he makes in the preface to *The Mock Doctor* we gather that he knew what he was about and that he was in Molière's debt for more than the plot of his farce. When, according to Fielding, the great French dramatist brought out his most profound play, *Le Misanthrope*, he was similarly embarrassed by its cool reception. "That excellent play was of too grave a kind to hit the genius of the French nation; on which account the author in a very few days, produced this farce [*Médecin malgré lui*]; which being added to his *Misanthrope*, gave it one of the greatest runs that any play ever met with on that stage."[21]

Fielding's play, by no means the first adaptation of *Médecin malgré lui*, stays fairly close to its original. Yet *The Mock Doctor* is not a mere translation. The process of cutting down Molière's three acts to one is of no significance since both plays are closely similar in length and structure. Still there are cuts and additions. In general, Fielding cuts out much of the elaborate stage business which in the French play gives us so fascinating a picture of the great playwright-farceur in action. Also omitted are several of the passages of staccato dialogue in which Molière builds up to violent physical action and some, though by no means all, of the satire on the medical profession. Fielding substitutes other materials to fill in the gaps left by these cuts: songs set to ballad tunes to replace the passages in dialogue; a brief but pointed attack on a particular physician, the notorious Misaubin, to whom the play is mockingly dedicated. The most significant change is to add new weight to the part of the woodcutter-physician's wife, for Fielding was

[21] Modern scholarship has dismissed as inaccurate this long-popular story of how Molière's popular farce kept his *Misanthrope* from sinking.

deliberately shaping the role to exploit once more the talents in song and comedy of the much admired Kitty Clive. With all the changes, Fielding still left Molière's play what it had been, a brief and lively farce, by no means devoid of character interest or sharp comment but having also a generous quantity of the disguises, the beatings, the vigorous physical clowning of traditional farce.

The changes made in *The Mock Doctor* for the benefit of Mrs. Clive are a mere nothing compared to those in the next farce by Fielding, *The Intriguing Chambermaid* (1734). Not only did he dedicate the piece in almost extravagant terms to the rising young star; he went a considerable step further. Again a French farce provides a basis, Regnard's *Retour imprévu*, a play already drawn on, without much success in the theatre, for the anonymous *Lucky Prodigal* (1715). Regnard's story, itself taken from Plautus, is built around the clever valet Merlin, who with Crispin had created a tradition in the French theatre. So much does Merlin dominate the play that his master and the other supposed principals fall under his shadow. To adapt the French piece to his needs Fielding was obliged to perform a major operation; either he must alter the play considerably to provide a new female-servant role for his favorite Mrs. Clive or he must make an even more radical change by replacing the valet with a soubrette. The second alternative proved the more attractive, and, in spite of the obvious difficulties, he made the shift. The venture proved so successful that *The Intriguing Chambermaid*, with the help of Kitty Clive's brilliant acting and fine voice, soon became a part of the permanent farce repertory.

Like its source, Fielding's play is a fast-paced intrigue farce, doubtless amusing, even charming, in performance but with little of the interest in character revelation or satirical comment that marks *The Mock Doctor*. As a sketch of the plot reveals, the whole play turns upon the glibness and the resourcefulness of the clever servant. A wealthy merchant unexpectedly returns from abroad and is on the point of discovering that the son with whom the care of his house and affairs was left has turned prodigal. Most of the movables have been pawned and the house is besieged by creditors. Meanwhile the son has also been trying vainly to win the consent of a wealthy widow in the neighborhood to marry her niece. Now the valet-turned-soubrette resorts to a whole series of clever lies to prevent the father's discovering the truth: the money a creditor asks for has been invested in the widow's house, now that she is ruined and has lost her mind; his own house must be exorcized of its ghosts before he can enter—the sounds of revelry within are readily translated into demoniacal laughter. With the appearance of the widow, the climax in beguilement is reached and Lettice's ingenuity is taxed to the utmost. Having already persuaded the merchant of the widow's insanity, she has no great difficulty in convincing the widow that the merchant has had a trifle too much of the tropical sun. The real problem is to keep either from entering the house. This she does for an extended period but the scene must inevitably come to an end when the truth comes out. When she sees that all is lost, Lettice withdraws with, "I have defended my pass as long as I can; and now I think it is no cowardice to steal off." With her disappearance most of the interest in the play evaporates, and we are hurried on to a weakly motivated happy ending. In the actual performances during the first run at Drury Lane the effect of Kitty Clive's withdrawal was perhaps largely offset by her returning to speak the clever prologue at the expense of Italian opera.

Though much of the farce of the 1730's and 1740's was running to intrigue and to French borrowings, English farce writers never made anything resembling a complete break with the native traditions of exaggerated character and gross physical action. Even where they borrowed a framework of intrigue from abroad they managed to assimilate their materials to such an extent that sometimes only an accident or an unusual amount of candor on the borrower's part will reveal the indebtedness. Two farces of these last two decades, one highly popular in London, the other far better known in Dublin, will illustrate.

In the summer of 1735 Henry Carey—by this time well known for a successful farce and a popular burlesque, somewhat less acclaimed for his more serious musical drama— produced his *Honest Yorkshireman*, an amusing work of thoroughly English flavor not too far above the level of such drolls as *The Generous Free-Mason*. The Yorkshireman of the title is Squire Sapscull, an incredibly oafish country squire who, with his equally loutish servant Blunder, has come up to London to marry the fair Arbella. Arbella prefers Gaylove, a young lawyer, but her Uncle Muckworm has ignored her wishes and promised her to the Yorkshire knight. Sapscull and Blunder are given some opportunity to show off their rusticity—admiring the sights of London, lamenting in speech and song the Lord Mayor's "crying down" of Bartholomew Fair—before they are descended upon by Gaylove and his clever servant, Slango. They are tricked out of their credentials and dressed up like apish fops. Eventually Sapscull is married off to Slango disguised as Arbella. All of this not very original horseplay is doubtless aided by the twenty songs Carey worked into his play.

Now while *The Honest Yorkshireman* is a thoroughly English play, it is clearly parallel with a farce by Molière which had been borrowed and reborrowed perhaps as often as any other French play, *Monsieur Pourceaugnac*. The closeness of the parallel can be demonstrated by an examination of the second piece I have mentioned, Thomas Sheridan's *Brave Irishman*, which is more obviously based on Molière's play. *The Brave Irishman* made its London debut as an afterpiece to *Hamlet* on 31 January 1746 at the Wells in Lemon Street, Goodman's Fields, but it had appeared ten years earlier in Dublin and seems to have already been well established in that city. It is an amusing little farce, no less interesting because it bears the imprint of at least four different national influences. It is based chiefly on Molière and on the one play by Molière, *Pourceaugnac,* which contains as much material taken directly from the Italian comedians as any other he ever wrote. In addition, there is a comic bit from Shakespeare and much of Irish nationalistic pride. It was in order to provide for this last element that Sheridan found it necessary to depart so far from his source. Hence an even more striking change takes place in the play, and stage-conventions of several generations' standing are flaunted. A brief résumé of the main scenes of the play will bring all of this out. At the beginning we have the standard situation: Lucy, daughter of old merchant Trader, loves Cheatwell, a penniless scamp, but must marry a provincial booby—corresponding to Pourceaugnac—the Irish Captain O'Blunder. O'Blunder arrives in London and acts the part of the uncouth outsider, while Cheatwell and his man Sconce put him through the same regimen Molière's booby is subjected to, including the ordeal in the madhouse so obviously borrowed from the *commedia dell'arte.* By the end of the play, however, the booby has been revealed as a magnanimous as well as brave Irishman, Cheatwell is shown up as a graceless rascal, and O'Blunder rather than Cheatwell wins the girl. The Shakespearean episode is quite brief, consisting of a scene, obviously based on *Henry V,* in which the Captain forces a cringing Frenchman to eat a potato, the national vegetable at which the foreigner has been jeering. It is small wonder that this farce had a warmer reception in Dublin than in London.

With the last play we are already in the closing decade of our period. By this time the farce afterpiece had clearly won its place in the theatrical bill and the farce repertory had settled down more and more to the repeated use of comparatively few pieces.[22] This does not mean that farce was entirely confined to the afterpiece though, with the exception of an occasional revival of a longer play with farce scenes, the trend was very much in that direction. Nor does it mean that no new farces were tried or that all new afterpieces were necessarily and consistently farcical. The success of such sentimental and didactic pieces as those written by Dodsley in the late 1730's, especially *The King and The Miller of Mansfield* (1737) and its sequel, encouraged new attempts in the same manner.

The first dramatic offering by David Garrick was of the didactic and mildly satirical kind. Though *Lethe, or Esop in the Shades,* which appeared two seasons before the actor's debut on the stage, was commonly called farce and is so labelled in Nicoll's handlist, it does not fall within the limits set here. As the subtitle clearly indicates, it belongs with those Lucianic pieces which had long been popular in English literature both on and off the stage. And, while it did not enjoy so great a popularity as some of Garrick's more farcical afterpieces it did very well for years.

But, as has just been suggested, Garrick did compose farces, two of the most popular ones appearing before midcentury. Thus he added to the standing of farce in still another way, just as he had already lent his prestige as an actor and was very soon to add that of manager. Both of Garrick's farces, *The Lying Valet* (1741) and *Miss in Her Teens* (1747), have significance enough to warrant detailed examination. Both indicate a trend toward a balance of intrigue and character, with possibly a greater emphasis on fast action and clever lines than on out-and-out slapstick. Both are adaptations of French intrigue-farces so that

[22] Professor Odell points out that the New York theatre in the eighteenth century not only borrowed its repertory of afterpieces from London but followed the practice of giving the same pieces over and over as well. *Annals of the New York Stage* (New York, 1927), I, 60.

Garrick tips the scales away from the native drama, though perhaps not seriously so.

The day after Garrick's sensational debut in *Richard III* at Goodman's Fields he wrote his brother Peter a letter telling of his success and added this interesting bit of news: "I have a farce (ye Lying Valet) coming out at Drury Lane." Evidently he had not gone quite so far as his note suggests in completing arrangements with Fleetwood and was able to retrieve the farce before the rival theatre could present it, for *The Lying Valet* made its bow at Goodman's Fields 30 November 1741, the author playing Sharp in his own play after having acted Chamont in the main piece, Otway's *Orphan*.

The Lying Valet is not actually a new play or even new to the English stage. In 1697 Motteux had adapted Haute-roche's *Souper mal apprêté* as the second act of his *Novelty*. Garrick's version is, however, much superior to Motteux's and deserved the vastly superior success it achieved. Like Fielding's *Intriguing Chambermaid* or the older *Anatomist* or the French valet-farce in general, it places the burden of the action on the servants of the play rather than on their masters. In doing so it follows a general direction English comedy had been moving in since at least the first appearance of *The Conscious Lovers* (1722). As Steele had indicated in both play and preface, the more genteel members of the cast of *The Conscious Lovers* were to concern themselves with "a joy too exquisite for laughter," leaving the less refined business of getting laughs more and more to the servants. I do not mean to suggest here that Gayless and Melissa in Garrick's farce indulge in heroics and sentiment. But they do retire somewhat into the background and permit the clever man and maid servants to carry on the laughable business of the farce.

The first of the two acts[23] composing this lively little play

[23] Though the two-act form, which was first used by Cibber in *The School-Boy* (1702), had some currency before 1740, after-

is taken over almost entirely by the servants, Sharp, the clever lying valet, Kitty Pry, the no less clever and very pert maid.[24] Their master and mistress provide the motivation but Sharp and Kitty are largely responsible for the action and the dialogue. The story—like that of the Regnard-Fielding play discussed above, obviously a Plautian one—involves the problems of a penniless gallant who wishes to hide the state of his finances from the wealthy young lady of his choice until after their marriage. Melissa is no Lydia Languish but she is too much in love with Gayless to believe him capable of deceit. Kitty is far wiser in men's ways and not at all blinded by love. She proves more than a match for the inventive Sharp and maneuvers him and Gayless into inviting the young ladies to a party which they have neither the intention nor the means of giving. In the second act Melissa abandons some of her love-beguiled manner and in a breeches part more than equals her servant in clever intrigue. Poor Sharp finds that every ingenious lie he tells only draws him in deeper and his master with him. At last, when the pair have been subjected to numerous indignities, Melissa relents. Now Garrick, who had fortunately been able to dispense with the usual out-worn testy father-in-law who opposes the match, is obliged to bring in a forgiving father, through a letter restoring Gayless to grace and

---

pieces were as likely to be in one or three acts. By mid-century, however, two acts had become more and more common for afterpieces. In the prologue to Garrick's *Peep behind the Curtain* (1767) the suggestion seems to be that the form had become a standard requirement:

> Bold is the man, and *compos mentis*, scarce,
> Who, in these nicer times, dares write a *farce*;
> A vulgar, long-forgotten taste renew;
> All now are comedies, five acts, or two.

[24] Both the name of the maid and the expansion of her role over what it had been in the original suggest that Garrick may very well, as his letter to Peter Garrick indicates, have prepared the farce for the Drury Lane company, especially with Kitty Clive in mind.

fortune, and all ends well. The dialogue is even superior to the fast and clever action. Altogether, Garrick could be as proud of the reputation his writing here earned him as of the plaudits he received from playing Sharp.

Though to our tastes an inferior play, *Miss in Her Teens* was quite as successful as *The Lying Valet*. There are several interesting parallels, aside from theatrical fortunes, between the two farces. Among those of least significance is the fact that this play also was first brought out at a rival theatre and not at Drury Lane, the house with which Garrick's name has been so inseparably linked. He had come into the Drury Lane company as early as the end of his first season, but for two seasons, 1745-46 and 1746-47, he had tried his fortunes elsewhere, first in Ireland and then with Rich's company at Covent Garden.[25] It was at the latter theatre that *Miss in Her Teens* was started on its long career. More significantly, this play too was borrowed from a French one, Dancourt's *Parisienne*. Both of Garrick's farces are notably fast-moving and clever in dialogue, though the later one is less brilliant and more dependent on slapstick and exaggerated character than *The Lying Valet*.

The prologue to *Miss in Her Teens*, supplied by "a friend," promises us something more than mere farce:

> Too long has farce, neglecting Nature's laws,
> Debas'd the stage, and wrong'd the comic cause;
> To raise a laugh has been her sole pretence,
> Tho' dearly purchased at the price of sense;
> This child of folly gain'd increase with time;
> Fit for the place, succeeded pantomime;

[25] A letter in *The Museum* for February 1747 tells of the great success Rich was enjoying with the help of such stars as Garrick, Quin, Mrs. Cibber, and Mrs. Pritchard. Most significant in this context is the statement that this unusual prosperity at Covent Garden was "without the assistance of almost a single dancer." A glance at the theatrical calendar partially confirms this. There were numerous afterpieces, farcical and non-farcical, offered at Rich's theatre this season but only a very few pantomimes.

Reviv'd her honours, join'd her motley band,
And song and low conceit, o'erran the land.
More generous views inform our author's breast,
From real life his characters are drest. . . .

A comment by a less friendly writer, appearing a few weeks after the premiere, denies that the play rises above the level of farce. The heroine is by no means so "natural" as the prologue insists. In short, this second commentator says, the success of the play depended more upon its author's skill in acting Fribble, plus Woodward's clowning in the part of Flash, in which exaggerated grimaces and some ridiculous items of costume added to the farce.[26]

An examination of the play bears out this latter contention. What Garrick did was to take Dancourt's play, already on the borderline between farce and comedy, and add to the farce. In his version we have a conventional intrigue and several farce turns which in actual performance must have been dominant. The plot concerns the rivalry of a superannuated lover Sir Simon Loveit and his soldier son Captain Loveit for the hand of the sprightly Miss Biddy Bellair. The rivals are, however, unaware of each other's identity until the very end of the play. Meanwhile Miss Biddy and her equally sprightly maid Tag manage to convince Biddy's Aunt, who is not required to appear on the stage, that such a December-May match as she had first approved would be foolish, and the ground is cleared for some comic business involving two inconsequential rivals for the young lady's hand. One of these is Fribble, an effeminate ass in the Fopling Flutter tradition but considerably more exaggerated than Etherege's famous original. Fribble is anything but a fighting man, but he allows himself to be maneuvered into a ridiculous battle with Flash, a *miles gloriosus*.[27] After these two have wrung the audience

26 C. T. Gray, *Theatrical Criticism in London to 1795* (New York, 1931), p. 98.
27 Walwyn, in his *Essay on Comedy* (1782), considers Garrick's

dry of laughter, Captain Loveit drives them off and, the young ladies having convinced Sir Simon that marrying Biddy would be a grievous error for him, father and son recognize each other and are quickly reconciled. Some highly amusing scenes and some of the best dialogue in the play come in the first act when the Captain's wily servant Puff encounters an old rival and friend Jasper and then his own wife whom he has deserted, Miss Biddy's maidservant Tag.

Flash superior to and less farcical, in the sense employed here, than Jonson's Bobadil though, oddly enough, he is careful to retain the conventional labels: "The farcical character of Flash must be, therefore, preferred to the comic character of Bobadil."

CHAPTER 9

CONCLUSION: THE STATUS OF FARCE

✦✦

> If comedy's their theme, 'tis ten to one
> It dwindles into farce, and then 'tis gone.
> If farce their subject be, this witty age
> Holds that below the grandeur of the stage.
> —Prologue to *The Beau's Duel* (1702)

✦✦

FROM all that has been said about the success of farce in winning a place in the theatrical bill by mid-eighteenth century it may seem superfluous to talk of its status. Still there is a very real difference between popular reception and critical standing. While farce as a distinct genre was gaining its hold on audiences—a hold it has never relinquished—it had no success in winning the esteem of critical writers. Only rarely was a voice raised in defense of so "low" a form of entertainment, and even on those rare occasions the defense was so lamely apologetic or the defender so little deserving of esteem that what was said could count for very little.

Again France provides an interesting parallel. Even though the French had long had the separate genre and had shown a greater receptiveness to the farce-playing Italian comedians, the writer and player of farces had no status with the critics. Long before Marlowe's scornful reference to "Jigging veins of rhyming mother wits" we hear Du Bellay and Jean de la Faille expressing contempt for the *badineries et sottises* of the early French popular drama. Even Molière, who did so much to gain a position for the popular dramatic genre, was repeatedly scorned for writing and playing farces and obliged at times to hide behind the more innocuous terms of *comédie-ballet* and *divertissement*. And

Molière could count on the support not only of the popular throng but of the *roi soleil* himself, for Louis XIV was
a lover of farce. In time, the status of farce was to improve.
The nineteenth century saw a writer of farce-comedy, Labiche, elevated to the Academy, not, however, without incident; and our own day has seen an important French
thinker, Bergson, devote his attention to slapstick in a pene-
trating study of laughter.

In England recognition was at least as slow in coming.
As late as the end of the eighteenth century there were
many more scorners than admirers. At least there were few
who dared express a regard for the "low" in print. The
youthful Byron voices the conventional attitude in his first
satirical work:

> Oh, Sheridan! if aught can move thy pen,
> Let comedy assume her throne again. . . .
> Give as thy last memorial to the age,
> One classic drama, and reform the stage.
> Gods! o'er these boards shall Folly rear her head,
> Where Garrick trod, and Siddons lives to tread?
> On those shall Farce display Buffoon'ry's mask,
> And Hook conceal his heroes in a cask?

Eventually the attitude toward farce was to undergo a
profound change in England, even to the extent of calling
forth extravagant praise. Seventy-five years after Byron's
scathing pronouncement was made we find Henry Morley
defending buffoonery, both that of the old London fairs
and that of the modern theatre and music hall:

> The "Humours interspersed" at the Fair with tales of
> Rome and Babylon, still live in the farces and burlesques
> which keep us merry at the theatres. We practise our-
> selves well in laughter over feigned absurdities, and we in
> the meantime learn to subdue with laughter also real ab-
> surdities of life, which, in a nation holding itself to be

wiser for its want of foolishness, would prompt only to follies that occasion tears and groans. Then let us not stand aloof magnificently from the nonsense of the Fair. The ludicrous things to be read in Manifestoes of its Ministers of Pleasure, are in the worthiest sense State Papers to us, if we understand them thoroughly. Such State Papers have done more good to England than will ever be done to her neighbour country by the programmes, with no fun in them, proceeding from the manager, who, regardless of expense, has produced the Tragi-Comedy of "the Empire" at his great Theatrical Booth somewhere in Paris.[1]

In our own day, too, farce has had its ardent defenders, as has been demonstrated by some of the remarks quoted in preceding chapters on the acting of Chaplin and other great modern farceurs. But this striking change in attitude could hardly have seemed predictable in the period under study, when almost no one dared raise his voice in defense of farce.

Perhaps nowhere more than in a discussion of critical attitudes is the lack of a precise terminology so grievously felt. When, as was indicated in Chapter 1, *farce* may refer to any one of half a dozen genres or traits, it is difficult to describe with complete confidence just what the general attitude toward farce as we understand it was. Still, with a little care some reasonably clear notion can be arrived at, especially since most of the disapproved qualities were shared both by farce in the restricted sense employed here and by the various types lumped together as farce.

One of the main points of contention had to do with "following nature," the *sine qua non* of so many eighteenth-century commentators, which in its most widely accepted sense meant staying within the bounds of the realistic and the plausible. Farce, with its tendency to overwork coinci-

[1] *Memoirs of Bartholomew Fair*, p. 330.

dence or fantastic disguise, was only somewhat less guilty than burlesque and pantomime. From Dryden on, we find numerous assaults on farce for its tendency to go beyond nature.

An even darker sin, in a century still under the influence of Aristotle and Horace, was the failure to combine edification with entertainment, a failure in which farce and pantomime were equally guilty. When, therefore, we hear the speakers in A Comparison between the Two Stages refer to foreign dancers and tumblers as players of "farce," we may regret that the term could not have been more precisely used, but we admit that the substance of the charge will apply equally well to real farce. Writers of serious plays were just as prone to classify farce writers with dancers or even less exalted members of the entertainment world. Shadwell, in the prologue to his Squire of Alsatia (1688), contends that

> If poets aim at nought but to delight,
> Fidlers have to the bays an equal right.

And nearly a century later we find a character in Hugh Kelly's School for Wives (1773) bringing the play to a close with the remark that "unless we learn something while we chuckle, the carpenter who nails a pantomime together will be entitled to more applause than the best comic poet in the kingdom."

One of the vaguest appellations, and consequently one of the most commonly used to damn farce, burlesque, or almost any genre, was the term "low," the one which irritated Fielding and Goldsmith so much. Where it has a discernible meaning it may refer to the social status of the characters in a play. As we have seen, there was a tendency to classify all plays which dealt with the lower classes as farce, and, though we cannot admit that such a classification ever had any real validity, we must agree that for the most part characters in farce belong in the lower strata of society. More commonly, however, "low" applies to coarseness of language and manners, and here again farce is at least as guilty as the other genres, with the possible exception of burlesque. Concern over vulgarity increased as the century progressed but it was present almost from the start. There is a nice touch of irony here as can be seen in those cases where writers of burlesques attacking the so-called baser forms of theatrical entertainment were themselves condemned as low. Something of the sort seems to have occurred to Shadwell when he included a burlesque against farce in his *True Widow* (1678).[2] Certainly it was the fate of Fielding, Ralph, and others in the 1730's when they attempted to ridicule pantomime or fustian tragedy.[3]

One looks in vain for any sort of kindly comment in the work of major writers. When Dryden or Pope or Johnson deign to take notice of farce at all it is usually to show their scorn. Even though Dryden contributed to the list of partly farcical plays, especially in adaptations from French comedy, he did so with a feeling of self-reproach. His highly significant remarks in the preface to *An Evening's Love* (1668) became, by repetition, a sort of official pronouncement on the subject. The most important passage will bear reproducing:

> But I have descended, before I was aware, from Comedy to Farce; which consists principally of grimaces. That I admire not any comedy equally with tragedy, is, perhaps,

[2] Shadwell had introduced a farce sequence into his play "to expose the style and plot of farce-writers, to the utter confusion of damnable farce, and all its wicked and foolish adherents." When, either because the audience misunderstood his intentions or because it disapproved of them, Shadwell's play was damned, he resolved in his next play, *The Woman-Captain* (1679), to comply with the demand for mere entertainment, though not with the best grace as his blustering epilogue shows.

[3] *The Grub-Street Journal* was especially severe on the burlesques by Fielding, Ralph, and Odingsells which appeared in March and April 1730, even though these writers shared the common purpose of attacking "debased entertainments."

from the sullenness of my humour; but that I detest those farces, which are now the most frequent entertainments of the stage, I am sure I have reason on my side. Comedy consists, though of low persons, yet of natural actions and characters; I mean such humours, adventures, and designs, as are to be found and met with in the world. Farce, on the other side, consists of forced humours, and unnatural events. Comedy presents us with the imperfections of human nature: Farce entertains us with what is monstrous and chimerical. The one causes laughter in those who can judge of men and manners, by the lively representation of their folly or corruption: the other produces the same effect in those who can judge of neither, and that only by its extravagancies.

Pope is less explicit on the subject but hardly less scornful. And he too had a hand in farce-writing when he clubbed with Gay and Arbuthnot in the ill-fated *Three Hours after Marriage*. He did not, however, publicly claim any share in the piece and may perhaps be exonerated from any serious association with a piece that was produced largely in the spirit of conspiratorial fun which marks so much of the work of the Scriblerus Club. Pope's few comments on farce are chiefly casual asides, of which his well known comment on current audiences and tastes in *The Epistle to Augustus* may serve as illustration:

> A senseless, worthless, and unhonour'd crowd,
> Who, to disturb their betters mighty proud,
> Clatt'ring their sticks before ten lines are spoke,
> Call for the Farce, the Bear, or the Black-joke.
> What dear delight to Britons farce affords!
> Ever the taste of mobs, but now of lords.

Even Henry Fielding, who could defend the "low" against high-minded critics or could turn his hand to a rousing farce, at times joined in the almost universal chorus of condemnation as when he closes the prologue to his *Modern Husband* (1732) with this sentiment:

> If then true nature in his scenes you trace,
> Not scenes that comedy to farce debase;
> If modern vice detestable be shown,
> (And, vicious as it is, he draws the town:)
> Though no loud laugh applaud the serious page,
> Restore the sinking honour of the stage:
> The stage, which was not for low farce designed,
> But to divert, instruct, and mend mankind.

In the face of so nearly uniform an opposition the writer of mere farce could hardly expect to be given serious consideration, and he did not ask for it. His tone, when he shows any concern at all over the lack of critical recognition, is frankly apologetic: "What I offer here," he says in effect, "is trash, concocted in haste for the purpose of mere light entertainment for those who have no objection to such frivolity. No one should make the error of taking it so seriously as to examine it critically." Not infrequently he added a little judicious flattery to help disarm the critics.[4]

The few attempts to speak out in favor of farce during the period are on the whole timorous or inept. The first and by far the most ambitious was by Nahum Tate, who in 1693, after he had succeeded Shadwell in the laureateship, reissued his nine-year-old *Duke and No Duke* with an elaborate preface on farce.[5] Tate's defense of the genre rests largely on two rather flimsy bases: an insistence that the fantastic treatment required is more difficult than the simpler realism of comedy and an alleged connection with

---

[4] Two of many examples which could be quoted appear in the prologues to *The Whim* (1734) and *The Double Disappointment* (1746). As the earlier of these prologues puts it, "A farce we know's beneath the critick's care."

[5] For the source of some of Tate's ideas see A. H. Scouten, "An Italian Source for Nahum Tate's Defence of Farce," *Italica*, XXVII No. 3 (September 1950), 238-239.

the ancients, a defense which parallels that of John Weaver for pantomime. To these Tate adds a form of *tu quoque* pleading when he points out various farcical scenes and characters in the highly respected works of Jonson and Shakespeare and suggests that "if we enquire into the best of our modern comedies, we should find the most diverting parts of them to be farce, or near a kin to it."

No one seems to have been willing to defend farce on merely esthetic grounds. *Utile dulci* was a highly stable compound in the eighteenth century, as has been pointed out, and no one dared eliminate the first element. Especially after the rise of a form of drama more directly concerned with edification than ever, sentimental comedy, the emphasis on the *utile* of Horace's recipe was even increased.

There are hints of a defense which is almost as frivolous, however, one which has a psychological or even physiological basis. Here and there farce is recommended, as it is in the remarks of Morley quoted above, on the grounds that it sweetens the temper. This line of approach—so impressive today when everyone is as obsessed by the fear of maladjustment as our forefathers were by original sin—was not strictly a new one but it certainly was not widely held. Though there are doubtless more examples of its appearance in pre-Commonwealth times, I have discovered but two. In the prologue to the popular mid-sixteenth-century play by Udall, *Ralph Roister Doister*, we find this interesting comment:

> For myrth prolongeth lyfe, and causeth health.
> Mirth recreates our spirites and voydeth pensiveness,
> Mirth increses amitie, not hindring our wealth,
> Mirth is to be used both of more or lesse,
> Being mixed with vertue in decent comlynesse.[6]

[6] Taking these lines out of context may be misleading. As the last line quoted here suggests, Udall is interested in the traditional mixture of "vertue and myrth."

A similar recommendation is to be found in Thomas Heywood's *Apology for Actors* (1612). Among the various ingredients of comedy he singles out "sportful accidents to recreate such as of themselves are wholly devoted to melancholy, which corrupts the blood, or to refresh such weary spirits as are tired with labor or study, to moderate the cares and heaviness of the mind, that they may return to their trades and faculties with more zeal and earnestness after some small, soft and pleasant retirement."

In the period under survey the possibility of such a defense is scarcely more than hinted at a few times. The first instance to come to my attention occurs in a strong and highly conventional defense of the Horation requirement of instruction coupled with entertainment. Charles Johnson, in the prologue to his *Wife's Relief* (1711), compliments the audience on its just reception of sound plays, such as those produced by "Avon's swan," but he qualifies his praise with a little blame:

> Yet bad ones oft succeed, and Harlequin
> Has trick'd your judgment, when he cur'd your spleen.
> That author shows the utmost pow'r of art,
> Who can at once instruct you and divert.

Four years later Christopher Bullock of the rival company shamelessly abandons any pretense of instruction on offering his *Woman's Revenge*. In the prologue he expresses a fear of being accused of partisanship in the heated struggle then going on between Hanoverians and Jacobites whereas nothing is farther from his mind,

> Because this farce, which he presents to night,
> He did upon an old foundation write;
> But his sole aim, is to divert your spleens,
> With follies of low life, and sportive scenes;
> Where, if there's humor, you'll forgive him sense;
> And 'stead of laboured lines, with homely mirth dispense.

These mere hints of "diverting the spleen" are elaborated into a claim or defense by Fielding in the preface to *Joseph Andrews*. True, the claim is made in favor of burlesque, but it seems almost certain that what Fielding says would apply equally well, or better, to farce as we have used the term here. After agreeing with Shaftesbury's contention that burlesque was unknown among the ancients, he parts company with the philosophical nobleman in expressing a favorable judgment on the form,

> and that not because I have had some little success on the stage this way; but rather as it contributes more to exquisite mirth and laughter than any other; and these are probably more wholesome physic for the mind, and conduce better to purge away spleen, melancholy and ill affections than is generally imagined. Nay, I will appeal to common observation, whether the same companies are not found more full of good humor and benevolence, after they have been sweetened for two or three hours with entertainments of this kind, than when soured by a tragedy or a grave lecture.[7]

In making this claim, however, Fielding would seem to be defending his own *practice* whereas in the lines from *The Modern Husband* previously quoted he is content to go along with the traditional statement of the *theory* of comic purpose. His ambivalence is quite typical. The rigidly

[7] Some twenty years after Fielding wrote his preface Joseph Reed summed up this view of the contrasting purposes of comedy and farce very neatly in the prologue to *The Register Office*:

> The bard, whose hopes on comedy depend,
> Must strive instruction with delight to blend.
> While he, who bounds his less-aspiring views
> To farce, the combrush of the comic muse,
> With pleasantry alone may fill the scene:
> His business chiefly this—to cure the spleen.

Again, however, we face an ironical situation, for *The Register Office*, though in only two acts, is really a little satirical comedy on the pattern of Jonson's *Alchemist*.

limited theory of the drama inherited from the renais-
sance—enforced by the reforming tendencies of an age
which could boast as its one contribution a middle-class,
moralizing drama—found no room for mere entertainment.
But, whatever the critical theory, the populace demanded
to be entertained. Farce, along with such other popular
forms as pantomime, filled that urgent if inarticulate demand. In fact, as has been previously indicated, farce was
able to win at least some freedom from the most severe
judgments, which were directed at pantomime. The anonymous author of *Stage Policy Detected*, published in 1744
when the so-called war against pantomimes was at its height,
volunteers to speak for the theatre-going public on this
matter:

> As to the town's not being satisfied with a play alone,
> had that, and not the sixpences,[8] been your motive for
> persisting in your pantomimes, it had been highly laud-
> able; but you are as sensible as I am, that there is scarce
> a single person in any audience, that would be much
> better pleased with the meanest farce than the best pan-
> tomime you can shew 'em: you'll say the farces are but
> few, and those the town tired out with the repetition of;
> but it may be answered, there are many others common
> and to be had any where, which it would be but a very
> little trouble to revive, and many of which would please,
> perhaps, as much as those you act so commonly: But a
> thing of much more consequence to the publick, is to
> demand, why have not authors better encouragement to
> write you new ones?[9]

[8] That is, six pences paid on what was called "the latter account,"
which refers to the practice of collecting that sum for people who
came into the upper gallery after the play just to see the "entertainment."

[9] In choosing farce over pantomime this writer is agreeing with
several others, notably Aaron Hill in *The Prompter*, No. 13 (24
December 1734). On the other hand, Tom Davies thought "pantomime . . . a kind of stage entertainment which will always give more

Oddly enough, the growing popularity of sentimental comedy tended also to strengthen the position of farce, for the suppression of laughter in favor of sighs and sententious dialogue in full-length plays forced the dramatist more and more into using the afterpiece as a refuge for laughter. In its earlier stages the drama of sensibility showed a tendency to allow at least minor characters to run to the ludicrous. Even as late as 1773 we find Hugh Kelly professing the intention "to steer between the extreme of sentimental gloom, and the excesses of uninteresting levity. . . ."[10] But with the closing years of the century the shades of Kotzebuean gloom closed in and levity was often banished to the afterpiece. As Thorndike has remarked of a leading exemplar of sentimental comedy who also turned out her share of farces, "Mrs. Inchbald seems to have compromised on a distinction similar to the famous romanticist separation of fancy and imagination. Fun and merriment might be given rein in such trivial and fanciful pieces as farces and petite comedies, but should have only a slight and secondary place in works of the imagination extolling, as the sentimental plays assuredly did, 'scrupulous purity of characters and refinement in sensations.' "[11]

Whether he was to be ignored by respectable critics or reduced to the tag-end of the theatrical bill, the writer of farces went about his business of turning out amusing plays and accepting the plaudits of his contemporaries—and their money—without any thought of a brighter or more lasting fame. He might, if he had been concerned enough to do so, have looked back at the ballad makers of an earlier day and found consolation in the fact that they were then—in the latter part of the eighteenth century, at least—coming into a belated recognition as by no means despicable among

---

delight to a mixed company than the best farce that can be written." *Memoirs of the Life of David Garrick, Esq.* (1780), I, 76.

[10] Preface to *The School for Wives.*

[11] *English Comedy*, p. 464.

poets. A century or so earlier, however, hardly any artist could have been more condemned—while his work was enjoyed. Professor Rollins sums up the attitude:

> Shakespeare knew dozens of ballads by heart: he and his fellow dramatists quote from ballads in nearly every play; and if occasionally they quote in ridicule, then their ridicule applies also to "John Dory," "George Aloe," "Little Musgrave," and "Mussleborough Field,"—traditional ballads now enshrined in Professor Child's *English and Scottish Popular Ballads*. The great Elizabethans did not dream of judging ballads as poetry—though indisputably they enjoyed reading and quoting them—and lost no opportunity of denouncing their authors. Ben Jonson, for example, flatly declared that "a poet should detest a ballad-maker," echoing Thomas Nashe's grave remark that if a man would "love good poets he must not countenance ballad-makers."[12]

Or a farce writer with a gift for divination might have found even greater consolation in the contempt shared in his own day by writers of novels. Richardson had a strong aversion to the label *novelist*, even while doing important pioneering work in the form for which he is greatly honored today. And even half a century later Jane Austen loses some of her characteristic aplomb when she interrupts her account of Catherine Morland for a not altogether ironic attack on novelists who are ashamed of the title. When, therefore, Dr. Johnson's character Dick Minim is heard to wonder "what was become of the comic genius which supplied our ancestors with wit and pleasantry, and why no writer could be found that durst now venture beyond a farce,"[13] he sounds strangely like Johnson's friend Goldsmith when, in his *Essay on the Theatre: or, A Comparison between Sentimental and Laughing Comedy*, he comments scorn-

[12] *A Pepysian Garland* (Cambridge, 1922), p. xii.
[13] *Idler*, No. 60 (9 June 1759).

fully on the slight creative powers required of the senti-mental writer: "Those abilities that can hammer out a novel are fully sufficient for the production of a sentimental comedy."

BIBLIOGRAPHY

Addison, Joseph, and Richard Steele. *The Spectator*, ed. G. A. Aitken. London, 1898.
———. *The Tatler*, ed. G. A. Aitken. London, 1898-99.
Akerby, George. *The Life of James Spiller*. London, 1729.
Albert, Maurice. *Les Théâtres de la Foire*. Paris, 1900.
Aristophanes: The Eleven Comedies. New York, 1943.
Ashton, Harry. *Molière*. New York, 1930.
Aston, Anthony. *Brief Supplement to Colley Cibber*. (Appended to Lowe's edition of Cibber's *Apology*, q.v.)
Avery, Emmett L. "Foreign Performers in the London Theatres in the Early Eighteenth Century." *Philological Quarterly*, xvi (1937), 105-123.
Avery, Emmett L., and A. H. Scouten. "A Tentative Calendar of Daily Theatrical Performances in London, 1700-1701 to 1704-1705." *PMLA*, lviii (1948), 114-180.
Bader, A. L. "The Modena Troupe in England." *Modern Language Notes*, l (1935), 367-369.
[Baker, D. E.] *The Companion to the Playhouse*. London, 1764.
Baker, Herschel. "Strolling Actors in Eighteenth Century England." University of Texas *Studies in English*, 1941, pp. 100-120.
Baldwin, T. W. *Shakspere's Five-Act Structure*. Urbana, 1947.
Barker, R. H. *Mr. Cibber of Drury Lane*. New York, 1939.
Baskervill, C. R. *The Elizabethan Jig*. Chicago, 1929.
Beattie, James. *Essay on Poetry and Music as They Affect the Mind; on Laughter, and Ludicrous Composition*. Edinburgh, 1776.
Behn, Aphra. *The Works of Aphra Behn*, ed. Montague Summers. London, 1915.
Bergson, Henri. *Laughter*. New York, 1911.
Bonnassies, Jules. *Les Spectacles Forains et la Comédie Française*. Paris, 1875.
Boswell, Eleanore. *The Restoration Court Stage*. Cambridge, Massachusetts, 1932.
Boswell, James. *Boswell's Life of Johnson*, ed. G. B. Hill and L. F. Powell. Oxford, 1934-50.
Boswell's Journal of a Tour to the Hebrides, ed. F. A. Pottle and C. H. Bennett. New York, 1936.
Bowen, Marjorie. *William Hogarth*. London, 1936.
The British Stage. 1724.
Brown, Thomas. *The Compleat Works of Mr. Thomas Brown*. (The third edition.) London, 1710.
Campardon, Emile. *Les Comédiens du Roi de la Troupe Italienne*. Paris, 1880.

———. *Les Spectacles de la Foire.* Paris, 1877.
Catalogue of the Larpent Plays in the Huntington Library, ed. Dougald MacMillan. San Marino, California, 1939.
Chambers, E. K. *The Elizabethan Stage.* Oxford, 1923.
———. *The English Folk-Play.* Oxford, 1933.
———. *The Mediaeval Stage.* Oxford, 1903.
[Chetwood, W. R.] *The British Theatre.* Dublin, 1750.
———. *A General History of the Stage.* London, 1749.
Cibber, Colley. *An Apology for the Life of Mr. Colley Cibber,* ed. R. W. Lowe. London, 1889.
Cibber, Theophilus. *The Lives and Characters of the Most Eminent Actors and Actresses.* London, 1753.
Colby, Elbridge. "A Supplement on Strollers." *PMLA,* xxxix (1924), 642-654.
Collins, William Lucas. *Aristophanes.* London, 1872.
A Comparison between the Two Stages, ed. Staring B. Wells. Princeton, 1942.
A Compleat List of All the English Dramatic Poets, appended to Thomas Whincop, *Scanderbeg.* London, 1747.
A Complete Key to the Last New Farce, The What D'y Call It. London, 1715.
Congreve, William. *Amendments of Mr. Collier's False and Imperfect Citations.* London, 1698.
Cooper, Lane. *An Aristotelian Theory of Comedy.* New York, 1922.
Crawford, J. P. W. *Spanish Drama before Lope de Vega.* Philadelphia, 1937.
Crichton, Kyle. *The Marx Brothers.* Garden City, New York, 1950.
Crowne, John. *The Dramatic Works of John Crowne,* ed. James Maidment and W. H. Logan, Edinburgh, 1873-74.
Davies, Thomas. *Dramatic Miscellanies.* London, 1785.
———. *Memoirs of the Life of David Garrick, Esq.* London, 1780.
Dennis, John. *The Critical Works of John Dennis,* ed. E. N. Hooker. Baltimore, 1939-43.
Downes, John. *Roscius Anglicanus,* ed. Montague Summers. London, 1928.
Dryden, John. *A Defence of an Essay of Dramatique Poesie,* prefixed to *The Indian Emperour.* London, 1668.
———. *A Discourse Concerning the Origin and Progress of Satire,* prefixed to *The Satires of Decimus Junius Juvenalis.* London, 1693.
———. *Of Dramatick Poesie.* London, 1668.
Duchartre, P. L. *The Italian Comedy.* London, 1929.
Eastman, Max. *The Sense of Humor.* New York, 1921.
The English Stage Italianiz'd. London, 1727.
Evelyn, John. *The Diary of John Evelyn,* ed. Austin Dobson. London, 1908.

BIBLIOGRAPHY

Faure, Élie. *The Art of Cineplastics.* Boston, 1923.
Fitzgerald, Percy. *A New History of the English Stage.* London, 1882.
Foote, Samuel. *The Roman and English Comedy Consider'd and Compar'd.* London, 1747.
Forsythe, R. S. *A Study of the Plays of Thomas D'Urfey.* Cleveland, 1916.
Fransen, J. *Les Comédiens Français en Hollande au XVIIe et au XVIIIe Siècles.* Paris, 1925.
Gagey, E. M. *Ballad Opera.* New York, 1937.
[Garrick, David.] *An Essay on Acting.* London, 1704.
————. *The Private Correspondence of David Garrick* [ed. James Boaden.] London, 1831-32.
Gayley, C. M. *Representative English Comedies,* Vol. 2. New York, 1913.
Genest, John. *Some Account of the English Stage.* Bath, 1832.
Gherardi, Evaristo. *Le Théâtre Italien de Gherardi.* Paris, 1700.
Gilbert, H. *Literary Criticism: Plato to Dryden.* New York, 1940.
Goldsmith, Oliver. "Essay on the Theatre; or, a Comparison between Sentimental and Laughing Comedy." *Westminster Magazine,* 1773.
Gray, C. H., *Theatrical Criticism in London to 1795.* New York, 1931.
Greig, J. Y. T. *The Psychology of Laughter and Comedy.* London, 1923.
Heywood, Thomas. *An Apology for Actors.* London, 1612.
Hill, Aaron. *The Dramatic Works of Aaron Hill.* London, 1760.
Hill, John. *The Actor.* London, 1750.
[Hippisley, John.] *A Dissertation on Comedy.* London, 1750.
Hooker, E. N. "Charles Johnson's 'The Force of Friendship' and 'Love in a Chest': a Note on Tragi-comedy and Licensing in 1710." *Studies in Philology,* XXXIV (1937), 407-411.
Hotson, Leslie. *The Commonwealth and Restoration Stage.* Cambridge, Massachusetts, 1928.
Huff, Theodore. *Charlie Chaplin.* New York, 1951.
Hughes, Leo, and Scouten, A. H. *Ten English Farces.* Austin, Texas, 1948.
Hurd, Richard. *A Dissertation Concerning the Provinces of the Several Species of the Drama.* (Appended to his edition of Horace's *Ars Poetica.*) London, 1753.
Isman, Felix. *Weber and Fields.* New York, 1924.
Jack, W. S. *The Early Entremés in Spain.* Philadelphia, 1923.
Jackson, Alfred. "London Playhouses 1700-1705." *Review of English Studies,* VIII (1932), 291-302.
————. "Play Notices from the Burney Newspapers." *PMLA,* XLVIII (1933), 815-849.

Kelly, J. A. *German Visitors to English Theaters in the Eighteenth Century.* Princeton, 1936.

Klemm, Werner. *Die Englische Farce in 19. Jahrhundert.* Bern, 1946.

Knight, Joseph. *David Garrick.* London, 1894.

Lacy, John. *The Dramatic Works of John Lacy,* ed. James Maidment and W. H. Logan. Edinburgh, 1875.

Lancaster, H. C. *The Comédie Française, 1680-1701.* Baltimore, 1941.

———. *A History of French Dramatic Literature in the Seventeenth Century.* Baltimore, 1929-42.

———. *Sunset.* Baltimore, 1945.

Langbaine, Gerard. *An Account of the English Dramatick Poets.* London, 1691.

Lanson, Gustave. "Molière et la Farce." *Revue de Paris,* III (1901), 129-153.

The Laureate, London, 1740.

Lawrence, W. J. "Early French Players in England." *Anglia,* XXXII (1909), 61-89.

———. "Early Irish Ballad Opera and Comic Opera." *Musical Quarterly,* VIII (1922), 397-412.

———. "The Mystery of 'The Stage Coach.'" *Modern Language Review,* XXVII (1932), 392-397.

———. "A Player-Friend of Hogarth." *The Elizabethan Playhouse,* 2nd series (1913), pp. 215-226.

Lea, Kathleen M. *Italian Popular Comedy.* Oxford, 1934.

Letter to My Lord——on the Present Diversions of the Town. London, 1725.

Letters of Wit, Politicks and Morality. London, 1701. (Appended to *The Dramatick Works of William Burnaby,* ed. F. E. Budd. London, 1931.)

Liebrecht, Henri. *Histoire du Théâtre Français à Bruxelles au XVIIᵉ et au XVIIIᵉ Siècles.* Brussels, 1923.

Little, D. M. *Pineapples of Finest Flavour.* Cambridge, Massachusetts, 1930.

McManaway, J. G. "Philip Massinger and the Restoration Drama." *ELH,* I (1934), 276-304.

Marvell, Andrew. *The Poems and Letters of Andrew Marvell,* ed. H. M. Margoliouth. Oxford, 1927.

Maxwell, Ian. *French Farce and John Heywood.* Melbourne, 1946.

Millett, F. B., and G. E. Bentley. *The Art of the Drama.* New York, 1935.

Moland, Louis. *Molière et la Comédie Italienne.* Paris, 1867.

Moore, J. B. *The Comic and the Realistic in English Drama.* Chicago, 1925.

Morley, Henry. *Memoirs of Bartholomew Fair.* London, 1880.

Nicholson, Watson. *Anthony Aston Stroller and Adventurer*. South Haven, Michigan, 1920.

——. *The Struggle for a Free Stage in London*. Boston, 1906.

Nicoll, Allardyce. *A History of English Drama 1660-1900*, vols. I-III. Cambridge, England, 1952.

——. *Masks, Mimes and Miracles*. London, 1931.

Norris, E. T. "The Original of Ravenscroft's Anatomist." *Modern Language Notes*, XLVI (1931), 522-526.

Northup, G. T. *An Introduction to Spanish Literature*. Chicago, 1936.

Noyes, R. G. *Ben Jonson on the English Stage 1660-1776*. Cambridge, Massachusetts, 1935.

Odell, G. C. D. *Annals of the New York Stage*, vol. I. New York, 1927.

Orrery, Roger Boyle. *The Dramatic Works of Roger Boyle, Earl of Orrery*, ed. W. S. Clark. Cambridge, Massachusetts, 1937.

Palmer, John. *Comedy*. London, 1914.

——. *Comedy of Manners*. London, 1913.

Parfaict, Claude, and François Parfaict. *Dictionnaire de Théâtres de Paris*. Paris, 1756.

——. *Mémoires pour Servir à l'Histoire des Spectacles de la Foire*. Paris, 1743.

Pepys, Samuel. *The Diary of Samuel Pepys*, ed. H. B. Wheatley. London, 1893-99.

Perwich, William. *The Despatches of William Perwich*. London, 1903.

Petit de Julleville, Louis. *La Comédie et les Moeurs en France au Moyen Âge*. Paris, 1886.

The Players: a Satire, London, 1733.

Privitera, J. F. *Charles Chevillet de Champmeslé*. Baltimore, 1938.

Rasi, Luigi. *I Comici Italiani*. Florence, 1897-1905.

Riccoboni, Luigi. *An Historical and Critical Account of the Theatres in Europe*. London, 1741.

——. *Observations sur la Comédie, et le génie de Molière*. Paris, 1736.

Rollins, H. E. "A Contribution to the History of the English Commonwealth Drama." *Studies in Philology*, XVIII (1921), 267-333.

——. *A Pepysian Garland*. Cambridge, England, 1922.

Rosenfeld, Sybil. "Shepherd's Market Theatre and May Fair Wells." *Theatre Notebook*, V (1951), 89-92.

——. *Strolling Players & Drama in the Provinces, 1660-1765*. Cambridge, England, 1939.

Schwartz, I. A. *The Commedia dell'Arte and Its Influence on French Comedy*. Paris, 1933.

Scouten, A. H. "An Italian Source for Nahum Tate's Defence of Farce." *Italica*, XXVII (1950), 238-239.

Seldes, Gilbert. *The Movies Come from America*. New York, 1937.
Sherburn, George. "The Fortunes and Misfortunes of Three Hours after Marriage." *Modern Philology*, xxiv (1926-27), 91-109.
Smith, D. F. *Plays about the Theatre in England*. New York, 1936.
Smith, Winifred. *The Commedia dell'Arte*. London, 1912.
The Stage Mutineers. London, 1733.
Steele, Richard. *The Correspondence of Richard Steele*, ed. Rae Blanchard. London, 1941.
Stone, G. W. "The God of His Idolatry." *Joseph Quincy Adams Memorial Studies*. Washington, 1948.
Summers, Montague. *A Bibliography of the Restoration Drama*. London, 1934.
————. *Restoration Comedies*. Boston, 1922.
The Theatrical Museum. London, 1776.
Thomas, Tobyas. *The Life of the Late Famous Comedian, Jo. Hayns*. London, 1701.
Thorndike, A. H. *English Comedy*. New York, 1929.
Tyranny Triumphant. London, 1743.
Walpole, Horace. *The Letters of Horace Walpole*, ed. Mrs. Paget Toynbee. Oxford, 1903-05.
Walwyn, B. *An Essay on Comedy*. London, 1782.
[Ward, Edward.] *The Dancing Devils*. London, 1724.
[————.] *The Dancing School*. London, 1700.
[————.] *The London-Spy: Compleat in Eighteen-Parts*. London, 1703.
Weaver, John. *The History of the Mimes and Pantomimes*. London, 1728.
Wheatley, H. B. *Hogarth's London*. London, 1909.
Wilcox, John. *The Relation of Molière to Restoration Comedy*. New York, 1938.
[Wilkes, Thomas.] *A General View of the Stage*. London, 1759.
Willis, Eola. *The Charleston Stage in the XVIII Century*. Columbia, South Carolina, 1924.
The Wits; or, Sport upon Sport, ed. J. J. Elson. Ithaca, New York, 1932.
Young, Karl. "The Influence of French Farce upon the Plays of John Heywood." *Modern Philology*, ii (1904), 97-124.

INDEX

Account of the English Dramatick Poets, 157
Actor, 25, 55-56, 197-198
Adams, John, 153
Addison, Joseph, 44, 45, 85
Adventures of Half an Hour, 41-42, 255
Aesop, 126, 226
Aitken, G. A., 85, 102
Akerby, George, 190, 191
Alard, Pierre, 96, 97, 100
Albert, Maurice, 211
Albumazar, 36, 69, 120, 145, 159-160, 233
Alchemist, 58, 145, 281
All without Money, 148, 150, 240
Amant ridicule, 65
Amendments of Mr. Collier's False and Imperfect Citations, 10
Amorous Prince, 162
Amorous Widow, 144
Amour médecin, 48, 145
Amphitryon, 15, 34, 240
Anatomist, 34-35, 48, 140, 148, 189, 194-195, 206, 235, 241-243, 267
Andersen, H. C., 236
Andronicus, 75
Angel, Edward, 47-48, 54, 134, 156, 157, 159-164, 234
Anne, Queen, 55, 184
Anti-Theatre, 190
Apology for Actors, 280
Apology for . . . Colley Cibber, 46, 78, 85, 87, 101, 103-104, 111, 155, 164-165, 167, 169-170, 173, 176, 183
Arbuthnot, John, 122, 249-252, 277
d'Argenson, 99

Aristophanes, 11, 35, 119-120, 145
Aristotle, 10, 113, 275
Arlequin à la guinguette, 107
Arlequin empéreur dans la lune, 115
Art of Poetry, 16
Arthur, John, 210
Ashton, H., 5
Assignation, 132, 168
Aston, Anthony, 165, 169, 174, 176, 184, 225-228
Aubert, Mrs., 12
Auction, 4
Auditor, 38
Austen, Jane, 284
Author's Farce, 12, 124, 125, 224
Avare, 143, 144, 145, 146
Avery, E. L., 80, 141, 211

Bacchus and Circe, 231
Bader, A. L., 136
Baggs, Zachary, 85
Bailey, Nathaniel, 14
Baker, Herschel, 203
Baker, Thomas, 177, 180
Baldwin, T. W., 61
Bannister, 79
Barker, Kathleen, 195
Barker, R. H., 77
Barnard, John, 222, 223
Baron, Catherine, 98, 99, 106, 107
Bartholomew Fair, 153, 193
Baskervill, C. R., 23, 70
Baucis and Philemon, 231
Bauday, King of, 101
Baxter, Mrs., 209
Baxter, Richard, 97-98, 100, 106-108
Bays's Opera, 125

Beattie, James, 19
Beau Demolished, 105
Beaumont, Francis, 53, 111
Beau's Duel, 272
Beaux Stratagem, 55, 179, 232
Beggar's Opera, 10, 90, 112, 122, 123, 189, 194, 197, 205, 213, 218, 219, 232, 256
Beggar's Wedding, 128
Behn, Aphra, 7, 26, 40, 41, 43, 49, 54, 59, 95, 100, 138, 139, 159, 162-163, 164, 166, 170, 187, 235, 236-240, 252
Bentley, G. E., 7
Berenice, 74
Bergere in the Temple of Flora, 230
Bergson, Henri, 34, 43, 50, 273
Betterton, Thomas, 76, 77, 97, 144, 148, 155, 177, 240
Biancolelli, Domenico, 47, 65, 135
Biographia Dramatica, 168
Birth of Venus, 230
Black Man, 71
Blakes, Charles, 195, 243
Blanchard, Rae, 105
Blount, Thomas, 13, 14
Boarding School, 38, 193
Boileau, Nicolas, 42
Boisrobert, François de, 65
Bonnassies, Jules, 98
Bonus, 230
Booth, Barton, 102, 110, 111
Boswell, Eleanore, 135, 136
Boswell, James, 198
Boswell's Life of Johnson, 13, 17
Bourgeois gentilhomme, 144
Boursault, Edme, 126, 182
Bowen, Marjorie, 207
Bragge, Benjamin, 217
Brave Irishman, 147, 264-265
Brett, Henry, 83-84
Breval, John, 7
Brief Supplement, 169
British Stage, 94, 118

British Theatre, 9
Brome, Richard, 133
Broun, Heywood, 52
Brown, John Mason, 19-20
Brown, Thomas, 60, 78, 212-213, 216, 222
Budd, F. E., 145
Bullock, 105
Bullock, Christopher, 4, 150, 186, 187, 188, 189, 203, 209, 252-255, 259, 280
Bullock, Hildebrand, 190
Bullock, William, 38, 44, 53, 54, 172, 174, 177-179, 184-185, 186, 187, 196, 216
Burbage, Richard, 170
Burnaby, William, 145, 182
Byron, Lord, 273

Caffé, 150
Caius Marius, 37
Callot, 46, 47, 196
Camp Visitants, 7
Campardon, Emile, 97, 98, 99, 107, 135, 215
Careless Lovers, 164
Carey, Henry, 59, 126, 151, 255-256, 263
Carrosses d'Orléans, 244
Cartouche, 9
Caryll, John, 43, 44
Casey's Court Circus, 71
Cataline, 163
Centlivre, Susannah, 8, 81, 145, 209
Cephalus and Procris, 115
Cervantes Saavedra, Miguel de, 43, 122
Chambers, E. K., 69, 70
Champion, 227
Chaplin, Charles, 34, 39, 47, 52, 61, 71, 117, 142, 155-156, 274
Chapman, 193, 195
Chapman, George, 187
Charke, 228

Charles II, 44, 45, 54, 72, 136-137, 157-158, 160, 234
Charley's Aunt, 36
Chaste Maid in Cheapside, 117
Cheater Cheated, 72, 117
Cheats of Scapin, 9, 15, 80, 92, 139, 145, 244
Cheats, or the Tavern Bilkers, 105
Cheshire Comics, 127
Chetwood, W. R., 116, 225
Child, F. J., 284
Chimera, 128
Choix de petites pièces, 258
Chrononhotonthologos, 126, 206, 255
Cibber, Colley, 38, 46, 54, 57, 58-59, 78, 81, 83, 85, 87, 101, 102, 103-104, 105, 109, 110-111, 112, 127, 149, 155, 164-165, 167, 169-170, 172, 173, 175, 176, 177, 181, 182-183, 184, 185, 243-244, 248, 252
Cibber, Susanna, 269
Cibber, Theophilus, 4, 59, 111, 116, 197, 201-202, 246
Cid, 258
Cinthio, Giraldi, 10
Circus, 39
City Farce, 10, 154
Clark, Bobby, 47
Clark, W. S., 131, 134
Claxton, 79, 80
Clinch, 78, 79, 80
Clive, Catherine Raftor, 150, 192, 196-199, 259, 262-263, 268
Clouds, 120, 145
Cobler, 230
Cobler's Opera, 128
Cobler of Preston (unspecified), 206
Cobler of Preston (Bullock), 36, 188, 189, 190, 252-254
Cobler of Preston (Johnson), 36, 189, 252-254

Cocoanuts, 52
Coffee House, 150, 153
Coffey, Charles, 9, 38, 128, 219
Cokain, Aston, 138, 238
Colby, Elbridge, 203, 206
Coles, Elisha, 14
Collier, Jeremy, 78
Collier, William, 85, 87, 101, 188-189
Collins, W. L., 11, 119-120
Comedian, or Philosophical Enquirer, 197
"Comedie Italienne," 246
Comédie sans comédie, 73
Comedy of Errors, 33, 69
Comical Revenge, 159
Comical Rivals, or the School-Boy, 9, 80, 81, 83, 92, 149, 175, 243, 244, 257, 267
Committee, 157
Comparison between the Two Stages, 15, 54-55, 78, 95-97, 100, 118, 177, 183, 275
Compleat Works of Mr. Thomas Brown, 78
Complete Key to the . . . What D'ye Call It, 12, 122
Complete Key to . . . Three Hours after Marriage, 140
Confederacy, 44
Congreve, William, 10, 15, 83, 124, 145, 209
Conscious Lovers, 34, 267
Contes aux heures perdues, 235
Constant Couple, 180, 192
Contrivances, 92, 151, 255-256
Cooke, Thomas, 123
Cooper, Lane, 10
Coppinger, Matthew, 212
Corey, John, 120, 145, 180
Corneille, Thomas, 147, 235
Cornish Squire, 147
Corregio, 196
Cotgrave, Randle, 13-14
Countrey Wit, 81, 133

Country Gentleman's Vade Mecum, 78
Country House, 9-10, 89, 92, 148, 244
Country Wake, 134, 175, 189, 191, 226, 240, 248, 249
Country Wife, 18, 107, 168
Covent-Garden Tragedy, 260-261
Cowley, Abraham, 72, 164, 233
Craftsman, 194
Crawford, J.P.W., 6
Crichton, Kyle, 52
Crispin Médecin, 35, 148, 241-243
Critic, 122
Cromwell, Henry, 16
Crowne, John, 133, 174
Cuckold in Conceit, 83
Cuckolds-Haven, 48, 166, 173, 240
Cure for Covetousness, 213
Curll, Edmund, 173
Cutter of Coleman Street, 72, 164, 233

Dacier, 75
Daily Advertiser, 195, 224, 225, 227, 228, 229, 230
Daily Courant, 4, 9, 27, 79, 85-86, 97, 98, 100, 107, 184, 216, 223, 226, 243
Daily Post, 9, 226
Daily Post-Boy, 223
Damon and Phillida, 92, 127, 205, 206
Damon and Pythias, 51
Dancing Devils, 118
Dancing School, 213
Dancourt, F. C., 81, 142, 148, 150, 244, 269, 270
Daniel, George, 212
Davenant, William, 72-74, 75, 148, 234
Davenport, Robert, 208

Davies, Thomas, 27, 55, 193, 200, 259, 282-283
Davys, Mary, 38
Defence of an Essay of Dramatique Poesie, 6
Defoe, Daniel, 190
Dennis, John, 15-16, 168, 177, 181
Devil of a Wife, 4, 128, 130, 134, 189, 217, 240, 254, 257
Devil to Pay, 9, 17, 36, 92, 128, 134, 192, 193, 197, 199, 206, 213, 219, 232, 257-259, 261
Devonshire Girl, 80
Diable à quatre, 258
Dictionnaire des Théâtres, 107
Dictionnaire portatif des théâtres, 67
Discourse Concerning the Original and Progress of Satire, 75
Dissertation on Comedy, 10
Dissertation on the Provinces of the Drama, 16
Doctor amoureux, 65
Doctor Faustus (Marlowe), 69, 234
Doctor Faustus (Mountfort), 43, 49, 95, 139, 166, 234
Doctor Faustus (Thurmond), 104, 108, 246
Dodsley, Robert, 92, 126-127, 170, 266
Doggett, Thomas, 37, 44, 174-177, 181, 183, 189, 192, 215, 216, 225, 240, 243, 248-249
Don Quixote (Cervantes), 254
Don Quixote (Durfey), 79, 240
Double Disappointment, 278
Downes, John, 44-45, 48, 78, 95, 159, 163, 172, 175, 183
Dragon of Wantley, 126, 255
Dramatic Miscellanies, 55, 259
Dramatic Works of Aaron Hill, 199
"Drunken Man," 193, 226
Drury, Robert, 135, 146

Dryden, John, 6, 14, 15, 17, 31, 33, 73, 75, 122, 132, 144, 147, 158, 168, 172-173, 205, 235, 240, 275, 276-277
Du Bellay, Joachim, 272
Duchartre, P. L., 46
Duck Soup, 34
Duffett, Thomas, 137
Dufresny, Charles, 250
Duke and No Duke, 17, 24, 36, 149, 238, 278
Dumb Lady, 48
Durfey, Thomas, 26, 32, 37, 38, 43, 72, 124, 132, 166, 170-172, 174, 193, 237-238, 240
Dutch Courtezan, 51, 63, 69, 72, 134, 187, 252
Dutch Lover, 54, 164
Dyer, 209

Earl of Marr Marr'd, 123
Eastman, Max, 50
Ecole des maris, 146
Edwards, John, 216
Edwards, Richard, 51
Elford, Mrs., 79
Elson, J. J., 23, 208
Empéreur de la lune, 247-248
Emperor of the Moon, 15, 40, 43, 46, 49, 95, 100, 101-102, 138, 149, 164, 166, 188, 238-240, 245, 248
Encyclopaedia Britannica, 18-19
English Stage Italianiz'd, 141
Englishman in Paris, 12, 17, 128
Englishman Returned from Paris, 12-13, 17, 128
Epistle to Augustus, 185, 277
Epsom Wells, 164, 178
Escapes of Harlequin, 231
Esope, 182
Essay on Acting, 59, 175-176
Essay on Comedy, 270-271
Essay on Laughter and Ludicrous Composition, 19
Essay on the Theatre, 284-285

Estcourt, Richard, 54, 101, 181, 189
Etherege, George, 159, 166, 225, 270
Etourdi, 132, 143, 144
Europe's Revels, 83
Evans, Mr., 80-81
Evans, Miss, 79
Evelyn, John, 74, 136
Evening's Love, 14, 147, 276-277
Everyman in His Humour, 31
Everyman out of His Humour, 137

de la Faille, Jean, 272
Fair Maid of the West, 221
Fairy Queen, 95
False Count, 7, 170
Fancy'd Queen, 146
"Farendt Schuler mit dem Teufelbannen," 236
Farinelli, 232
Farquhar, George, 38, 43, 81-82, 135, 149, 177, 180, 244
Fashionable Lady; or Harlequin's Opera, 118, 125
Fatal Jealousie, 37
Fatouville, Nolant de, 40, 115, 138, 139
Faure, Elie, 47, 155
Faust, 142
Feign'd Astrologer, 147
Feign'd Curtizans, 170
Feint astrologue, 147
Female Vertuoso's, 144, 240
Fenton, Elijah, 109
Fielding, Henry, 11, 12, 20, 62, 91, 93, 113-114, 118, 121, 123-125, 128, 146, 150, 197, 205, 227, 229, 250, 259-264, 267, 268, 275, 277-278, 281
Fielding, Timothy, 219
Fields, W. C., 47
Fine Lady's Airs, 178, 180

Fiorilli, Tiberio, 31, 47, 65, 135-136, 138, 163
Fitzgerald, Percy, 102, 109
Fleetwood, John, 103, 112-113, 199, 267
Fletcher, John, 53, 72, 111, 133, 209
Floorwalker, 34
Flora, 92, 205, 206, 221
Flying Post, 79
Fog's Weekly Journal, 127, 222
Fool's Preferment, 166, 238
Foote, Samuel, 12-13, 17, 93, 128, 201
Force of Friendship, 86
Forc'd Physician, 213
Fortune Hunters, 41
Fourberies de Scapin, 42, 75, 143, 144, 149
Fox, 145
Franklin, Benjamin, 125
Fransen, J., 136, 205
French Dancing Master, 157
French Doctor Outwitted, 195
Frogs, 35
Fryar Bacon; or, The Country Justice, 215
Fuzelier, Louis, 216

Gagey, E. M., 7, 134-135, 256
Gammer Gurton's Needle, 23, 60, 69
Garrick, David, 7, 8, 9, 17, 58-59, 81, 103, 126, 128, 150, 156, 192, 199-202, 229, 230, 241, 243, 260, 266-271, 273
Garrick, Peter, 200, 267, 268
Gasperini, 80
Gaultier-Garguille, 64
Gay, John, 12, 90, 121-123, 128, 140, 154, 197, 218, 229, 249-252, 277
Gayley, C. M., 39
General History of the Stage, 116

General View of the Stage, 17, 44, 58, 118, 128, 175
Generous Choice, 34
Generous Free-Mason, 42, 220-221, 264
Genest, John, 55, 165, 168, 172, 180, 184, 186, 187, 188, 190, 193, 194, 195, 225, 254-255
Gentleman Dancing-Master, 138, 163-164
Gentleman's Magazine, 67
George, Prince, 84
"George Aloe," 284
George Dandin, 144
Gherardi, Evaristo, 21, 115, 135, 137, 139, 140-141, 249, 250
Gibraltar, 181
Giffard, W., 220
Gilbert, A. H., 10
Glossographia, 13
Goldsmith, Oliver, 13, 275, 284-285
Gorge, Mrs., 79
Gorgibus dans le sac, 42
Gray, C. T., 270
"Great Claus and Little Claus," 236
Great Favourite, 6
Greene, Robert, 69
Greenwich Park, 243
Greig, J. Y. T., 25
Griffin, Benjamin, 38, 122, 150, 177, 186-188, 254
Grimm brothers, 236
Gros Guillaume, 45, 64
Grub-Street Journal, 213, 220, 221, 222-223, 276
Guardian, 8, 72, 233
Guarini, Giambattista, 10
Guinguette angloise, 108, 116
Guinguette: or, Harlequin Turn'd Tapster, 107
Guzman, 47, 131, 134, 234

Hackabout, Kate, 219
Hamlet, 21, 165, 207, 265

Haines, Joseph, 157, 166-169, 182, 188, 222
Hall, Jacob, 211
Hallam, 228
Hanging and Marriage, 59
Happy Despair, 230
Harlequin Doctor Faustus. See Doctor Faustus (Thurmond).
Harlequin Hermit, 231
Harlequin-Hydaspes, 12, 123
Harlequin Jack Sheppard, 111
Harlequin Restored, 224
Harlequin Sorcerer, 103, 112, 224
Harlequin Statue, 231
Harlequin Student, 118
Harlot's Progress, 229
Harper, 209
Harper, John, 38, 116, 117, 192, 193, 194, 218, 259
Hauteroche, Noel de Breton, Sieur de, 35, 66, 142, 148, 150, 240, 241, 267
Haynes, Mrs., 79
Henri IV, 211
Henry V, 224, 265
Henry VIII, 259
Henry and Emma, or the Nut-Brown Maid, 127
Heraclitus Ridens, 184
Heywood, John, 68-69
Heywood, Thomas, 280
Higgins Variety, 85-86
Hill, Aaron, 86, 140, 188, 199, 245-248, 282
Hill, John, 55, 197-198
Hippisley, John, 47, 55, 193-195, 201-202
Historia Histrionica, 78
Historical and Critical Account, 5, 45
History of Mimes and Panto-mimes, 97, 98
Hitchcock, Alfred, 25
History of the English Stage, 173
Hart, Charles, 76, 159

Hob, 134, 190, 192, 213, 248-249, 257
Hogarth, William, 11, 207
Honest Yorkshireman, 92, 133, 206, 224, 264
Hook, James, 273
Hooker, E. N., 16, 86
Horace, 16, 61, 275, 279
Hospital for Fools, 7
Hotson, Leslie, 23, 70, 77, 78, 242, 244
Houghton, 116
Howard, Edward, 14-15, 160-162, 164, 170
Howard, Robert, 6, 157
Hubert, André, 37
Huff, Theodore, 34, 39, 52, 71
Hughes, John, 53, 54
Hughes, Leo, 6, 13, 51, 131, 147, 190, 238-239, 252
Humour of the Age, 177-178
Hunt, Mrs., 57-58
Hurd, Richard, 16-17
Hurlothumbro, 127
Hymen's Temple, 231

Idler, 284
The Importance of Being Earnest, 49-50
Inchbald, Elizabeth, 283
Inconstant, 81-82, 180
Inimicizia tra i due vecchi, 35
Injur'd Love, 175
Injured Virtue, 186
Intriguing Chambermaid, 20, 92, 150, 192, 193, 259, 262-263, 267
Irish Evidence, 212
Isman, Felix, 33

Jack, W. S., 6
Jack Juggler, 69
Jackson, Alfred, 79, 97
James II, 54, 75
Jane Shore, 223
Jephtha's Rash Vow, 184

Jevon, Thomas, 4, 128, 156, 165-166, 168, 169, 217, 238, 239, 240, 254, 257
Jodelet, 65
Jodelet maître, 148
Johan Johan, 69
"John Dory," 284
John Swabber, 40, 51, 71
Johnson, Benjamin, 181, 189, 222, 252
Johnson, Charles, 86-87, 189, 252, 280
Johnson, Samuel, 3, 10, 13, 14, 16, 17, 62, 198, 276, 284
Johnson, Samuel (of Cheshire), 127
Jonson, Ben, 16, 31, 32, 54, 60, 106, 132, 133, 145, 153, 162, 256, 271, 279, 281, 284
Jordan, Dorothy, 192
Jordan, Thomas, 117
Joseph Andrews, 281
Journal of a Tour to the Hebrides, 198
Journey to Bristol, 133, 194
Judgment of Paris (anonymous), 127
Judgment of Paris (Congreve), 83
Jupiter and Juno, 224

Kaufman, G. S., 52
Keene, Theophilus, 105
Kelly, Hugh, 275, 283
Kelly, J. A., 115
Kemble, J. P., 246
Kemble, Roger, 206
Kemp, William, 170
Kentish man, 78
Kid, 117
Killigrew, Thomas, 139, 157
King and the Miller of Mansfield, 92, 126, 206, 266
King Lear, 207
Kirkman, Francis, 71
Klemm, Werner, 14

Knight, Joseph, 201

Labiche, Eugène, 273
La Chapelle, Jean de, 43, 149, 244
Lachi, F., 35
Lacy, James, 9
Lacy, John, 26-31, 48, 54, 155, 156, 157-159, 233, 234
La Grange, Charles de, 64, 66
Lamb, Charles, 237
Lancaster, H. C., 5, 45, 65, 99, 134, 138, 205, 216, 236
La Motte, Houdar de, 67
Langbaine, Gerard, 27, 131, 145, 157, 235
Lanson Gustave, 5, 37, 39, 46, 64-65, 134
Laureate, 112
Lawrence, W. J., 3-4, 81-82, 135, 136, 194, 245
Lea, Kathleen M., 35
Leacock, Stephen, 50
Le Blanc, Abbé, 195-196
Lee, 218
Leigh, Anthony, 34, 37, 38, 48, 54, 155, 157, 165, 166, 169-174, 177, 178, 181, 193, 235, 238, 239
L'Sac, Monsieur, 79
Letter to My Lord, 188
Letter-Writers, 260
Letters of Wit, Politicks and Morality, 145
Letters on the English and French Nations, 196
Lethe, 7, 17, 126, 128, 266
Liebrecht, Henri, 135-136, 205
Life of . . . Jo. Hayns, 167
Life of Mr. James Spiller, 191
Little, D. M., 201
"Little Farmer," 236
"Little Musgrave," 284
Lives and Characters, 111
Lloyd, John, 127

London Cuckolds, 24, 37, 144, 210, 235-237
London Magazine, 222
London Merchant, 127, 213
London-Spy, 174
Lottery, 11, 92, 128, 260
Louis XIV, 5, 64-65, 139, 140, 167, 252, 273
Love for Love, 174, 176, 226
Love for Money, 37
Love in a Chest, 38, 86
Love in a Riddle, 127
Love in a Sack, 42, 187, 255
Love in a Wood, 187, 255
Love Lost in the Dark, 208
Love Makes a Man, 177, 182, 185
Love without Interest, 145
Lover His Own Rival, 206
Lover's Opera, 92, 206
Love's Contrivances, 8, 81, 145, 226
Love's Last Shift, 79
Loves of Mars and Venus, 148, 241, 242
Lowe, R. W., 78, 85, 95, 169
Loyal Protestant and True Domestick Intelligence, 212, 234
Lucian, 113, 114, 126
Luckey Chance, 166
Lucky Discovery, 133, 206, 210
Lucky Prodigal, 150, 189, 249, 262
Lying Valet, 150, 193, 200-201, 266-269
Lyly, John, 62

Macbeth, 181
Macclesfield, Earl of, 27
McManaway, J. G., 208
Mad Captain, 135
Madam Fickle, 32, 171
Maidment and Logan, 26-27, 174
Maintenon, Madame de, 252
Maison de campagne, 81, 244

Malade imaginaire, 146
Mamamouchi, 144, 164, 235
Man of Mode, 38, 166
Man of Taste, 146
Manly, J. M., 39
Mann, Horace, 113
Manning, Francis, 34
Man's the Master, 148
Marchand ridicule, 236
Margery, 126
Mariage forcé, 144, 145, 149
Marianne, 109
Maris, Mrs., 209
Marlowe, Christopher, 234, 272
Mars and Venus, 104, 105, 108
Marsh, Henry, 71
Marston, John, 51, 63, 69, 72, 133, 134, 187, 252, 253
Marvell, Andrew, 136, 137
Marx, Groucho, 34
Marx, Harpo, 28
Marx Brothers, 28, 52
Massinger, Philip, 186, 208
Maxwell, Ian, 69
May Day, 187
Médecin malgré lui, 48, 143, 149, 261-262
Mémoires pour Servir, 98, 99, 116
Memoirs of . . . David Garrick, 200, 283
Merry Devill of Edmonton, 39, 69-70
Merry Milkmaid, 208
Metamorphosis, 120, 145
Middleton, Thomas, 117
Midsummer Night's Dream, 95, 114
Miller, James, 7, 146, 150, 154
Millett, F. B., 7
Misanthrope, 42, 143, 261
Misaubin, John, 261
Miser (Fielding), 197
Miser (Shadwell), 144
The Miser; or, Wagner and Abericock, 116

Miss in Her Teens, 150, 266, 269-271
Miss Lucy in Town, 260
Mr. Anthony, 47, 163, 164, 234
Mr. Turbulent, 166
Mitchell, Julian, 33
Mock Doctor, 92, 146, 197, 206, 259, 260-262
Mock Marriage, 177
Modena, Duke of, 136
Modern Husband, 278, 281
Mohocks, 121-122, 154
Mohun, Michael, 76, 159
Moland, Louis, 134
Molière, 5, 42, 43, 46, 64-65, 74, 75, 120, 121, 132, 133, 134, 139, 141, 142-147, 148, 149, 150, 197, 213, 235, 240, 244, 249, 250, 251, 261-262, 264-265, 272-273
Molloy, Charles, 249, 250
Momies d'Egypte, 250
Monmouth, Duchess of, 251
Monmouth, Duke of, 45, 204
Monsieur Porceaugnac, 144, 145, 146, 147, 149, 264-265
Moore, J. B., 61-62
Morley, Henry, 215, 216, 217, 224, 273-274, 279
Morrison, 206
Most Knowing, Least Under-standing, 140, 247-248
Mother-in-Law, 146
Motteaux, Mrs., 227
Motteux, Peter Anthony, 41, 43, 80, 95, 97, 139, 148, 150, 240, 241, 267
Mottley, John, 123, 197, 259
Mountfort, William, 43, 95, 139, 166, 234, 243
Mournful Nuptials, 232
Mucedorus, 70, 214
Much Ado about Nothing, 132
Mummies of Egypt, 207
Munden, Joseph, 192
Murphy, Arthur, 8

Muse of New-Market, 203, 208, 209, 212
Museum, 269
"Mussleborough Field," 284
Mylius, Christlob, 115
Mynn, Mrs., 217

Nabbes, Thomas, 208
Nashe, Thomas, 284
Nancy; or the Parting Lovers, 206
Natural Magick, 139
Necromancer; or, Harlequin Doctor Faustus, 108, 109, 116
Newman, 249
Newton, Thomas, 201
Nicholson, Watson, 127, 222, 225
Nicoll, Allardyce, 18, 21, 45, 46, 77, 95, 97, 128, 131, 136, 138, 139, 154, 174, 204, 209, 229, 250, 266
Nicomède, 65
Nivellon, Louis, 96-97
Noah, 68
Noce Angloise, 116
Nokes, James, 34, 36-37, 44-45, 47-48, 49, 59, 134, 155, 157, 160-162, 163-164, 165, 166, 169-174, 177, 178, 181, 187, 193, 194, 196, 234, 235, 238
Norfolk, Duke of, 204
Norris, E. T., 139, 194
Norris, Henry, 44, 45, 47, 54, 55-56, 154-155, 174, 177, 179-181, 183, 187, 189, 192, 215, 249, 252
Norris (the younger), 228
Northern Heiress, 38
Northup, G. T., 6
Novelty, 41, 43, 80, 95, 97, 139, 148, 240, 267
Noyes, R. G., 59, 222

Observations sur la comédie, 129
Odell, G. C. D., 225, 266

Odell, Thomas, 128
Odingsells, Gabriel, 125, 126, 276
Of Dramatick Poesie, 73
"Of Pantomimes," 113
Old Batchelour, 168
Old Debauchees, 260
Old Man Taught Wisdom; or, The Virgin Unmask'd, 92, 206, 260
Old Troop; or, Monsieur Raggou, 26-31, 32-33, 39, 158-159, 234
Oldys, William, 173
Ormond, Duke of, 204
Oroonoko, 191
Orphan, 267
Orrery, Roger Boyle, Earl of, 47-48, 131, 134, 163, 234
Othello, 13
Otway, Thomas, 37, 74-75, 86, 122, 139, 143, 145, 166, 244-267
d'Ouville, Antoine le Metel, Sieur, 235, 236

Pack, George, 249
Paget, 225
Palmer, John, 18, 63
Parfaict, Claude and François, 98, 99, 107, 116
Parisienne, 150, 269
Parker, 216
Parting Lovers, 230
Pasquin, 20, 227, 229, 259
Pathelin, 64
Patron, 128
Payne, Henry Nevil, 36
Peep behind the Curtain, 268
Pellegrin, S. J., 107
Penelope, 12, 123
Pepys, Samuel, 8, 9, 74, 95, 157-158, 159-160, 167, 211-212, 233-234
Perplexed Couple, 38, 249

Perseus and Andromeda, 114-115
Perwich, William, 167
Peterson, Joseph, 210
Petit de Julleville, Louis, 19
Philips, John, 123
Phillips, Edward (dramatist), 256
Phillips, Edward (lexicographer), 13-14
Philpott, James, 209
Picture; or, Cuckold in Conceit, 7, 146
Pinchbeck, 228
Pinkethman, William, 38, 46, 53, 54, 55, 57, 59, 80, 101-102, 145, 154-155, 156, 168, 169, 170, 172, 174, 175, 176, 177, 178, 179-180, 181-186, 188, 189, 191, 192, 196, 215, 216, 222, 252
Pinkethman (the younger), 220
Plain Dealer, 143, 168, 226, 243
Plautus, 33, 61, 262, 268
Play, a Satire, 127
Play Is the Plot, 7
Players, 256
Play-House to be Lett, 73-74, 75-76, 80, 143, 144
Plot, and No Plot, 16, 168, 177
Politick Whore, 208
Pope, Alexander, 122, 185, 249-252, 276, 277
Potter, John, 90
Précieuses ridicules, 5, 6, 45, 146
Presumptuous Love, 114
Prison-Breaker, 219
Prisoner's Opera, 229
Pritchard, Hannah, 269
Privitera, J. F., 66
Prompter, 146, 282
Prophetess, 111-112
Provoked Wife, 246
Pyramus and Thisbe, 114

Quacks, 145

Quaker's Opera, 219
Quin, James, 269
Quinault, Philippe, 73

Racine, Jean, 74
Rainton, 116
Ralph, James, 118, 125, 126, 147, 276
Ralph Roister Doister, 23, 60, 69, 279
Rambler, 3, 10, 13, 62
Rape of Proserpine, 90, 111
Rasi, Luigi, 135, 136
Ravenscroft, Edward, 34-35, 95, 139, 144, 164, 166, 195, 210, 235-237, 238, 241-243
Ravissement d' Hélène, 216
Rawlins, 144
Recruiting Officer, 135, 180, 191, 194
Reed, Joseph, 281
Reform'd Wife, 182
Register Office, 281
Regnard, J. F., 142, 150, 197, 249, 250, 262, 268
Rehearsal, 12, 121, 122
Rehearsal at Goatham, 122
Relapse, 107, 176
Retour imprévu, 150, 197, 249, 250, 262
Revenge, 166, 187, 240, 252
Rex and Pontifex, 127
Reynolds, 219
Riccoboni, Luigi, 5, 45, 129, 194-195
Rich, Christopher, 77, 83-85, 101, 106, 182, 183, 188, 244
Rich, John, 9, 82, 88, 89, 90, 91, 100, 102-105, 108-109, 111-112, 114, 116, 125, 149-150, 177, 186, 187, 188, 189, 191, 192, 199, 219, 225, 269
Richard III, 267
Richardson, Samuel, 284
Richelieu, Armand-Jean Du Plessis, Cardinal de, 64

Richmond Heiress, 175
Rival Fools, 177
Rivals, 34
Robin Hood, 40, 220, 221
Robinson Crusoe, 190
Roger, 116
Rollins, H. E., 23, 70, 71, 284
Romagnesi, M. A., 136
Roman and English Comedy, 201
Romeo and Juliet, 37
Romulus, 67
Roscius Anglicanus, 44-45, 54, 78
Rosenfeld, Sybil, 92, 123, 174, 184, 203, 204, 205, 207, 209, 210, 211, 225, 229, 230-231
Roundheads, 41
Rousseau, J. B., 150
Rover I, 164, 170
Rover II, 26, 43, 49, 59, 139, 164, 236
Rowe, Nicholas, 223
Rule a Wife, 181, 188
Ryan, Lacy, 128
Rymer, Thomas, 13

Sachs, Hans, 236
Sackville, Charles, 31
Saffry, Mrs., 212
St. George for England, 214
"Sally in Our Alley," 255
Sauny the Scott, 233
Scaramouch, 95, 144, 166, 235
Scarron, Paul, 148, 235
School-Boy. See Comical Rivals.
School for Wives, 275, 283
Scipio's Triumph, 221
Scott, Thomas, 177
Scouten, A. H., 51, 80, 147, 190, 238-239, 252, 278
Schwartz, I. A., 134
Second Shepherds' Play, 40, 68
Seldes, Gilbert, 61
Settle, Elkanah, 168, 214, 216-217

Sganarelle ou le cocu imaginaire, 5, 74, 143, 144, 146
Shadwell, Thomas, 8-9, 32, 43, 132, 144, 145, 159, 164, 178, 238, 275, 276, 278
Shaftesbury, Anthony Ashley Cooper, Third Earl of, 281
Shakespeare, William, 33, 35, 36, 51, 53, 60, 86, 106, 122, 132, 133, 134, 142, 199, 204, 232, 233, 253-254, 256, 265, 279, 284
Sham Doctor, 206
She Stoops to Conquer, 13
She Ventures and He Wins, 37, 175
She Wou'd If She Cou'd, 225
Sheppard, Jack, 111, 219
Sherburn, George, 251
Sheridan, R. B., 121, 273
Sheridan, Thomas, 147, 264-265
Shirley, James, 133
Shoulder Arms, 40
Shuter, Edward, 195, 224
Sicilien, 133
Siddons, Sarah, 273
Siege of Bethulia, 221
Siege of Troy, 214, 216-217
Silent Woman, 16, 31, 145
Simpkin, 71
Simpleton the Smith, 21-23, 24, 38-39, 60, 63, 71
Simpson, 184, 216
Singspiele der englischen Komödianten, 70
Sir Giddy Whim, 8
Sir Harry Wildair, 81, 180
Sir John Cockle, 92, 266
Sir John Falstaff in Masquerade, 127
Sir Martin Mar-all, 144, 172
Sir Salomon Single, 43, 44, 149
Six Days Adventure, 162
Skipwith, Thomas, 83-84
Slip, 189, 203
Smith, D. F., 121

Smith, R. J., 184
Smugglers, 128
Sorin, 97-98, 100, 106-108
Souldiers Fortune, 144, 166, 173
Souper mal-apprêté, 150, 240, 267
Southerne, Thomas, 173
Southwark Fair, 219
Spanish Fryar, 172, 173, 226
Spectator, 44, 53-54, 86, 102, 177, 179, 181
Speculatist, 141
Spiller, James, 38, 47, 59, 101, 169, 177, 186, 187, 188-191, 194, 254
Squire of Alsatia, 165, 275
Squire Trelooby, 145, 175
Stage Coach, 4, 43, 81-82, 83, 85, 86, 87, 92, 149, 175, 192, 206, 210, 244-245
Stage Mutineers, 256
Stage Policy Detected, 282
Stair, John Dalrymple, Earl of, 106-107
Standhaffte Mutter der Machabeer, 70
"Statue at Charing Cross," 136
Steele, Richard, 53-54, 55, 85, 90, 105-108, 109, 112, 176-177, 178-179, 181, 185, 267
Sterne, Laurence, 5
Stone, G. W., 92
Strolers, 193, 206
Strolers Pacquet open'd, 209, 210, 213
Subligni, Madamoiselle, 80
Sullen Lovers, 8, 95, 159
Summers, Montague, 45, 54, 78, 95, 138, 166, 174, 195, 235
Swiney, Owen, 83-85, 87, 101, 145, 188

Tabarin, 42, 64
Talkers, 43
Tambourine of Tambourines, 230

Taming of the Shrew, 8, 35, 36, 134, 233
Tanner of York, 92
Tarlton, Richard, 153
Taste, 12
Taswell, 195
Tate, Nahum, 48, 131, 138, 166, 173, 238, 240, 278
Tatler, 53, 54, 85, 106, 178-179, 185
Tavern Bilkers, 98, 105, 108
Tempest (Dryden-Shadwell), 164
Temple of Diana at Ephesus, 231
Terence, 61
Thaler, Alwin, 203
Theatre, 185
Théâtre Italien, 21, 137, 138, 139, 140, 249, 250
Theatrical Museum, 193
Theobald, Lewis, 103, 112, 114, 115, 122
Thersites, 69
Thomas, 209
Thomas, Tobyas, 167
Thorndike, A. H., 18, 61, 283
Three Entertainments, 246
Three Hours after Marriage, 41, 53, 57-58, 122, 123, 140, 249-252, 277
Thurmond, John, 108, 111-112, 116, 246
Tillie's Punctured Romance, 61
Tillotson, John, 53
Toby and Ezekiel, 172
Tom-Essence, 144
Tom Jones, 62, 259
Tom Thumb, 12, 122, 124, 206, 259
Tom Tyler, 69
Tomkis, Thomas, 120, 133, 145, 159, 233
Town-Talk, 106
Toy-Shop, 92, 126, 206

Trapolin creduto principe, 138, 238
Trick upon Trick, 252
Trifles, 127
Trip to Portsmouth, 209-210
Trissino, Giangiorgio, 10
True and Famous History of Semiramis, 215
True Widow, 238, 276
Tumble-Down Dick, 114, 118
Turlupin, 64, 65
Turner, L. G., 195
Twin Rivals, 38, 177
Two Angry Women of Abington, 69
Tyranny Triumphant, 188, 243

Udall, Nicholas, 279
Underhill, Cave, 37, 49, 53, 156, 160-162, 164-165, 169, 181, 235

Vanbrugh, John, 9, 44, 81, 82, 83, 126, 145, 148, 182, 244
Venice Preserved, 226
Victor, Benjamin, 194
Villiers, George, 12
Vintner in the Suds, 206
Violante, Mme., 91
Virgin Martyr, 186
Virgin Unmask'd. See *Old Man Taught Wisdom*.
Virtuous Wife, 37, 170-171

Walker, Essex, 209
Walking Statue, 41, 86, 88, 140, 188, 190, 206, 210, 245-248
Walker, T., 3
Walker, Thomas, 219
Walpole, Horace, 13, 112-113, 257-258
Walsh, William, 145
Walwyn, B., 270-271
Ward, Edward, 78, 174, 213-214
Ward, Henry, 210
Wat Tyler, 220

Way of the World, 153
Weaver, John, 97, 98, 104, 105, 108, 113-114, 279
Weber and Fields, 33
Weddell, Mrs., 155
Wedding, 92
Weekly Packet, 105
Wells, S. B., 78
West, Richard, 258
What D'ye Call It, 92, 122, 123
Wheatley, H. B., 11, 108, 193
Whim, 278
Whimsical Death of Harlequin, 107
Whincop, Thomas, 197, 259
Whole History of Herod and Marianne, 221
Wife well Manag'd, 206
Wife's Relief, 280
Wilcox, John, 132
Wile (Wild), Jonathan, 219
Wilkes, Thomas, 17, 44, 58, 118, 127-128, 175
Wilks, Robert, 55, 102, 105, 110, 180
Willis, Eola, 225
Wilson, John, 27

Wincheslea, Anne Finch, Countess of, 251
Wit at a Pinch. See *Lucky Prodigal*.
Wit of a Woman, 4
Wits, 21, 70, 71, 207, 208
Wits Led by the Nose, 41
Witts, 72-73
Wives Excuse, 173
Woman Captain, 276
Woman's Revenge, 4, 38, 187, 189, 252, 280
Womans Wit, 83, 175, 243
Womens Conquest, 14-15, 160-162, 164
Woodward, Henry, 195, 270
Woodward, John, 251
World in the Moon, 168
Wright, James, 78
Wright, Thomas, 144, 240
Wycherley, William, 18, 124, 138, 143, 187
Wynn, Ed, 47

Yarrow, Joseph, 210
Young, Karl, 68-69

Zypherus and Flora, 230